How to Be a Lawyer

How to Be a Lawyer

THE PATH FROM LAW SCHOOL TO SUCCESS

Jason Mendelson
Alex Paul

Published by John Wiley & Sons, Inc., Hoboken, New Jersey.
Published simultaneously in Canada.

For general information on our other products and services or for technical support, please contact our Customer Care Department within the United States at (800) 762-2974, outside the United States at (317) 572-3993 or fax (317) 572-4002.

Wiley also publishes its books in a variety of electronic formats. Some content that appears in print may not be available in electronic formats. For more information about Wiley products, visit our website at www.wiley.com.

Library of Congress Cataloging-in-Publication Data is Available:

ISBN: 9781119835813 (Hardback)
ISBN: 9781119835837 (ePDF)
ISBN: 9781119835820 (epub)

COVER DESIGN: PAUL McCARTHY
COVER PHOTOS: COURTESY OF THE AUTHORS/CONTRIBUTORS

SKY10034101_042122

Jason would like to dedicate this book to his wife and best friend, Jenn. Her love, support, and encouragement are the best gifts a guy could get.

Alex would like to dedicate this book to his wife, Carolyn, who supported him in law school and has been by his side through good times and bad, always a loving partner and best friend.

CONTENTS

About the Authors

Jason Mendelson (jasonmendelson@gmail.com, @jasonmendelson) is a former venture capitalist, co-founder of a technology company, lawyer, and a software engineer.

Jason is a founding partner of Foundry Group, a Boulder, Colorado–based venture capital firm that focuses on making technology investments and identifying and supporting the next generation of venture fund managers.

In addition, Jason is a co-founder of the startup SRS Acquiom and was a managing director and general counsel for Mobius Venture Capital. Prior to this, Jason was an attorney with Cooley LLP. Early in his career, Jason was a software engineer at Accenture.

Now Jason spends his time as an up-and-coming musician (under his stage name Jace Allen) and author. Jason also is involved in several criminal justice reform initiatives.

Jason is a co-founder of Breakthrough and is on the board of the Leeds Business School at University of Colorado. Jason holds a B.A. in Economics and a J.D., both from the University of Michigan.

Alex Paul (alex@wealthgatetrust.com) is a lawyer-entrepreneur reimagining wealth management and philanthropy for himself and others.

Alex founded Wealthgate Trust Company (a Nevada-registered trust company) and Wealthgate Family Office (a SEC-registered investment advisor in Boulder, Colorado) to provide bespoke trust administration and independent investment management solutions for ultra-high-net-worth families seeking to protect and sustain generational wealth so they may achieve their financial and philanthropic goals over decades and generations.

Inspired to redefine how philanthropy is implemented in family offices, Alex co-founded Giving Place, a technological solution that navigates the challenges of large-scale family philanthropy. Giving Place harnesses technology to generate transparency, efficiency, and measurable impact for philanthropic families.

Alex is also treasurer/director of LENA, an operating nonprofit that seeks to close the gap between haves and have nots by using technology to improve early childhood language development.

Having managed the Boulder, Colorado, office of Harrison & Held, he is now of counsel. His practice focused on estate planning, charitable giving, technology, and other business matters. He previously served as outside corporate counsel for Renaissance Learning, a public K-12 educational software company. Alex holds a B.A. from Lawrence University and a J.D. from Northwestern University School of Law, and has served on the NU Law Board since 2004. After graduating from NU Law, he served as Judicial Clerk to Justice Jon P. Wilcox of the Wisconsin Supreme Court and entered private practice in Wisconsin before moving to Colorado in 2003.

Acknowledgments

We wouldn't have been able to write this book without the able assistance of many people.

First, to all our guest authors: you made this book. We learned more from your chapters than even we could have imagined, and many of your stories gave us the opportunity to get to know you better. Thank you, friends.

A special shoutout to Dave Beran, who spearheaded the chapter on being the calmest person in the room. Dave, you've always been that person to us and we thank you for your time and wisdom. And thanks for the proofreading and editing. You are good stuff.

Jason would individually like the thank the University of Colorado Law School, and especially Brad Bernthal, for letting Jason teach all these years. Those interactions with students were the inspiration for this book. Also, Jason would be remiss if he didn't thank his former firm, Cooley LLP, and all of the friends and colleagues he has met along the way during his legal career.

Alex would like to specifically thank his parents, Terry and Judi, who inspired him to go to law school and become an entrepreneur, while providing incredible opportunities. He'd like to thank his children, who keep him excited about building for the future. He'd also like to thank Lou Harrison, co-founder of Harrison & Held, who taught him how to practice law with integrity and humor. Finally, he would like to thank Northwestern School of Law and its leadership team for a great legal education combined with amazing opportunities for practical experience.

This book wouldn't be possible without the risk-taking nature of our publisher Bill Falloon over at Wiley. He gave Jason a shot with his first book *Venture Deals: How to Be Smarter Than Your Lawyer and Venture Capitalist* and for some reason decided to double down there. Thanks Bill.

We've met a lot of lawyers and clients during our professional journeys. Some great, some decent, some terrible, but all important in educating us along our winding paths. You all taught us (whether you knew it or not!) in ways we could have never learned on our own. Thank you. Yes, even to some of you jerks out there.

Why We Wrote This Book

This book was written by 28 people who went to law school. We are of different ages, sexes, races, and went to law schools that rank in the hundreds to the top five. We have had jobs ranging from general counsels of billion-dollar companies to hanging out our own shingles right after law school. Collectively, we practice in almost every area of the law.

Despite our diversity, we share the strong opinion that most law schools fail to prepare students for the real world of actual lawyering. Law schools are great at graduating students and terrible at graduating lawyers. We were all frustrated in our progression from students to practitioners and relived those frustrations when we hired, worked with, mentored, and interacted with others coming out of law school.

Jason Mendelson, one of the lead authors of this book, has been a lawyer, software engineer, startup co-founder, venture capitalist, and worked with and hired hundreds of lawyers in all shapes and sizes. He has had good experiences, bad experiences, and, like many in the legal profession, a long memory. Maybe most importantly, Jason taught as an adjunct professor for a decade at the University of Colorado Law School. In that decade he spent as much time mentoring law students on how to best transition to the real world as he did imparting legal and business knowledge. Ironically (or maybe not so), most of the professional academics in the law school did little to nothing to aid in student transition. Even worse, some openly were not fans of Jason's pragmatic approach.

Alex Paul, the other lead author, has worked in law and business for over 20 years, covering a range of legal specialties from litigation, intellectual property, corporate and securities law, nonprofit law, tax, and estate planning. In business, both as corporate counsel and an entrepreneur, Alex has supervised leading attorneys in all those specialties as well as others such as water law, real estate, and banking law. Alex has seen a trap that too many smart and sophisticated lawyers fall into: myopia. That is, attorneys suffer personally and professionally by being siloed early on because they specialize in one area of the law and one type of client shortly after law school. Because of that, they unfortunately view every problem through the lens of their specialty and become limited in their ability to do broader yet necessary things like serve as a true fiduciary, run their law firm successfully, or simply be happy and thoughtful people. Given that law schools don't teach the subject "after law school," this book is an attempt to solve this problem. Alex doesn't want to see the next generation of lawyers make the same mistakes as others in the past.

To be clear—this book is not intended to be a book about law school bashing. Law schools aren't bad. Rather, they are archaic institutions still believing that a student goes to law school, takes the classic curriculum, and a job magically appears at the end of the scholastic journey. Or maybe if your circumstances are a bit more challenging, you can use the school's career placement center's assistance. Perhaps this was truer 30 years ago, but these days only a small handful of law students win this lottery.

Given the changing nature of job discovery for law students, it is even more important they "hit the ground running" when they do find that right opportunity. Yes, there will be a plethora of statutes, regulations, tactics, strategies, client management, and other important concepts to learn, but stepping into a new career completely blind is a recipe to, at best, frustrate your employer and clients and to, at worst, be shown the door quickly.

To add to the problem, the stakes for post-graduation success have never been higher. Every year, about 35,000 people graduate from U.S. law schools. On average, these individuals have racked up close to $150,000 in debt for this privilege. Across the country, only about 80% of these people find a job within six months and nearly 10% never find a job as a lawyer. Some estimates say that average yearly turnover is between 15% and 30% and interviews with hiring partners at major law firms say it now takes two to three years on average to properly train people coming out of law school so that they may actually be additive to their firms. More than half of the junior lawyers do not keep their jobs. This attrition and turnover collectively costs firms about $9 billion each year. These statistics are unlike any other professional degree where graduates transition much more easily from school to the real world.

In our research, we found no class, book, webinar, website, or other source of material that specifically or effectively explains how to be successful with a law school degree. And yet, the problem of transition from classroom to practice is huge. This book aims to fix this problem.

We wrote this book with three audiences in mind. Obviously, the largest target audience is people currently in law school. We recommend reading this book as early in your law school career as possible and refreshing your recollection as you narrow down what your intended career path may look like. We also wrote this book, however, with the pre-law student in mind as well. The practice of law has changed greatly over the past few decades. The type of person who succeeds has changed, as well. No longer are grades, knowledge, and tactics enough to get by. We'll say this many times in the book: great lawyers must be people persons. Being a lawyer is service business. To all of you thinking about law school out there: this book will give you great insight into what the practice of law is really about. Lastly, there will be folks who've graduated and stumble upon this book, as well. We've made this book relevant to you, too.

We worked to write this book as simply and efficiently as possible, as well. We are all still scarred from the amount of text we unnecessarily read while in law school. We empathize firsthand and don't want to add to that burden. If we don't have something important to say, we won't make you read it.

The first part of this book lays out our theories of the case. The second part is the pragmatic section where we'll go out on a limb and give you concrete advice in what to do and what not to do. The last part of the book will wrap up and apply what we've discussed to the real world. Along the way we hope to make you more thoughtful and a bit uncomfortable. We believe that what we've put on these pages can start you on the path to becoming a great (and hopefully happy) lawyer.

CHAPTER

1

The Divide Between Law School and Lawyering

There is very little in common between law school and lawyering. Law schools are great at teaching case law and theory, but generally poor in how to apply either to real-world situations, as almost all law school situations involve a courtroom. Courtroom situations are by far the least common situation for most lawyers. Also, law schools teach nothing about how to work with clients outside of a narrowly tailored ethics class, which, while vital, is only a small part of the picture. Mock trials are just that: mock. And for those of us who made the switch from mock to real, we realized very quickly that life outside the four walls of law school is a completely different beast.

Why aren't people skills, psychology, and negotiations manda-tory subjects? This isn't computer science. Remember this: lawyers are called "counselors" for a reason. Any good attorney is as much an armchair support system as they are a statute-application machine. Lawyering is a people business. It's about listening, empathizing, syn-thesizing information, and problem solving. None of these things are taught in law schools to the extent needed once you are a bar-carrying legal eagle.

This isn't to say law schools are useless or bad. In fact, a good law school can teach you a skill set that is incredibly valuable for both legal and nonlegal careers. We assume that this skill set is also highly valuable in illegal professions, but none of us have particular experience there. If you are struggling with the definitions of "legal,"

5

"nonlegal," and "illegal" then you either haven't gotten to law school yet or you did poorly on the logic games part of the LSAT.

We believe that most law schools hold a unique distinction of teaching three years of valuable academic knowledge with almost zero practical knowledge. We can't think of another professional graduate school that leaves one so practically ill prepared. Think about your friends who go to medical school, obtain a master's in social work, or get an M.B.A. Okay, just kidding about the M.B.A. But otherwise, these friends walk right out of their graduate program into the world and work. Sure, it takes some time to get up to speed. But lawyers? Even in the best-case scenario, partners at law firms claim that it takes two to three years before an associate is truly ready to practice (and in many cases even longer before they're allowed to speak directly with clients). Note, however, that these same partners have no issue charging their clients for your multi-year apprenticeship.

Why is this the case? Simply put, professional graduate schools other than law schools employ teachers and professors who have actual and bona fide real-world experience. Whereas other professional graduate schools celebrate individuals who have succeeded in their real-life professions, most law schools have a bit of underlying loathing to those professors who have street cred. In fact, most of the professors who have real lawyering experience are relegated to lecturers, adjunct, or secondary professorship roles.

This problem will never go away. Innovation in law schools is about as likely as innovation in government, prison systems, and healthcare administration. These are caste systems with generations of built-in bureaucracy and rules, and in the case of academia, tenure. When one considers the real overlord of law schools in the United States, then innovation prospects dim considerably. Who is the overlord, you may ask? Simple—it's the *U.S. News & World Report* rankings. And how much innovation do you think they foster when they are still counting physical library space and volumes in their rankings? Hello, the Internet is calling. It's real, not a fad, and we think it'll catch on. Perhaps that physical library space could be better used.

So, we now come to the "divide," which is the reason we wrote this book. The gap, if you will, is created between law school and the point at which you actually begin serving a client one day. When we use the word "divide" in this book we are actually talking about two divides. The first is the gap you need to fill when working with clients. The second is the divide existing between you and your superiors at whatever job you take. You can disregard this second divide if you graduate law school and hang up your own shingle, but solo practice is not an option for most right away. (As an aside, one of the guest chapters later is from two people who went straight from law school to starting their own firm.)

Let's start with an example pertaining to something that all lawyers and clients are acutely aware of: money. We'll use an example at one end of the spectrum, but it applies to the majority of lawyers starting their practice.

Imagine that Janice is the CEO of a new startup in Chicago, Illinois. She is 30-something, just raised $750,000 from friends and family, and has a great new idea in the natural foods space. She is experienced and has had two previously successful companies. She's also smart so she hires a well-known and reputable law firm to represent her and the company. You are a first-year associate at the firm and have been there for two months.

Janice and her co-founder Jimi each make $100,000 a year. Your starting salary is $185,000 fresh out of school. You went straight from undergrad to law school, so this is your first real job. Your billing rate is $525 an hour. Note that this salary and billing rate isn't even top of market as of 2022 when this book was published. The partner you work for bills out at $1,500 an hour and the result is that Janice prefers to call you over the partner.

Janice calls you wondering if you could advise her on whether she should issue options or restricted stock units to her first couple of employees. Being so green, you have absolutely no clue what she is talking about. You scribble something down and tell her you'll get back to her shortly. She's mildly frustrated that it will take another call to resolve her question, as she's busy running the company, but asks you to call her as soon as possible.

You do a Google search to figure out what the terms mean, and you set off to the partner's office to ask them their advice on how to answer Janice's question. Ten to 15 minutes later you are back at your office, call Janice and give her the advice.

(Shameless plug: if you are thinking about going into startup counseling, consider buying Jason's book *Venture Deals: Be Smarter Than Your Lawyer and Venture Capitalist, Fourth Edition,* available wherever fine books are sold.)

One month later, Janice gets the bill for her questions. You billed 30 minutes for $225 and the partner tacked on 12 minutes for $300 for a grand total of $525. Janice is not pleased. She calls her friend Carlos, who is also a CEO and uses the same firm. Carlos says that he coincidentally had the exact same question, but when he called his associate at the firm (who is a third-year associate) he got an immediate answer and it didn't even show up on a bill. Now Janice is several less degrees of pleased and starts cursing the legal profession as her nice but "know-nothing" first-year associate makes almost double what she makes and billed her for something her friend didn't get billed for. You don't hear from her for a while, as she begins to use "self-help" from the Internet.

No one can blame you for not knowing the answer right away. You just started your job. But this is one example of the divide and it happens over and over. You are charging rates as a professional, but no one has taught you how to work with a client. You could have handled the situation much better. Over the course of this book, we'll give you tips and strategies that most likely would lead to a better outcome in this scenario.

And the partner? They are asking themselves whether it will take you two or three years to really get up to speed. Divide number two is in the books.

One thing that few readers of this book will realize is how much larger the divide has become as lawyer salaries have outpaced inflation and salaries in other fields. And not by just a little bit. When Jason started as a first-year attorney in September 1998, his salary at a big law firm was $71,000. By February of the next year, it was $125,000 as the first of many "salary wars" occurred in the legal field. And what happened to junior folks' take-home pay bumped up all the way to the senior lawyers as well. In the past, a senior law firm partner might make twice what a CEO client would make. Now that ratio has increased to over ten times. Think about this—first-year associates are making more than most executives of the clients they service. With this regime, the expectations as to your knowledge, service level, and the attention to your billing statements has exponentially increased. As a first-year lawyer, you effectively have a target painted on your back.

And while you might not go to a large law firm and instead perhaps into government, nonprofit, criminal defense, or a variety of other legal professions, many lawyers have seen their salaries increase in a way that other professions have not. Wherever you end up, the expectations will be higher than they were thirty years ago simply because of the amount of money you are being paid. You may go work for the Michigan Department of Labor after law school and your client may be the state, but the divide between your supervisors will be just as real as in our example above.

In short, expectations have increased while the law school experience has remained the same. So, the big question is, how do we collapse the divide, especially when you are still in a steep learning curve mode?

Our belief is that there are four core concepts to focus on immediately when transitioning out of law school. Even better, consider these concepts to be a lens when you take any law school class. In the next chapter, we'll discuss these four core concepts: empathy, listening first, asking questions, and always usually giving advice.

2

The Core Concepts of Lawyering

What does a good lawyer do? Depending on who you ask, people may be quick to point out that lawyers should vigorously defend and represent their clients as fiduciaries to the extent that the law and legal ethics provide. Generally, law schools are in business to teach these broad principles and while they certainly aren't wrong, they miss the point of what day-to-day lawyering looks like. Also, clients don't think about their legal relationship this way. Most clients (at least most we know) want their issues handled quickly, financially efficiently, and without unnecessary drama. Unfortunately, sometimes these expectations are at direct odds with one another.

When we set out to write this book, we asked ourselves, "What really are the core concepts of being a lawyer?" What was interesting to us is that few people we spoke with focused on legal knowledge, intelligence, or even experience. Successful lawyers and clients alike kept focusing on the soft skills. What soft skills does every great lawyer need to succeed? After many discussions with lawyers and clients, and thinking about our own careers, we came up with four key concepts:

1. Empathy.
2. Listen first, talk second.
3. Ask questions, especially when you don't know the answer.
4. Always (usually) give advice.

Note that these concepts are in a particular order. We would suggest that you approach clients, colleagues, and bosses with these in mind.

Empathy

When we talk about the divide, the single biggest gap is a lack of empathy from the lawyer to their client and junior lawyers to senior lawyers. You'll note that we are not focusing on anyone's empathy toward you. It's not that it isn't important, but rather you already know what type of empathy you need to feel your best and we don't know you. But also, let's face it, in many situations as a junior lawyer, people don't want to think about your needs. If you haven't heard this before, then get used to it.

We are trying to show you the other side so that you aren't surprised. And with all our collective years in the legal business, we feel qualified to talk about clients and senior lawyers.

Okay, so what is empathy? According to the dictionary, the definition of empathy is "the ability to understand and share the feelings of another." There are also three kinds of empathy, which we'll explore now.

The first type of empathy is called *cognitive empathy*. This is simply understanding how another person feels and what they might be thinking. This is the ability to take the perspective of another or walking in someone else's shoes, so to speak.

The second type of empathy is called *emotional empathy*. This is when someone feels physically along with another person as if their emotions are shared. A good example of this is what some people might feel (e.g., cringing or wincing) when they see a wreck in a car race, someone being thrown from a bull, or perhaps even tripping and falling while walking down a sidewalk. There was a joke in here about how Jason dances, but he kept taking it out of the drafts.

The third type of empathy is called *compassionate empathy*. This is when not only does a person understand and feel for someone's situation, but also is moved to then act and help that person.

At this point, it's appropriate to take a deep breath, relax, and think about how you've previously experienced (or not) these three types of empathy. It's also a probably a good idea to ask yourself how emotionally comfortable you are with each of these concepts (one, two, three. . .). Okay. Break's over.

We believe that the vast majority of new lawyers lack empathy toward their clients and bosses. Some of this is due to the mental, physical, and emotional strain of being a new lawyer. Some of this is due to working too hard, being too tired, and worrying about paying off student loans. Some of this due to people entering the profession who are not naturally empathic humans. Some of this is because law school beats it out of you over three years.

Whatever the case is, this lack of empathy is perhaps the biggest wedge between lawyer–client relationships. And it doesn't help you get ahead when your boss doesn't feel like she is getting this acknowledgment as well.

When Jason was a venture capitalist, he was amazed by how many times he would hear a junior lawyer complain about how "stupid" the client was. Most of the time this was a junior lawyer disparaging a CEO who had just laid everything on the line in founding a startup, a proposition that more than 50% of the time ends in complete failure. In return, Jason would hear from the startup CEO that their lawyer "frustrated them" or "didn't listen well." Because of this, the CEO was reticent to call the lawyer and thus didn't seek legal help when they probably should have, leading the junior lawyer to have clean-up work, which reaffirmed their belief that the CEO was stupid.

This is a relatively small example of the issue, but let's take an empathetic lens to the CEO's reality. An empathetic person, who had even a small clue about what startup CEOs deal with on a regular basis, would know:

1. Being a CEO is a very lonely job. You can't really talk to anyone at the company about your fears, as you don't want to freak anyone out. The result is the CEO has few, if any, open and honest relationships.
2. Being a CEO means you are, literally, responsible for every employee's (and their families') paycheck and medical benefits, among other things.
3. No one really ever wants to call their lawyer. It's costly and means there is an issue they can't handle themselves.
4. Startups are notoriously under resourced. They don't have enough money, time, and people. Every good CEO Jason ever met along the way carries this burden with them.

5. CEOs are focused manically on the business, as they should, and not the detailed legal stuff the young lawyer is focused on.
6. The CEO probably spends a ton of time as unofficial counselor to other executives of the company.

Now these factors don't even account for any current situation the CEO is dealing with. Perhaps the product isn't working correctly, their largest customer just left to go with a competitor, they are running low on cash, or they just got a terrible review online. If you think for a moment about the systemic issues, coupled with any acute problem, it's no wonder that startup CEOs suffer so frequently from mental burnout and health issues. We haven't even begun to talk about how these take tolls on their personal and family lives.

And here the young lawyer thinks the CEO is an idiot, because they aren't focusing enough on the things the lawyer thinks they should. Like the legal stuff is what the CEO wants to keep front of mind when every day is a tightrope walk across lava? Hmmmm. Maybe the lawyer should try to become a person who helps the CEO feel less lonely. Maybe the lawyer should start with empathy and not intellectual criticism, and maybe then the lawyer might start to understand what the CEO is going through. And maybe then the divide between the client and lawyer will lessen. Maybe the lawyer will build a real and trusting relationship with the CEO.

What about your boss? They've got it easier than you, right? They make more money, have more experience, and have more job security. They might even be making money off of you, depending on what your job is. But perhaps their elevated status comes with extra pressures you can't imagine. Maybe the law firm partner has been told that without a certain number of new clients this year, they will be shown the door, or worse yet, the firm isn't doing as well as you think it is and without those additional clients, there will be layoffs that will include your position.

Maybe the government lawyer you work with is constantly on the treadmill to be reappointed despite changing administrations, or maybe they even have to be elected to their office every few years. Maybe the immigration partner is terrified their whole practice is going to be upended by new federal policy. The scenarios are endless, but one thing we know: as you mature in your profession, life gets more, not less, complicated. The issues become bigger, the stakes larger, and your personal life more interesting.

If you are thinking, "I didn't go to law school to become a psychologist," then we have bad news: you have no choice. Seriously, if you think you can "Hollywood lawyer" your way to success by being tough, argumentative, dismissive, and smart, you are wrong. Only a few nonempathetic lawyers we know have become successful, and they are all on Wall Street.

You can think of empathy as "bedside manner." Doctors learned long ago that the best way to avoid malpractice lawsuits was to improve their (apparent) empathy with their patients. Customers like to feel special. People paying you want to believe you aren't just competent, but that you actually care about them and their issues.

While we've seen very few law students come out of school as empathetic lawyers, we've seen a few who are naturally programmed this way. As you start your career, try to practice empathy by thinking deeply about what motivations people have that you can't see on the surface. Do research on your colleagues and clients and construct a narrative of what might be driving their behavior instead of simply writing them off. As you get good at this, you'll have much better relationships and feel much about your decisions when you actually do decide to deem someone an idiot, because let's face it—they are out there too. And always remember, clients and partners are like icebergs; what you can see is only a fraction of what they have going on below the surface.

One last word on empathy. Remember the three types that we discussed above? Cognitive, emotional and compassionate? Realize which one you are using and feeling. Cognitive should always be turned on, as it's the only way to really be on the same "playing field" as someone else. Emotional is much less voluntary. You can't choose to feel another's emotion. If you live your life being a regular emotional empath, you may find yourself feeling burdened by other people's issues. Imagine if you internally carried every client's issues as your own. That is a surefire way to burnout. Similarly, if you apply compassionate empathy to every issue, there will be a lot of people thinking, "I didn't want you to fix my problem. I just wanted you to listen." This last point can be very relevant in close personal relationships as well. Note that high amounts of emotional and compassionate empathy seem to go hand-in-hand with successful criminal defense lawyers. The bottom line is that some of this analysis will depend on what area of law you pursue; fortunately, our guest chapters dive into this by chosen professions.

We empathize that this section is a bit deep and for some of you, not the easiest or most enjoyable read. Remember, if you don't identify with being empathetic, or do see yourself this way, but you tend to get busy and forget to be empathetic, it's okay. We believe that you can work and practice to get better. And remember, you just got through one of the densest sections of this book and we are just getting started! We didn't leave the punchline for last, rather as a filter for the rest of the book. Go stretch your legs, pet your animal companion, grab a drink, or watch *Tiger King 2* for the second time and we'll move onto the other core concepts of lawyering that we promise won't be nearly as thick.

Listen First, Talk Second

Listening first is a really good habit to acquire as a lawyer. It's tough to screw up if your lips aren't moving. In fact, very good litigators use the fact that most people don't like silence to carve up their adversaries during depositions. It's also a marvelous way to practice empathy and make people happy. Clients and bosses like to feel heard and the best method to facilitate this is for you to not talk. There are two different ways to approach this concept: listening out of necessity and listening as a strategy.

Listening out of necessity is listening when you are trying to get all information and facts on the table so that you may best analyze a situation. Consider this similar to reading the facts of a case before you dig in on what you think the outcome should be. While email dominates much more than it did 20 years ago, most major conversations with clients and colleagues are usually still verbal. One, it's way more efficient, and two, it doesn't leave a paper trail, which can be important for gnarly situations. Note that it's your responsibility to dig out all the facts and issues of a situation. If the client wants to use email, but you think you aren't getting the full picture, pick up the phone. But here's a pro tip: only do this if you have to. Maybe the email suggests that the client is super busy. Again, empathy matters.

Listening as a strategy is also very important. This is the situation where you've "been there, done that" and you know what's coming. Why not butt into the conversation, look smart, and solve the problem? If you work for a law firm, you just saved the client two minutes of billings! And, if you are in New York at a top firm, this savings is roughly equal to three nice Avery IPAs in Boulder, Colorado (if you thought there would be no math in this book, we apologize). The problem is the client feels like you didn't listen, and no one likes this feeling. Think about a conversation where your significant other and you talk over each other. Even if one or both of you were correct, it still doesn't feel good to be unheard.

The smart play is to listen. Listen because you'll get more relevant data. Listen when you think you already know it all because maybe there is a twist in the facts you aren't considering. Even if you are 100% "in the know," listen because it makes you look good, compassionate, and thoughtful. Listening builds trust. Listening makes you at least appear calm.

Ask Questions

Okay, you've mastered empathy. And you've listened correctly. The client, boss, or whomever is thinking, "Wow, this person is really mature and put together for a junior lawyer!" Now what? It's time to talk. You have a choice: Do you start with recommendations and analysis, or do you ask questions? Our advice is the latter.

It is rare that someone gives you all the data you need to solve a problem. Very rare, in fact. Our experience suggests that if you think you have all the data you need, it's because you aren't thinking broadly enough about the issue at hand or are missing something. If questions initially don't come to mind, we suggest you look inward and ask yourself, "What am I missing here?" Remember, if it is that simple, they wouldn't be asking you.

The question could be as easy as asking the senior law firm partner, "When do you want this done and how many hours do you want me to allocate to this?" It's amazing to us how few junior attorneys ask this question. The question seems basic, but the response is super important. If you are late on the project, the partner and client are angry. If you bill an unexpectedly high number of hours, then it's even worse.

We've said this before and we'll say it again: don't fall into the trap of feeling like you have to prove your intelligence by jumping too quickly to conclusions and advice. No one expects you to be like that from day one out of law school so don't fall for the false assumption. Do a quality job in the time allowed and get it right. Nothing is worse than screwing up a project and having to do it again. Remember, you're unlikely to outsmart the senior lawyer the vast majority of times.

There is one more way to look at our point. Remember the most famous Hollywood lawyers and detectives? The ones who are famous for "always winning?" Think about how much time the dialogue is them asking questions, versus them stating conclusions.

Always (Usually) Give Advice

Let's take a mental check here. Empathy? Got it. Listening? Yep. Ask questions? Got this one, too. The last core concept is the idea that you should always give advice.

Wait. . .What?

You should be thinking, "Wait. How do I always give advice when I'm fresh out of school and don't really know what I'm doing?" Most junior lawyers focus on this question and decide not to give advice. They tell the client, "I'll get back to you," or they wait two days to return an email and frustrate the person who sent the communication. This also applies to getting back to bosses and senior lawyers.

Let's put this another way: you start at your law firm billing out at $300 to $600 an hour and you've just spent 20 minutes on the phone with a client. While you've done a good job with the other three core concepts, you get done and say, "Thanks, I'll get back to you." From the client's perspective, this is what they are thinking:

1. I just spent $100 to $200 and got nothing. Not even a morsel of an answer?
2. Did they hear what I was telling them?
3. Why am I paying for someone who doesn't know anything and then will have to go the partner and double bill me?
4. Why can't I get a more experienced lawyer who can help me?

These are all bad thoughts to have as a client. We've been clients as well and have had them. Patience only goes so far with today's billing rates and salaries. The problem is that you really don't know what you are doing and may be scared to react. What should you do?

We've found that there is a relatively simple technique that can make the client feel good about the conversation, make you look smart, and preserve your options to change your mind later once you get up to speed on the subject matter. That technique: give advice in the form of a question (at this point, we should all take a moment of silence for Alex Trebek).

Here is how it works: Once the discussion around the scenario has ended and you have asked your relevant questions, ask the client, "In a perfect world, how would you like to see this issue resolved?" This simple question will give you a ton of data, not only about the issue, but about the client themselves. When they answer you'll know how reasonable they are, if they are emotional about the issue, and what their optimal solution is, which is a great starting point for your research.

When we've asked this question as junior lawyers, here are some actual quotes from clients:

"I don't want to pay any taxes on this transaction."
"I want a younger workforce and want to fire older and slower workers."
"I don't want my spouse to know about this."
"I want to threaten a lawsuit to make this company accept my acquisition offer."
"I don't want to turn over documents to the other side."
"I want person X to do Y or I'm going to the police."

Each of these quotes should raise red flags. Whether the client's goals are allowable is an easy legal answer regardless of the actual fact patterns (which we assure you were somewhat complicated). Regardless of your knowledge of litigation, criminal, employment, mergers, business, or family law, the hairs on the back of your neck should be saying, "Uh, you can't do that."

Despite you potentially not knowing the actual laws in any of these areas, you still can provide advice. You can still help solve the problem, which is what the client wants. Before you think that these are implausible scenarios, they aren't. You learned some things in law school and those who didn't go to law school don't have that background. While these are more extreme cases, the point is that by asking what the goals are and using your intuitive brain, you may be able to give advice while buying yourself some time. In these cases, perhaps your answers could be the following:

"I don't want to pay any taxes on this transaction."

Answer: "I understand your goals and I will do everything to minimize the tax impact on you."

"I want a younger workforce and want to fire older and slower workers."

Answer: "I hear your frustration, but employment discrimination is illegal, and I don't want you to get in trouble. Let me work out an employee performance plan that you can use to evaluate everyone on a case-by-case basis."

"I don't want my spouse to know about this."

Answer: "I understand, and I want to assure you that my fiduciary responsibility is to you, but there are nuances here that I want to make sure we abide by. I'll get back to you shortly."

"I want to threaten a lawsuit to make this company accept my acquisition offer."

Answer: "I understand how important this transaction is to you. I would consider whether suing them would make for a healthy combined company after the sale. We also need to be careful of ethics laws. Let me do a bit of work and get back to you."

"I don't want to turn over documents to the other side."

Answer: "I understand the sensitivity of these documents. As you probably know, there are a lot of laws around when we can and cannot withhold documents. I want to give you all the nuances regarding these and will send you an email that you can read and we can discuss."

"I want to person X to do Y or I'm going to the police."

Answer: "Involving the police is a serious step. We need to be thoughtful about this and I want to talk to our contacts at the firm before we take any action."

Each of these scenarios is steeped in dense case law. And by no means is the complete answer our one-sentence response. You likely will have little or no knowledge of the particular law and cases but use your law school intuition. Common sense goes a long way, and if you can show that you are "on the case," recognize the issue, and can provide a little off-the-cuff guidance, you'll quickly earn the trust and respect of your client. They key is not just giving up and saying, "I'll get back to you." If you can, give the client a nugget to chew on while you are getting up to speed. The issue is when you get overwhelmed in the fact pattern and give up until you can start your research. In each of these cases, you can ask the client their goals, and in many cases, know if they are on the right track or not.

The title of this section is "Always (Usually) Give Advice." If you are totally stuck and overwhelmed, err on the side of caution and don't give advice. That is why we put the word "usually" in the title. We've found that many junior lawyers separate themselves from others who are good at this last concept early in their careers.

For those of you who will bill hours, note that being good at these four concepts makes your billing rates more justifiable to your clients. You'll find much less pushback (and maybe even none) if your clients feel good about their interactions with you.

As we've wrapped this section up, we invite you to read the rest of the book with these concepts as filters for the rest of the material. But more importantly, if you are still in school, how do you apply these concepts to your coursework? What can you take away from your particular classes that will allow you to succeed on the soft skills side of being a lawyer? We advise you not just to think about fact patterns and the application of laws but also to take the time to think about how you would empathize, listen, and ask questions of the parties involved. Then you'll be ready to really solve the problem and give advice.

In the next two chapters we are going to dig into what you might get out of particular classes that will help you in the real world.

Understanding the Importance of Law School Rankings on Your Future

While we wish we could tell you that law school rankings don't matter, that isn't true. They do. It's commonly acknowledged that rankings matter more for law school than any other professional school outside of business schools.

Let's be blunt. We believe students should go to the highest ranked law school where they're accepted, with due consideration of three variables: cost (weighing scholarship and financial aid packages), location, and size. Given how expensive law school can be, cost may rule the day and we wouldn't argue against that. Furthermore, location is important. Many employers only recruit from the geographical location of where your law school is situated. Finally, you've been to school before. Size may matter to you.

As we've said before, being a lawyer is a skilled trade. The experience is much less about "fit" than college. The goal of law school is to get a job, and eventually one that you love doing every day. And there's a direct pipeline from higher ranked law schools to top law positions across the country.

Rankings matter because they allow firms to outsource their HR departments to law school admissions offices for recruitment. It sucks. It's not fair and it's stupid, but if no one has told you yet, we are.

By recruiting from a few schools within a particular ranking cluster and often with a geographical focus, firms dramatically reduce their recruitment costs. It's as simple as that. But it's a numbers game and the uniformity of law school curriculum, combined with consistency of grind needed to succeed as a junior lawyer, allows for a codependent relationship between firms that hire lawyers and law schools. And it's not just firms. The same is true with judicial clerkships, which tend to be even more tribal.

If you are reading this before law school, do everything in your power to crush the LSAT. It's the key metric that admissions people look at. Also there appears to be a correlation between LSAT performance and law school performance. How we know this, we are not allowed to tell you, but we've seen some convincing data from a very good law school on this subject. The LSAT is also your most manipulatable data point to get scholarships and more generous financial aid packages. Just about anyone can improve their LSAT score 10 to 20 points with preparation, which on the edges can be the difference between a tier 1 and a tier 3 law school.

For the majority of you reading this book, you've chosen your school and the ranking is what the ranking is. If you are in a top 20 law school, you probably can knock on any employer's door with the right grades and get a response. If you are top 40, it's a bit harder, and so on. So, what do you do if you are worried about your law school ranking?

Remember that these rankings only affect the first job you get out of law school. After that, no one will care where you went, it's all about how well you performed as a lawyer. So, the ranking is only a momentary concern. We both have worked for and hired great and terrible lawyers from top ranked and lower-ranked law schools. For us in hiring (not subject to tribalism in a Big Law hiring committee), the school is but one data point among many others. Yes, it's interesting, but no, it doesn't seal the deal.

Most importantly, the very best lawyers (which includes our guest authors) are the best because of what they've done and how they've done it, not where they went to school. Great lawyers are not ones who we stop and think about where they went to law school. Did they go to Yale or Cappodocia State Law? We just remember that they did a great job for us and feel fortunate to work with them again. The key is to learn in law school what you can (and learn it well) and then figure out how to apply that to the real world. That's why we've written this book.

We spoke to a hiring partner at a Global 50 law firm and asked if there was any correlation between making partner and which law school a person went to. This firm hires from all over the world. It hires from U.S. law schools ranked 1 to 126. The answer was "no." Not only was there no correlation according to this person, but people from lower ranked schools tended to turn over less in the early years.

If you are feeling anxious about your law school ranking for the job you are looking for, we recommend networking your way into the employer long before you actually need a job. Find a way to give them something interesting to look at. Perhaps try to show them that you have the missing soft skills that so many junior lawyers lack. Get some experience outside the law school that indicates you could be valuable early in your career. In other words, be like Avis and try harder. You'd be surprised how many lawyers who went to highly ranked schools don't.

A couple of words about Big Law, which has a negative reputation to many people in law school. We would argue to not dismiss Big Law out of hand. Done correctly, it can be some of the best training for whatever you eventually want to do while getting paid handsomely. Also, you can leave at any time, and you have yet another thing on the resume to market. Putting yourself into a large student debt portfolio while dismissing the most lucrative part of the market may not be the best business model.

In our experience many folks who want to do public service pay off their debts and then can go do what their calling really is. Whatever you choose, remember that your first job out of school is only that. Get the job, become a great lawyer, and figure out what the game plan is later.

4

Classic Coursework (What Is It Good For?)

Depending on where you go to school, who you have as a professor, and what your own personal interests may be, you will have a wildly varying experience taking the "classics" at law school. Perhaps, inherently, you find yourself intrigued by rabbi trusts, fertile octogenarians, hairy palms, firework explosions on train platforms, or the seemingly infinite ways to define a human death, but what's it all worth when you are at your first job out of school?

This chapter gives advice on what practical knowledge could come out of these classes. In other words, "Okay, I'm dying sitting through civil procedure. Is there anything I could use to make myself a better lawyer once I graduate?"

We won't waste your time with the obvious: if you want to be a constitutional lawyer, pay attention in con law, okay? If you want a fancy billboard one day that has your picture on it, torts and civil procedure might just be your jam. We are going to try to unpack what could be important taking the mandatory classics for when you aren't practicing in that particular area.

Keep our four core concepts in mind and ask yourself the following: How is what I'm learning today potentially applicable to solving a client problem tomorrow?

Note that there are also some variances in which of these classes are mandatory depending on where you go to law school.

Torts

Of all the classics, at least torts is the funniest, right? But if you aren't going into personal injury law, it's irrelevant, right? Wrong. Believe it or not, torts are prevalent in legal areas such as trusts and estates, business, and acquisitions. In short, people do bad things to one another, and it shows up all over the place in the real world. Think of it this way. Torts is really about one party (or parties) doing something that hurts another party (or parties) either intentionally or unintentionally.

And let's face it, people do stuff to one another all the time. What you may not realize is that there is probably a tort for that. Your banking client calls a customer of their competitor and talks them into changing banks while talking trash about the competitor? It could be a tortious interference with a business relationship and subject to treble damages! Ouch. The list is long. Most law schools focus torts on personal injury, but in the real world, it's actually widely applicable.

Also in torts, one studies negligence, which includes the concept of foreseeability. Again, law schools tend to focus on things like malpractice or poor Mrs. Palsgraf, but not how foreseeability matters so much in how contracts are drafted. For instance, the best contracts are ones where parties have their interests aligned, rather than an agreement trying to force good behavior. In both situations, the ability for a lawyer to foresee the potential misalignment of incentives and how a counterparty could game a business arrangement is key.

As far as the product liability section of torts goes, enjoy it for the stories and think how lucky you are that driving a car is infinitely safer today than it was 90 years ago.

Bottom line: Torts is super useful to build your intuition and ability to see around corners for future issues. Issue spotting (past, current, and future!) is a key trait in how to best think like a lawyer.

Contracts

Oh, contract law class. What you *could* have been. But you weren't. This pertains to our law schools and from reviewing current course outlines at several well-known schools. Apparently, we weren't alone.

Let's review. Most contracts classes teach that a contract is about mutual assent, expressed by a valid offer and acceptance; adequate consideration; capacity; and legality. Then you try to test these limits and learn about illusory promises, consideration (or lack thereof), and the parole evidence rule.

You study case law, actual contracts, and then debate in class whether the paper would stand up in court.

And almost none of these matters in the real world. Let's look at the data.

First, only 0.1% of contracts entered into actually go to court, according to Contract Assistant, a contracts management platform company. While the data is less public, it appears that somewhere around 9% of contracts, however, have some form of dispute where one party calls the other party to complain. This is way short of filing a lawsuit. In areas such as mergers and acquisitions, however, the dispute percentage is 25% to 35% according to SRS/Acquiom, the leading merger and acquisition platform that coincidentally was co-founded by Jason.

What we have seen is the following: almost never are the disputes around mutual assent, expressed by a valid offer and acceptance; adequate consideration; capacity; and legality. Let's face it: the bar is pretty low to create a binding contract. Disputes aren't about *if* there is a contract, but rather *what* does the contract mean. Who is right and who is wrong about the interpretation of a valid contract? What *should* be taught in law school is how to better construct and draft contracts to minimize disputes. This isn't about advanced drafting, either, because most experienced lawyers can use English as a weapon to twist meanings. We're talking about knowing the key concepts. Keep these four things in mind right out of the gate and you will be automatically way ahead of other lawyers:

1. Constraining behavior and the alignment of incentives.
2. Transaction costs.
3. Agency costs and information asymmetry.
4. Reputation constraints.

As we dive into these in detail, we borrow heavily from Jason's other book *Venture Deals: How to Be Smarter Than Your Lawyer and Venture Capitalist, Fourth Edition* (Wiley).

Constraining Behavior and Aligning Incentives

Any good contractual relationship strives to be a win-win situation for both parties, where each party is incentivized to act in each other's best interests. Many things can drive this. It could be that the business relationship is so important to both parties, so everyone will be a good actor. There can be reputational constraints involved. However, neither of these have any legal teeth to make sure everyone behaves. Consequently, contracts were developed to make sure that if something went awry, that good behavior, to some extent, would be enforceable. Think of it this way. The contract is the backstop if folks can't play nice.

While it's nice to think that people are generous of spirit, it's a fact of life that most people, especially in a business context, are driven by self-interest. That's not a bad thing, but it's useful to always keep this in mind. The first thing to think about is, how aligned are people's motivations at the beginning of the relationship? The more alignment, then the smoother the relationship should be. The less there is, then proper contract drafting is even more important. So, if you are wondering "how much lawyering" you should put into a contract, consider this: Is this a "win-win" relationship (like a joint business venture) or is this a "winner take all" relationship (like a settlement agreement)?

We encourage you to deal with misalignments like this openly and directly. Ultimately, if you can't reach an agreement on how to address them, the situation will be bounded by the contractual terms that you have agreed to beforehand. Because of this, it is critical to think about how contracts constrain bad behavior and align incentives. Whenever you are trying to figure out if a particular term is good or bad for you, consider how this will either proactively or negatively decrease the ability for people to behave poorly, or whether the term improves the alignment of your incentives with your counterparty.

If something feels out of whack and you think a particular provision divides the sides' incentives, be careful about accepting it. It's in this vein that you have a very powerful negotiating tool. You don't have to say, "I don't want this term." Instead, try the approach of, "Wait a minute, this term starts the relationship by dividing us and resulting in our incentives being misaligned."

Outside of these considerations, every good contract should deal effectively with transactions costs, agency costs, and information asymmetries, which we'll discuss next.

Transaction Costs

There are different definitions of transaction costs, but for our purposes transaction costs are the cost—in both time and money—associated with creating a relationship between two parties. For instance, in closing a venture deal between an entrepreneur and a venture capitalist, transaction costs will include not only the costs of lawyers for both sides but also the costs of meetings, the time involved to complete due diligence, and every step of the process from that first meeting to the signed definitive documents.

When entering a contractual relationship, consider that all good contracts minimize current and future transaction costs. This might mean you choose a different structure on a deal because the structure, itself, is cheaper to paper than another structure. Always consider the value you bring to a contract. If the value of the contract is $10,000 consider how many hours are appropriate versus a merger worth $100,000,000.

We find future transaction costs to be even more important to consider. For instance, you should negotiate a detailed merger letter of intent (LOI) to avoid too much negotiation ambiguity while drafting the definitive documents. As you have more negotiating power during the LOI stage, what would take two hours to negotiate now could save you tens of hours later. In short, you are defining the relationship up front so that you don't have to run up huge costs, both in time and money, figuring who has which rights and who receives what consideration.

Agency Costs and Information Asymmetry

Agency costs are costs associated with an agent acting on behalf of a principal. Some of these costs are direct. If we hire a stockbroker to buy stocks for us, we must also pay them a fee to complete the trade. Some of these costs are indirect and hard to spot.

Let's use the example of a "walking dead startup company." This is a company that is still in business, but just limping along with no clear path to an outcome. It would probably be in the startup investors' best interest if the company shut down so the investors could recoup whatever money is left in the bank account and take the tax loss.

Let's consider the investors the principal in the scenario. The CEO of the company, however, has other incentives. He still has a decent salary and gets to walk around town with his CEO business card. His incentive is to keep the company alive as long as possible. The CEO in this case is the agent.

Regardless of the amount of time the investors and the entrepreneur spend together, there is no way either party will know as much about the other's business—and motivation—as they know about their own. This information asymmetry, like agency dynamics, results in a misalignment of incentives.

Consider how contractual provisions could help alleviate this conflict. A contractual right to a board seat for the investors would be helpful. An odd number of board members, with at least one independent board member might be useful. Perhaps a term that says the company will give investors their money back in X years would protect against this situation.

Reputation Constraints

If you are playing a long-term game, reputation constraints can be even more important than a specific term in a contract. For instance, the venture capital industry is small, and reputation matters a lot. Bad behavior gets talked about, even if it's done behind closed doors and not out in the open. The smaller the ecosystem, the more this phenomenon exists, so as you focus on smaller geographies, the importance of reputation increases.

While there are some people who care less about their reputation than others, your reputation will be established over a long period of time. No contract is airtight, but how you deal with ambiguity and conflict will help define your reputation. This impacts both entrepreneurs and investors.

When considering how to create a contract, again, forget about most everything you learned in class and ask yourself: Does reputation matter to both of these parties? Will reputation constrain bad behavior here, or not? If we take the joint venture scenario where the relationship is a true win-win, then perhaps we have less to concern ourselves about. If this is a divorce (personal, business, or otherwise), then perhaps neither party cares about their reputation. The really interesting situations are where only one party cares about their reputation. These situations are ripe for abuse by the noncaring party.

Bottom line: Contracts isn't just for business lawyers. It's great for anyone who deals with relationships, so long as you consider the filter of our four concepts for contracts. If you get caught up in the technicalities of the law school class, it's a bore and seems irrelevant to most.

Civil Procedure

Frankly, we can't figure out who this is useful for unless you are going to be a litigator. Jurisdiction and evidence, with a focus on discovery and venue, are relevant in other legal areas, but they are usually better learned in those contexts than this one. We are sorry that we don't have more for you here.

Bottom line: If you are going into litigation, pay close attention. If not, consider taking this pass/fail if you can, and relax a bit. However, if your law school has an excellent professor of federal jurisdiction consider taking it. Understanding the rules of federal jurisdiction is vital for many areas of law, including intellectual property.

Property

This is another class that we are going to struggle with advising you what to get out of it. Unless you are going into property law and/or trusts and estates, this class is another mandatory head scratcher. If we squint, we can tell you that some of the logic games of figuring out who owns a piece of property due to an imperfect fee simple granted by a fertile octogenarian who enacted a rabbi trust might help you become a better critical thinker, but other than that, we are mostly clueless.

On a personal note, we would tell you to pay attention to the major concepts so that if you buy a house one day, you'll better understand the real estate contract, but other than that, at least it's more fun than civil procedure. We highly recommend a course in real estate transactions taught by a practicing adjunct.

Bottom line: Most of us found this class easier and more interesting than civil procedure. It's also often a more important subject matter on most state bar exams, so there is that.

Criminal Law

While you may believe this is only useful if you become a criminal defense attorney, a prosecutor, or a judge, keep in mind that being a lawyer is a lot like being a doctor (or owning a pickup truck). Once friends and family know you've graduated (or even before), they will start asking you for help all the time. To these people all doctors and lawyers should know everything about medicine and law, respectively. Jason's father, who was a radiologist, also got questions about cats and dogs. Anyways, just know that as a lawyer, you'll get asked a lot of random things. And this is where the value of criminal law can come in for everyone. Plus, in line with our overall advice, don't assume in law school that you will never practice or need some knowledge of a specific specialty.

We hope you won't get asked a lot of questions about manslaughter or homicide, but there's a good chance you'll get questions about search and seizure, Miranda rights, Fourth Amendment rights, and DUIs. If nothing else, pay attention to the differences between manslaughter and murder as there are some interesting interplays with how foreseeability works in torts. Also understand the differences between criminal and civil actions that deal with the same subject matter, as you'll look smarter when reciting the latest celebrity blowup on TMZ. Lastly, criminal procedure is more useful in this context than civil procedure, and also more interesting.

Bottom line: Every lawyer needs to know something about criminal law even if it's not what you practice. It's the "price of admission" to be able to call yourself a lawyer amongst friends and family. Putting aside the glib nature, if you are at all interested in criminal justice reform (what Jason spends a lot of his time on these days), then this class is a good foundation. You may not ultimately practice in the area, but you may decide to dedicate some of your time to issues around justice reform.

Constitutional Law

If you had asked us prior to the mid-2010s and the onslaught of social media what good constitutional law could be for non-con law lawyers, we would have said something to the effect of, "Every democracy needs well-informed citizens to keep that democracy strong."

And then we would have made a quip of the lack of jobs in this area and kept this section as short as our Civ Pro section.

Alas, a lot has changed. It feels like con law is now also part of the "price of admission" of being a lawyer. It's not just correcting your friends on Facebook who swear their First Amendment rights are being trampled upon by their private employer. It really is about being a well-informed citizen who can understand the real issues between the debates yelling we hear on cable news channels.

Invariably you are going to get into discussions with friends, family, clients, bosses, and others on this topic. Keep in mind that it isn't just about knowing the right answer but also about being able to lay out a thoughtful analysis in an empathetic way. Being a know-it-all won't help here or get you ahead; rather you need to be able to deliver the material in a mature way so that people will look up to you.

Bottom line: Con law is great for understanding what your rights really are. It's also useful to make yourself super frustrated reading social media posts about "people's rights" and "free speech." This class is also adept at teaching you the fastest way to get into a fight during a family dinner party. Use you power wisely.

Legal Methods/Writing/Research

If your Methods class was anything like ours, it was very heavily biased toward litigation. And because of this, some of us didn't value it highly enough when we were enrolled. Bad on us.

Writing is more important than ever, as email has taken over as the primary form of communications. When Jason (who is a little older than Alex) started his first law firm job, there were barely computers on desks and email was "new." Paper cover letters to documents were still being written by first-year lawyers and reviewed by senior associates before they were whisked away by couriers who were running around town delivering packages. Talk about transactions costs!

Well, today, even a green first-year lawyer is sending emails to clients. Proper written communication is essential. Use your experience in this class to pay attention to words, because every one of them usually counts for something.

When it comes to blue book citations, grin and bear it if you aren't going to use these professionally. Only thing to pick up here is that all lawyers need to pay attention to detail. Otherwise, sorry.

Bottom Line: Writing is more important than ever. Take this opportunity to practice and learn.

Evidence

Evidence may seem only valuable to litigators, but that is short-sighted. We know that evidence is important in every facet of the legal profession because it governs what material will or will not get into a legal proceeding. Because of this, evidence laws also allow one party to exert pressure on another party prior to any legal proceeding. You can only imagine some of the things we've seen that people don't want the public to know about.

So whatever area you practice in, consider from day one what materials may or may not make it into a courtroom. Think about things like your own personal document retention policy earlier in your career. While much of your materials will likely be protected by attorney–client privilege, some of it is not, as loose email communications might include a party on the email chain that is not protected by privilege, thus, blowing the privilege.

Protect your clients and add value by encouraging robust document retention policies. This is a relatively easy area of the law that can be self-taught yet highly valuable from day one to your new client, regardless how junior of a lawyer you may be. Plus, the great thing about this area is that your expertise or position doesn't really matter. Pretty much every lawyer must manage documents correctly if she wants to be successful (or at least not commit malpractice). Don't wait to find your mistake. In the worst of these situations, we've seen lawyer work product produced in a trial and even worse, the lawyer called as an actual witness in a case. Yuck.

Bottom line: Even if you aren't going to be a litigator, please please please pay attention to how evidence works. All lawyers, their communications, and their work product have the possibility of ending up in court. Hope for the best, but plan for the worst.

Ethics and Professional Responsibility

This course is mandatory for a reason: it's all about you keeping your bar card, staying out of jail, and not showing up in the news for the wrong reasons. Unbelievably, there are a surprising number of lawyers who screw this stuff up.

Some didn't pay attention in class, some don't think things through, and some are just plain bad lawyers. In any event, while a lot of this is common sense, some is much more nuanced so pay attention.

This class may be boring and seemingly obvious, but there are two things to which you should pay particular attention. The first is conflicts of interest. The concept seems so simple, correct? Wrong. What do you do when you represent a company, and the CEO tells you to do something that you feel is not in the best interest of the company? For instance, the CEO says, "Please prepare a new employment agreement for me that doubles my salary." Is that in the best interest of the company? Do you have a conflict? We'll go into this and other scenarios in depth later in the book but for now consider that some conflicts are not so obvious.

The second is around the attorney–client relationship. It's imperative to know when you've created one, when you haven't, and when it's a bit ambiguous. Remember that it is from the client's, not your, eyes that determine whether there is a relationship. This means that you need to be careful of that three-drink advice you gave someone at a bar. You may have created a relationship that you don't want to have.

Bottom line: This class is the building block for many nuanced real-life situations. While most of these classes are limited to "just the facts," realize that the subject matter extends much more broadly than a law school professor is probably used to teaching. Throughout this book, we'll bring these issues into real-life examples.

Having finished up with the mandatory classes, let's dig into electives you might want to consider.

CHAPTER 5

Choosing Proper Electives

We believe the practice of law, whether full time as an attorney or part time as an entrepreneur, CEO, or politician, is a trade like any other. Therefore, law school properly done is professional training, not an intellectual odyssey or journey of self-discovery. While those things can happen, they're side benefits, not the purpose.

Somehow this can get confused in law school. Perhaps this happened long ago when the practice of law was more elitist and many law professors viewed themselves as philosophers rather than professional guides and mentors. Perhaps this is due to the Socratic method or the unintended consequences of unaccountable tenure, but this confusion has inflated costs and created a glut of unemployable lawyers. Being strategic and tactical in choosing your electives will help you avoid becoming one of these unfortunate souls.

When choosing electives, keep three things in mind. First, make sure you choose and take each class with the four core lawyering concepts as your filter; second, make sure you take classes that help you solve problems; and third, take a negotiations (i.e., alternative dispute resolution) class regardless of your legal interests.

With that in mind here is our elective choosing algorithm:

1. Conduct proper due diligence to protect and maximize your most valuable asset.

   The key to choosing proper electives is due diligence. It's shocking how many smart law students place so little value on the most valuable asset any of us have: time. Be jealous of your time, and only spend it with the very best your school has to offer.

Diligence should begin as soon as you have chosen your school. Scour social media and professional networks for recent alumni of your chosen school. Begin networking with those in your city or state, inviting them to a coffee or to provide career advice via Zoom. You should ask which professors and adjuncts they liked, who they didn't, and what are the top three classes they recommend you take. In line with this book, ask more generally for advice on how to be successful in your school.

Diligence continues when you arrive on campus. Networking is key to any successful law school career and should be one of your top priorities from the start. Join organizations that have second and third years at members, hopefully working collaboratively in a setting like a legal clinic or journal. Ask every second or third year you meet who they liked, who they didn't, and why.

See if your law school has student rating data on professors or adjuncts. And if not, ask why not, as you are the customer. Regardless, look for online networks that rate professors, which should be reviewed skeptically if they allow anonymous ratings or comments. But review all available resources and make informed decisions.

2. Choose courses by teacher/professor first, subject second.

As the law is all very interconnected and interrelated, and the skill set applicable across all subject areas, we believe you should select electives based on the quality of the teacher, not the type of content. Spending your time with the very best your school has to offer is key to maximizing your opportunity set. Put another way, great teachers teach you a lot more than just the subject material. They'll teach you how to think, talk, debate, laugh, learn, and perhaps feel what it is like to be in the moment as an interested attorney, not a bored law student.

Real Estate Transactions by an adjunct and Administrative Law by a tenured professor are two courses Alex chose with this method, and those experiences continue to pay dividends today, despite very little work with the direct content of each. Jason took a course called Blood Feuds about Icelandic law.

These experiences of learning from master teachers were worth way more than any particular subject matter.

3. Prioritize top adjuncts.

As two very competitive people, we don't view tenure as a positive for the business of law schools. However, we're stuck with it, so make the best of it. Certainly, during your first year mostly you will have the standards with tenured or tenure-track professors, and plenty of opportunities to take classes with those you enjoy the most in year two or three. It's the adjuncts where there are considerable arbitrage opportunities.

By finding the best adjuncts at your school, you can leverage your school's reputation for your benefit. That's because it's prestigious for practicing attorneys to teach a course in your law school, which enhances their brand. It's a level of competition and market selection that is more absent from the internal politics of tenure track positions and professorships. Our advice for choosing top adjuncts extends to choosing a law school that hires adjuncts from the real world in subject areas that you find interesting. Finally, because being an adjunct is hard work and time consuming (as Jason has experienced firsthand), the ranks are consistently refreshed, helping the content to be more relevant and timelier.

4. Don't specialize too early.

None of us know what we don't know. While a truism, keep this in mind while in law school. A lot of times, students come with some preconceived notion as to what type of lawyer they want to be. They choose a specialty early (say second year or before) based on limited anecdotal evidence rather than data, and eliminate whole areas based on nothing more than conjecture. For example, tax law might sound boring at first blush. However, once you realize that tax law is really about human behavior, incentives, unintended consequences, and power, it becomes a lot more relevant and interesting. Of course, you need a good professor to teach it this way.

Instead, strive to be a great lawyer, which among other things means versatility and not being siloed. All areas of the law overlap, and to be successful, you need to understand those overlaps. Our era of hyper-specialization is driven by efficiency in allocation of resources, not by maximizing your individual potential to be a great lawyer. Realize the considerable pressure to specialize early on isn't helping your particular brand and fight it.

You will meet students who have a clear path right away. Perhaps they are the offspring of a corporate lawyer or litigator who knows from day one they want to follow in a parent's footsteps. That's great, but we believe that even those who know what their specialty is would benefit from greater breadth. You learn how to practice law by practicing law, not by being in law school. Rather, law school is your opportunity to enhance what will be the substance of your brand, and you should use it to broaden rather than narrow your reach.

5. Look for opportunities outside the building: clinic, externships, other colleges.

We both had extraordinary experiences outside of the classroom. While at Northwestern, Alex worked in the Legal Clinic, assisted on death penalty cases to overturn wrongful convictions, and represented juvenile clients in juvenile detention within Cook County Jail. Those experiences provided more insights into procedure than any course in the area. Working at the SEC Division of Enforcement helped Alex gain a fundamental understanding of administrative law, government power, and a deep sense of fiduciary duty. Externships will supercharge your understanding of certain positions and lead to job offers, all while placing you in an uncomfortable yet safe supervised position, thereby maximizing learning. In fact, Alex still relies on contacts created while at the SEC.

Jason got out of the law school to take business school classes in accounting and venture capital. He didn't even know what venture capital was and took the course because he was a former software engineer who wanted to learn about startups. Four years later Jason was hired at a venture capital firm. Later, he was promoted to head up all operations including finance. Going back to our specialization paragraph, this breadth of choice opened Jason up to his future career.

What Should You Get Out of Law School?

Throughout this book, we refer to hard and soft skills you'll need to acquire and develop to be a great lawyer. Later, we dive into other strategies for doing well and not making common mistakes.

A short chapter on what you should get out of the law school experience is helpful to better frame the objective. Note that each of the items are discussed in other parts of this book, but here are all our thoughts in one place. Consider this your checklist that you'll use to build your future practice.

We divided these into "hard" versus "soft" skills, but let's face it, many of these are both. Please be patient with our categorizations, but realize you'll need all of these in your toolbox if you want to be your best.

And the punchline? Note that you'll need a lot more things than the skills you'll learn in law school to actually succeed.

Hard Skills Necessary to Be a Great Lawyer

- Ability to solve problems and think analytically.
- Legal knowledge in your practice area *and* all practice areas that touch on your specialty (if you have one at all).
- Ability to negotiate and debate.
- Strong communication skills, both oral and written.
- Strong research skills.
- Experience and ability to work in a team setting.

Soft Skills Necessary to Be a Great Lawyer

- Empathy.
- Ability to listen first and then talk.
- Ability to ask good questions.
- People management.
- Conflict resolution.
- Self-organization.
- Good health, both mental and physical.
- Ability to work under pressure.
- Enthusiasm to always be learning.
- Passion for the job.
- Creativity.
- Good judgment.
- Resiliency in the eyes of failure or other hardship.
- Knowing when to trust or distrust.
- Perseverance and an ability to grind through lots of work.
- Strong integrity (however you define that).
- Positive attitude.
- Ability to disconnect.

Other Stuff You'll Want to Be a Great Lawyer

- An evolving and strong professional and personal network.
- Mentors who want to see you succeed.
- An identity outside of being a lawyer.

At this point, we are done focusing on school. Let's talk about what happens after you graduate.

7

Be a Fiduciary

You learn about being a fiduciary in law school. Depending on who teaches the subject, this term can sound boring, scary, or confusing. Law schools are poor at teaching this subject in context and it's too bad because it is essential to your role as an attorney.

Think about this: becoming a lawyer confers a unique state-granted privilege to act as a fiduciary for someone else. This is not an agent or a broker but a fiduciary. Wow. This is an honor and a privilege. It's one of the most rewarding things we do as lawyers.

Okay, so you've heard the word before. It's discussed in your corporate law and ethics classes, but often buried among other important topics. Too often it's couched in terms of someone else acting as a fiduciary, not you, and it's unfortunately included when learning about agents or brokers. There are courses on agency law, which used to be mandatory, but are now mostly optional, and still do not directly address what it means to be a fiduciary.

When you act as a fiduciary, you are in an essential position of trust for someone else and are charged with making decisions on their behalf in their, rather than your own, best interests. Yeah, it's a mouthful. Please go back and read that last sentence two more times.

Being a fiduciary is at the heart of being a lawyer. It's a vital legal and ethical relationship that's also integral to being a good CEO, board member, banker, investment advisor, partner, and just a competent person in our abstract complex world.

Ultimately, what it means to be a fiduciary is to use your specialized skills, access, and resources to act on behalf of another in their best interests, or how that person would act on their own behalf if they had your education, skills, access, or resources.

Four principles to keep in mind in your capacity as a fiduciary:

1. Know if you're acting as a fiduciary and on whose behalf.
2. Slow down.
3. Seek advice and help.
4. Always put your clients' interests ahead of your own.

Principle 1: Know If You're Acting as a Fiduciary and on Whose Behalf

When you act as an attorney for someone, you are a fiduciary. You are a service provider. Your client is the customer. But unlike the person selling you the latest iPhone at your local cellular store, you must not only treat them like a customer, you must always have their interests above your own.

On paper, this is easy, but in the real world it gets complicated quickly due to differing communication abilities, access, competing interests, and misalignments of incentives. You'll hear a lot about elements of what comprises a fiduciary duty. You may hear about duties of loyalty, care, good faith, lawful action, confidentiality, etc. Depending on what type of fiduciary you are, for example, a lawyer, board director, or trustee, some or all of these may come into play. But we don't want to overload and confuse you like law school. Let's just focus on simply being prepared and acting in the best interests of someone else.

Here are two hypotheticals to illustrate these complexities.

Example A

You're a second-year law student taking a clinic, supervised by a local attorney who is donating their time and graded by a full-time law school professor. You like both the professor and local attorney and may hit the attorney up for a job when you graduate. Your law school's clinic is currently working several complex habeas death penalty petitions at the federal appellate level. This is the number one focus during weekly clinic meetings, and the professor is recruiting all available resources to focus on these high-profile cases.

One case assigned to you is a 14-year-old juvenile in detention due to a previous gun charge, who is currently facing a car theft charge. The juvenile has a third-grade reading level and has been recently diagnosed with borderline personality disorder and ADHD, but with limited treatment options in juvenile detention. The prosecutor presents an offer and the professor encourages you to persuade the juvenile to take it and move on to the next case. The local attorney wants you to spend more time researching before coming to a decision. It's close to semester finals and you sit in your room wondering what to do.

Example B

You're a junior associate tasked with helping a senior partner on an acquisition. Your client is an internet security company looking to buy another firm in its industry. Your client was recently part of a majority purchase by a private equity firm. The private equity firm owns 55% of your client, the CEO owns 10%, and the remainder of the firm is owned by wealthy individuals and family offices with little expertise in the space.

The CEO and your senior partner are good friends, and the CEO is seeking to divest a substantial business line of the company to raise cash for this contemplated acquisition. Since your client just completed the private equity firm deal, you wonder if divesting a big part of the business is what the private equity owner would want the CEO to do. To make matters more interesting, the company the CEO wants to buy is also owned by the same private equity firm.

Perhaps you see the issues quickly, perhaps not. What you need is a framework to address and best manage the fiduciary issues before you give legal advice.

Our framework:

1. Who is the client?
2. Who is representing the client and/or giving guidance to you?
3. What conflicts of interest could this person have?
4. What conflicts of interest might you have?

Let's use our hypotheticals to work through the framework.

1. Who is the client?

In Example A, it's the juvenile. In Example B, it's the internet security company. That's obvious, but then you look to the next question.

2. Who is representing the client and/or giving guidance to you?

Unlike a simple situation where a person hires you to defend them in a lawsuit and they give you direction, these cases are a bit different. In Example A, the juvenile may not be able to give you any direction, so you are getting advice from both the local attorney and the professor. In Example B, the CEO is giving you direction. The senior partner is most likely giving you guidance as well. This leads to the next question.

3. What conflicts of interest could this person have?

In Example A there are potential conflicts with the professor trying to move work off her plate. Getting this case done leaves more resources for others. The local attorney could have a conflict depending on her relationship with the prosecutor.

In Example B, the CEO owns 10% of the company. They may or may not be aligned with the wishes of the majority owner, the private equity firm. If they are not, you have a problem. Even if they are, the private equity firm and CEO may not be aligned with the rest of the shareholders. This isn't a case where the majority of ownership is all that matters. It's what is best for your client—the company—that matters. If there was situation where the CEO and private equity firm wanted to do something in their best interests to the detriment of the rest of the shareholders, you have a real issue. Also, the senior partner and CEO are good friends, which can play into the conflict dynamics here. Okay, now let's look to the last part of the framework.

4. What conflicts of interest might you have?

In Example A, your potential conflicts are that you might want to get a job with the local attorney and, therefore, overweight the advice she gives you. You want to look good in front of her, so why not agree with her? Your other issue is that finals are right around the corner, and you need to turn your time and attention to exams. Lastly, the professor oversees your grade and why go against her advice?

Example B is the classic potential conflict of you trying to impress the senior partner and the CEO as the junior person while not paying attention to the actual client, the company. You get trapped thinking they are all one in the same. Sometimes they are. Sometimes they are not. The salient point is to recognize that you owe a fiduciary duty to the company, an abstract entity with numerous stakeholders (shareholders, officers, and employees). The CEO and PE firm speak for the company at times, but possibly against it at times, without ever letting you know there's a subtle switch. Be hypervigilant, and always consider whether there is a fiduciary duty in play.

Principle 2: Slow Down

Rarely is speedy decision-making required. Quick thinking, on the other hand, is a regular occurrence, especially for litigators. But even litigators have time to organize relevant facts, step into another's shoes, effectively analyze the situation, and reach a thoughtful decision. More formally, this is called the duty of care, and it's vital to being a fiduciary.

In today's constant communication world, texts, emails, Slacks, and Voxes encourage speed, which tends to reduce thoughtfulness. This is especially true under pressure from clients, bosses, and yourself. The concept of failure being celebrated or encouraged by some ecosystems (like startups) is not an option as a fiduciary.

While we encourage rapid learning and measured risk taking, you don't get a free pass as a fiduciary if you are moving too fast or don't take the proper care on a matter. A corollary is to not get overcommitted. We've all done this, and it often leads to shortcuts.

Don't take on a fiduciary relationship unless you can devote the necessary time to it.

Slowing down and taking time also means doing due diligence. Diligence is one of the first tasks any lawyer should do and is a valued skill no matter what your practice area may be. Suffice to say is that figuring out what you know, what you don't know, and where you need help are key aspects to understanding any decision you are going to make on behalf of someone else. Take the time to do it.

Principle 3: Seek Advice and Help

Related to slowing down and diligence is seeking advice and help. While always applicable, this is particularly important when acting as a fiduciary because our egos get in the way of seeking help, especially when it reveals inexperience. You can make disastrous career-ending mistakes by failing to seek help. Heed Principle 2, above: speed often compounds mistakes and makes it more unlikely to seek appropriate advice and help. Take time to seek necessary advice, which in a firm setting is free (even if you have to pay for it, it's worth every penny). If not in a large firm, reach out to your local bar association and your personal network. Maintain connections with your professors in your relevant area. At least Google it, okay? But also don't forget to listen to your stomach that you are in over your head and take action to correct it.

Principle 4: Always Put Your Clients' Interests Ahead of Your Own

This is the single most important principle and solves most fiduciary problems if faithfully implemented. Step into your client's shoes, examine every angle of the situation from their perspective, and determine what is best for her or him. Like Principle 3, this involves checking your ego; like Principle 2, it requires devoting time to the relationship. While acting as a fiduciary, continually ask this question: What would I want an expert to do for me if I was the client? Or put another way, use absolute tunnel vision to analyze what is best for your client. Forget about everything else. Now open up the aperture and ask if anything makes you feel uncomfortable about that vision given the exogenous pressures you have around you. And don't forget that simply the appearance of you acting on your own best interests will likely sink a career or a relationship. Give everything the "smell test."

While we've tried to teach you a bit about being a fiduciary, remember that not all situations involving clients mean you are a fiduciary. The biggest instance is negotiations around billing arrangements and fees. In this instance, you have no duty to the client (absent of bar ethics considerations) and are free to put your interests first.

In addition, do not fall into the trap that you owe a duty to opposing counsel. Many junior lawyers get lulled into a state where they want to please the other side or not upset them. These conflict-avoidant attorneys need to remind themselves where their real duty rests. It still surprises us how many lawyers fall into this group.

Finally, be careful who you become friends with. Again, perceptions matter. If you are a criminal defense attorney who regularly golfs with an assistant district attorney, realize that this perception may not be appreciated by your clients. Yes, you can claim that a good working relationship is important, but consider optics and how that might be perceived as a potential conflict.

CHAPTER 8

A Short Primer on Negotiations

Neither law schools nor any state laws mandate any sort of practical experience as part of the law school curriculum. What's up with that? Further, it pains us that law schools don't mandate a class on negotiations. Seriously? Is there a lawyer (or a person, really) on Earth who doesn't negotiate on some level? If nothing else, taking a course on negotiations will make life easier if you have a child or a poodle someday. We've already begged you to take this class—just do it!

It will only be to your benefit should you decide to load up on simulation experiences like mock trial or negotiations. Take practical clinics and get a start on representing actual civil clients. Do anything you can to practice before you practice. Better to learn to shave on your own face before you take the razor to your employer's, or worse, your client's. Our view is that people don't regret it in the future. Employers, knowing the gap we are trying to partially solve in this book, don't really care what classes you take because they know you probably didn't learn anything immediately useful. So— take something useful.

Back to negotiations. It is indefensible that law schools do not make this a core class taught by their best professors. You will negotiate something every day of life, whether at work or on the used car lot in attempts to secure that low-mileage and clean Subaru Outback. Below are our thoughts on negotiations. A bit of this is plagiarized from Jason's book *Venture Deals: How to Be Smarter Than Your Lawyer and Venture Capitalist*, but Wiley is the publisher of both books so let's do that.

If you had a great negotiations class, then this chapter serves as a good summary and place for you to learn some new tricks. If you weren't so lucky, then consider this your *Cliff Notes* version of what we wish we had known a long time ago. What follows is about finding a job, and we can guarantee that a job interview is as much of a negotiation as anything else.

Negotiation Tactics

Keep in mind that no matter how smart you are and how much experience or knowledge you have, you must be able to negotiate. It's one thing to be clever or think you are right. It's another to convince someone else to agree with you. No matter what area of the law you go into, you will find yourself negotiating. Despite what we see in movies, most negotiations are between parties wanting to resolve an issue together and come to an agreement. Yes, there are plenty of winner-take-all situations in litigation, but the majority of negotiations involve two parties trying to work together for both to be better off.

There are plenty of treatises on negotiations; however, this chapter walks through negotiation tactics that have worked well for us over the years. We go through a range of negotiation tactics to use in your life, and we illustrate some of the different types of characters you'll meet along the way.

What Really Matters?

Let's assume a situation where you represent party X. Party Y is represented by an attorney as well. Before you begin any negotiation, ask yourself these questions:

1. Will the parties have an ongoing relationship? In other words, is this negotiation the beginning of a relationship that the parties are trying to formalize?
2. Is this negotiation a one-time situation where each party will go its separate way (i.e., litigation, divorce, or even a company acquisition)?
3. Does reputation matter to the parties or lawyers involved?

If the answer to question 1 is yes, then consider the negotiating style most appropriate. Is a scorched-earth approach where you win every point and drive up legal fees on both sides the best idea? No, it's not and you'll damage your reputation in the process. In the worst situations, we've seen deals fall apart simply from bad attorney behavior. There is an old saying, "You never make money on terms." This can be particularly true in venture financings. If the company at issue turns out to be the next Google, then it's largely irrelevant what the deal documents say. Everyone gets rich. And if it's Theranos, it's the same story on the other end of the spectrum. Everyone loses their investment.

If you answer no to question 1 and yes to question 2, then you no longer care about party X and party Y getting along afterward. You have more latitude to torture the opposing attorney, so long as your client is willing to pay for it and it's legally ethical.

Lastly, know what you agreed to. It sounds obvious, but it's amazing how many lawyers think they negotiated for A, the other side thinks it is B, and the clients want C. Remember, humans are bad witnesses. Check out the early 1990s courtroom classic *My Cousin Vinny* if you don't believe us.

Bottom line: Pay close attention at all points during a negotiation.

Preparing for the Negotiation

The single biggest mistake people make during negotiation is a lack of preparation. It's incredible that people will walk blindly into a negotiation when so much is on the line. Failing to prepare is preparing to fail.

Some lawyers fail to prepare because they feel they don't know what they should prepare for. We'll give you some ideas but realize you probably know how to negotiate better than you think. You already negotiate many times a day during your interactions in life, but most people just do it and don't think too hard about it. If you have a spouse, child, auto mechanic, domesticated animal, or any friends, chances are that you have dozens of negotiations every day.

When you engage in negotiations, have a plan. Have key things that you want, understand which terms you are willing to concede, and know when you are willing to walk away. If you try to determine this during the negotiation, your emotions are likely to get the best of you and you'll make mistakes. Always have a plan.

Next, spend some time beforehand getting to know with whom you are dealing. Some people are so easy to find that you can perform a simple Google search and instantly know everything about them. For instance, Jason, in his past life as a venture capitalist, kept a blog, tweeted a lot, and wrote a book. He was very vocal about the stupidity of negotiating certain terms, as they are just a waste of a startup's money. If you were going to engage Jason, 10 seconds spent on a Google search would have told you exactly what he thought. You don't have to agree with him, of course, but when you send him a markup of his term sheet nitpicking it to death, he immediately looks down upon you. And after the venture financing is completed and he is on the board of the company, the first thing he does is start to look for a new attorney for the company.

If you learn about and get to know the other side ahead of time, you might also be able to play to their strengths, weaknesses, biases, curiosities, and insecurities. *Scientia potentia* est (translation: knowledge is power). Granted, you don't have to take advantage of your knowledge and gain the upper hand, but wouldn't it be great to have a ripcord to pull if things get hairy? As you learn more about the other side, try to imagine what they are doing to prepare for the negotiation. What motivates them? What are their incentives? What are their insecurities? Have multiple theories about the other side's point of view and be prepared to act on any in real time.

Remember: everyone has an advantage over everyone else in all negotiations. Goliath appeared to be an immovable and unstoppable force unwilling to negotiate, but David knew a few things the big man didn't. Life is the same way. Figure out your superpower and your adversary's kryptonite.

If you are a first-year associate negotiating a term sheet against a 40-something, well-weathered, and experienced lawyer, what possible advantage could you have? The veteran lawyer clearly understands the terms better. She also has a ton of market knowledge. Sounds pretty bleak, right?

Well, yes, but don't despair. There is one immediate advantage you probably have: time. If we generalize, it's easy to come up with a scenario in which the other lawyer has a family, lots of other clients, and a slew of obligations that seep into life as you age. In fact, you found her Facebook page and you confirmed it. You, on the other hand, likely have one singular focus: this client and this negotiation.

You can afford to make the process a longer one than the other lawyer might want. In fact, most experienced lawyers really hate this part of the process and will bend on terms to aid efficiency, although some won't and will nitpick every point.

Perhaps you'll want to set up your negotiation call at the end of the day, right before the lawyer's family dinner. Or maybe you'll sweetly ask the other lawyer to explain a host of terms that you "don't understand" and further put burdens on their time. Think this doesn't happen? One day Jason was mentoring a bunch of entrepreneurs and teaching them these tactics. A few months later, Jason's venture firm sent a term sheet to invest in one of the entrepreneurs. Of course, the CEO waited until two hours before Jason left on vacation to negotiate the term sheet. Jason failed to recognize this as their strategy and figured it was bad luck with timing. As a result, he faced time pressure that was artificially manufactured by a 20-something first-time entrepreneur.

There are advantages everywhere. Is the other side a huge UCLA fan? Chat her up and find out if she has courtside seats to the game. Are they into a charity that you care about? Use this information to connect with her so she becomes more sympathetic to you. While simple things like this are endless, what matters is that you have a plan, know the other side, and consider what natural advantages you have. In a perfect world, you won't have to use any of these tools, but if you need them and don't bring them to the actual negotiation, it's your loss.

A Brief Introduction to Game Theory

Everyone has a natural negotiating style. These styles have analogues that can either work well or poorly in trying to achieve a negotiated result. It's important to understand how certain styles work well together, how some conflict, and how some have inherent advantages over one another.

Before we delve into that, let's spend a little time on basic game theory. *Game theory* is a mathematical theory that deals with strategies for maximizing gains and minimizing losses within prescribed constraints, such as the rules of a card game. Game theory is widely applied in the solution of various decision-making problems, such as those of military strategy and business policy.

Game theory states that there are rules underlying situations that affect how these situations will be played out. These rules are independent of the humans involved and will predict and change how humans interact within the constructs of the situation. Knowing what these invisible rules are is of major importance when entering into any type of negotiation.

The most famous of all games is the prisoner's dilemma, which you've seen many times if you've ever watched a cop show on television. The simple form, as described in the Stanford Encyclopedia of Philosophy, follows:

> *Tanya and Cinque have been arrested for robbing the Hibernia Savings Bank and placed in separate isolation cells. Both care much more about their personal freedom than about the welfare of their accomplice. A clever prosecutor makes the following offer to each. "You may choose to confess or remain silent. If you confess and your accomplice remains silent, I will drop all charges against you and use your testimony to ensure that your accomplice does serious time. Likewise, if your accomplice confesses while you remain silent, they will go free while you do the time. If you both confess, I get two convictions, but I'll see to it that you both get early parole. If you both remain silent, I'll have to settle for token sentences on firearms possession charges. If you wish to confess, you must leave a note with the jailer before my return tomorrow morning."[1]*

The classic prisoner's dilemma can be summarized as shown in the following table.

Classic Prisoner's Dilemma

	Prisoner B Stays Silent	Prisoner B Betrays
Prisoner A Stays Silent	Each serves 8 months	Prisoner A: 12 years Prisoner B: goes free
Prisoner A Betrays	Prisoner A: goes free Prisoner B: 12 years	Each serves 5 years

What's fascinating about this is that there is a fundamental rule in this game that demonstrates why two people might not cooperate with one another, even if it is clearly in their best interests to do so.

If the two prisoners cooperate, the outcome is best, in the aggregate, for both. They each get eight months of jail time and walk away.

---

[1] See: http://plato.stanford.edu/entries/prisoner-dilemma/.

But the game forces different behavior. Regardless of what the co-conspirator chooses (silence versus betrayal), each player always receives a lighter sentence by betraying the other. In other words, no matter what the other guy does, you are always better off by ratting him out.

The other rule to this game is that it is a *single-play game*. The participants play the game once and their fate is cast. Other games are *multiplay games*. For instance, there is a lot of interesting game theory about battlegrounds. If you are in one trench fighting and we are in another, game theory would suggest that we would not fight at night, on weekends, on holidays, and during meals. Why not? It would seem logical that if we know you are sleeping, it's the absolute best time to attack.

Well, it's not, unless we can completely take you out with one strike. Otherwise, you'll most likely start attacking *us* during dinner, on holidays, or while we are watching *Billions*. And then not only are we still fighting, but now we've both lost our free time. This tit-for-tat strategy is what keeps multiplay games at equilibrium. If you don't mess with us during our lunch break, we won't mess with you during yours. And everyone is better off. But if you do mess with us, we'll continue to mess with you until you are nice to us again.

When you are considering which game you are playing, consider not only whether there are forces at work that influence the decisions being made, like the prisoner's dilemma, but also how many times a decision will be made. Is this a one-shot deal? Or will this game repeat itself, lending increased importance to precedent and reputation?

Negotiating Win-Win Agreements

Situations where everybody can be better off is one of the easiest games there is. Yes, dear lawyer friend, despite what law schools teach you, sometimes people cooperate, get along, and everyone is happy and better off! Also, you don't negotiate in a vacuum like your hypothetical fellow criminal co-conspirator. Finally, and most important, this is not a single-instance game. Therefore, reputation and the fear of tit-for-tat retaliation are real considerations.

Let's take the context where two parties are setting up a business relationship. Since they will need to spend a lot of time together post investment, the continued relationship makes it important to look at the financing as just one negotiation in a very long, multiplay game. Doing anything that would give the other party an incentive to retaliate in the future is not a wise, or rational, move.

Further, this deal is but one of many you hope to complete as a lawyer. Therefore, you should be thinking about reputational factors that extend well beyond this particular interaction. Having a negative reputation is trouble in the long run.

Not all lawyers recognize that each negotiation isn't a single-round, winner-take-all game. The more experience lawyers have, the better their perspective is, but this lack of a longer-term view is not limited to junior lawyers. When we run across people like this, at a minimum we lose a lot of respect for them and occasionally decide not to do business with them.

Negotiating Other Games

Not all games are win-win. There are many different types of games, but two others make interesting counterpoints to the financing game. Let's start with the polar opposite of the win-win game. The winner-take-all game is the classic high-stakes litigation situation. You are being sued by a patent troll or have some type of "bet-the-company" situation. In this game, reputations matter little, and results are all that count. You should prepare yourself for what will be an emotionally taxing, time draining, long and drawn-out battle. Don't assume that the other side will have the same moral code that you do, as lying generally isn't illegal except under oath. Even then, we've all seen people lie in a courtroom deposition. These cases usually involve lawyers becoming that attack dog that you envision in the movies. This is not fun. But beware, don't bring a knife to a gun fight.

The second case is where you have an extremely adversarial situation, but reputations still matter. The classic version of this is when a company founder is fired. There will be plenty of hard feelings and lots of emotions. However, as ugly as it may get at times, this isn't a winner-take-all scenario. Both the company and the departed founder have mutual interests in that they both want their reputations to survive intact and it's highly likely that the departed founder will keep some equity in the company. Therefore, the game constrains behavior to some extent. While not everyone needs to be friends post financing, civility will hopefully win out. In these cases, we normally see lawyers engage with respect, but firmness on their positions.

As we close out our thoughts on game theory, remember, you can't change the game you are in, but you can judge people who play poorly within it. And having a game theory lens to view the other side is very useful.

Negotiating Styles and Approaches

Every person has a natural negotiating style that is often the part of their personality that they adopt when they are dealing with conflict. Age, race, gender, upbringing, mood on a particular day, the relationship you have with your significant other and kids, the relationship you had with you parents and siblings, and many other things play into how you negotiate. Remember, you started negotiating as soon as you were born, and all of these experiences have made you who you are.

There is new research showing that gender can have a large effect on negotiations. Harvard Business School reports that women don't negotiate their job offers like men for fear that the reputation damage they will face upon starting their new job will be much higher than if they were men. There is also data that seems to suggest that men are more comfortable with men who negotiate hard versus women and thus there can be socials costs for women who negotiate.[2]

We hope that by being as transparent as we can in this book about the terms, the issues, and the ways to negotiate, that we can break down some of these barriers. We'd encourage everyone to take an inward look at themselves before they engage with the other side, regardless of who they are, and make sure your biases aren't negatively impacting your approach to a negotiation.

As with anything, few people are great at several things. In the world of negotiations this means that most people don't have truly different modes for negotiation, but that doesn't mean you can't practice having a range of different behaviors that depend on the situation you are in.

Most good negotiators know where they are comfortable, but also know how to play upon and against other people's natural styles.

---

[2] https://hbr.org/2014/06/why-women-dont-negotiate-their-job-offers

Following are some, but not all, of the personalities you'll meet and how you might want to best work with them.

The Bully (aka UAW Negotiator)

The Bully negotiates by yelling and screaming, forcing issues, and threatening the other party. Most folks who are bullies aren't that smart and don't really understand the issues; rather, they try to win by force. There are two ways to deal with bullies: punch them in the nose or mellow out so much that you sap their strength. If you can out bully The Bully, go for it. But if you are wrong, then you've ignited a volcano. Unlike the children's playground, getting hit by The Bully during a negotiation generally doesn't hurt; so unless this is your natural negotiating style, our advice is to chill out as your adversary gets hotter.

The Nice Guy (aka Used-Car Salesman)

Whenever you interact with this pleasant person, you feel like they are trying to sell you something. Often, you aren't sure that you want what they are selling. When you say no, The Nice Guy will either be openly disappointed or will keep on smiling at you just like the audience at a Tony Robbins event. In their world, life is great as long as you acquiesce to their terms (or buy this one-owner 2017 Kia Sorento). As the negotiation unfolds, The Nice Guy is increasingly hard to pin down on anything. While the car salesman always needs to go talk to their manager, The Nice Guy negotiator regularly responds with, "Let me consider that and get back to you." While The Nice Guy doesn't yell at you like The Bully, it's often frustrating that you can never get a real answer or seemingly make progress. Our advice is to be clear and direct and don't get worn down, as The Nice Guy will happily talk to you all day. If all else fails, don't be afraid to toss a little bully into the mix on your side to move things forward.

The Technocrat (aka Pocket Protector Person)

This is the technical nerd. Although they won't yell at you like The Bully and you never wonder if there is a real human behind the facade like you do with The Nice Guy, you will feel like you are in endless detail hell. The Technocrat has a billion issues and has a hard time deciding what's actually important, since to them everything is important for some reason! Our advice is to grin and bear it and perhaps play Fortnight while you are listening to the other side drag on. The Technocrat tends to cause you to lose your focus during the negotiation. Make sure you don't take your eye off the ball by remembering what you care about and conceding the other points. But make sure you cover all the points together, as The Technocrat will often negotiate every point from scratch, not taking into consideration the give-and-take of each side during the negotiation. Sometimes this role is simply that: a role. Many folks have endless energy for this stuff and will use this tactic to simply tire you out. If you watch *What We Do in the Shadows*, this is Colin Robinson. If you don't want that show, do yourself and favor watch it.

The Wimp (aka George McFly)

The Wimp may sound like the perfect dance partner here, but they have their own issues. Our bet is that you can take their wallet pretty easily during the negotiation, but if you get too good a deal, it will come back to haunt you. And then you get to live with them on your board of directors once you close your financing. With The Wimp, you end up negotiating both sides of the deal. Sometimes this is harder than having a real adversary.

The Curmudgeon (aka Archie Bunker)

With The Curmudgeon, everything you negotiate sucks. No matter what you arrive at is horrible, and every step along the way during the negotiation will feel like a dentist tugging on a tight molar at the back of your mouth. Unlike The Bully, The Curmudgeon won't yell; and unlike The Nice Guy, they will never be happy. While it'll seem like they don't care too much about the details, they are just never happy with any position you are taking. The Curmudgeon is also not The Wimp. They've been around the block before and will remind you of that every chance they get. In a lot of ways, The Curmudgeon is like a cranky grandparent. If you are patient, upbeat, and tolerant, you'll eventually get what you want, but you'll never really please them because everyone (and everything) pisses them off.

Smooth, Steady, and Smart (aka Dianne Lockhart from The Good Wife)

The last of the personalities is the person who really has it all. This person can shape-shift into one or more of the personas above but has a natural calm brilliance that makes for a strong adversary. Smooth, Steady, and Smart spends the right amount of time preparing, knows all the points at play, and has done their homework on you. They are so confident of their work product that they ooze a legitimate calm like they are walking in a park. If you've done your homework, the two of you probably will engender immediate respect and sometimes even trust. This is the best of all worlds and truly leads to a win-win outcome. On the other hand, if you haven't done your homework, Smooth, Steady, and Smart will steamroll you while making you feel good about it. Later on that evening, you will feel differently as you commiserate with yourself over your favorite adult beverage.

Wait. What about Someone Who Is Actually Normal?

What about the normal person? You know, the transparent, nice, smart, levelheaded person you hope to meet on the other side of the table? Though they exist, everyone has some inherent styles that will find their way into the negotiation, especially if pressed or negotiations aren't going well. Make sure you know which styles you have so you won't surprise yourself with a sudden outburst. You'll also see a lot of these behaviors come out real-time in board meetings when things aren't going quite as well as hoped.

If you are capable of having multiple negotiating personalities, which should you favor? We'd argue that in a negotiation that has reputational and relationship value, try to be the most transparent and easygoing you can be. Let the other person inside your thinking and get to know you for who you really are. If you are playing a single-round game, like an acquisition negotiation with a party you don't ever expect to do business with again, do like Al Davis said: "Just win, baby." As in sports, don't ever forget that a good tactic is to change your game plan suddenly to keep the other side on their toes.

Collaborative Negotiation Versus Walk-Away Threats

Of all the questions people ask about negotiations, the most common is when to walk away from a deal. Most people's blood pressure ticks up a few points with the thought of walking away, especially after you've invested a lot of time and energy (especially emotional energy) in a negotiation. In considering whether to walk away from a negotiation, preparation is key here. Know what your walk-away point is *before* starting the negotiation so it's a rational and deliberate decision rather than an emotional one made in the heat of the moment.

When determining your walk-away position, consider your *best alternative to negotiated agreement,* also known as BATNA. Specifically, what is your backup plan if you aren't successful reaching an agreement? The answer to this varies wildly depending on the circumstances. Understanding BATNA is important in any negotiation, such as an acquisition (walk away as a standalone company), litigation (settle versus go to court), and customer contract (walk away rather than get stuck in a bad deal).

Before you begin any negotiation, make sure you know where your overall limits are, as well as your limits on each key point. If you've thought this through in advance, you'll know when someone is trying to move you past one of these boundaries. It's also usually obvious when someone tries to pretend they are at a boundary when they really aren't. Few people are able to feign true conviction.

At some point in a negotiation, you'll find yourself up against the wall or being pushed into a zone beyond where you are willing to go. In this situation, tell the other party there is no deal, and walk away. As you walk away, be very clear with what your walk-away point is so the other party will be able to reconsider their position. If you are sincere in walking away and the other party is interested enough in a deal, they'll be back at the table and will offer you something you can stomach. If they don't reengage, the deal wasn't meant to be.

Finally, don't ever make a threat during a negotiation that you aren't willing to back up. If you bluff and don't back up your position, your bargaining position is forever lost in this negotiation. The seventeenth time we hear "and that's our final offer," we know that there's another, better offer coming if we just hold out for number 18.

Building Leverage and Getting to Yes

Besides understanding the issues and knowing how to deal with the other party, there are certain things you can do to increase your negotiation leverage. Perhaps you decide to anchor on a set of terms? Anchoring means to pick a few points, state clearly what you want, and then stick to your guns. If you anchor on positions that are reasonable while still having a little flexibility to give in the negotiation, you will get close to what you want as long as you are willing to trade away other points that aren't as important to you.

As with any type of negotiation, it helps to feed the ego of your partner. Figure out what the other side wants to hear and try to please them. People tend to reciprocate niceties. For example, if you are dealing with The Technocrat, engage them in depth on some of the deal points, even if the points don't matter to you, in order to make them happy and help them feel like you are playing their game.

When you are leading the negotiation, we highly recommend you have a strategy about the order in which you will address the points. Let's assume you have a document that you and opposing counsel are looking at. Maybe it's an outline of a settlement agreement. Your options are to address them either in the order that they are laid out in the document or in some other random order of your choosing. In general, once you are a skilled negotiator, going in order is more effective, as you won't reveal which points matter most to you. Often, experienced negotiators will try to get agreement on a point-by-point basis to prevent the other party from looking holistically at the process and determining whether a fair deal is being achieved. This strategy really works only if you have a lot of experience, and it can really backfire on you if the other party is more experienced and takes control of the discussion. Instead of being on the giving end of a divide-and-conquer strategy, you'll be on the receiving end of death by a thousand cuts.

Unless you are a very experienced negotiator, we suggest an order where you start with some important points that you think you can get to yes quickly. This way, both parties will feel good that they are making progress toward a deal. Then dive into the minutiae.

All of these tactics and theories assume that you are negotiating with a rational actor, one who does what is in their own (or their client's) best interests. An irrational actor (think toddler or those who act like them) will not offer an expected response to given inputs. In these cases, our strong opinion is to become an expert at empathy, much like you would negotiate with your three-year-old to go to sleep.

With our negotiation skills in hand, let's go find a job.

CHAPTER

Preparing for the Job Hunt

This book is not about finding a job after law school. This book is about becoming a great lawyer. That being said, we empathize with anyone trying to find a first job after law school. Well, maybe not everyone. For those of you at a top-10 law school who finish top of class, we have less empathy, but we have a ton of respect for what you did.

We know a thing or two about not only getting that first job but, more importantly, hiring people for that job. We've also talked to our colleagues to get their feedback as well. Here are some helpful tips on going from a student in law school to a lawyer with gainful employment.

You on Paper

Okay, paper may be out, but ensure your resume, cover letter and LinkedIn profile portray the version of you that employers will find most attractive. And you must have both a resume and a LinkedIn page. Many employers only care about your LinkedIn profile, so don't think you can get away without one.

As for resumes, it must be perfectly written with no mistakes. One typo is usually enough for disqualification. Use active verbs to describe your experiences and that all bullet points start with an active verb. We've seen people lose jobs simply because their bullet points start with different parts of speech. Your resume should focus on work experience, anything you've done creatively, and anything you've done to make your community a better place. The resume must also give the reader some idea of who you are outside of being a lawyer. What interests do you have? What hobbies to you have? Remember you are applying for a job to work side-by-side with these people. You'll spend more time at work than outside of it, so showing that you are fun and interesting are important, but you still need to remind potential employers know you are serious, too. It's a balance, so pay attention to it.

Cover letters are where you can "let your hair down a little" and show personality. It's also an opportunity to show what kind of emailer you will be and how clear you communicate. Your cover letters must be tailored to the particular employer instead of recycling the same verbiage for each role. Why are you a good fit for this position? We have noticed that fewer cover letters are getting passed along internally at companies, so make sure your resume stands on its own just in case.

Consider paying a few bucks to have a professional designer take your content and make it pop. When one is reviewing tens to hundreds of resumes, it really stands out having a resume that just looks different than the boring standard format. We've seen folks have great luck with designers on 99designs.com. If you don't want to pay, that's cool, too. Try out Canva.com, which has some really nice templates and it's free.

Specifically to LinkedIn, don't be the 85% of people applying who crop some selfie they took standing next to their dog or significant other in front of some outdoor scene. Do not wear sunglasses. Get a friend to take your phone and take your picture. Put on some casual, yet professional clothes and look directly into the camera. Your goal is to show an employer that you are nice, smart, and don't have four heads and two horns. Smile as you like or show a little grin—whatever feels natural to you. Or, think about smiling while listening. As they say, a picture is worth a thousand words. Take this seriously.

Social Media

We'll remind you later, but social media is discoverable by any potential employer. They probably won't look at it unless you get past the resume and LinkedIn stage, but it must portray the version of you that is employable.

Telling the Story

Assuming you get through the resume stage, you'll get an interview. Remember that you are selling yourself—clearly articulate your story as to why you are a great hire for this opportunity. The number one mistake is when the interviewee doesn't do enough research on the person, company, or firm they are talking to and look stupid. If you won't do great research on the person you are speaking to, how do they trust you to do the same on behalf of their clients?

We highly recommend you conduct practice interviews with a classmate. Try to throw each other off. Ask the hard questions you don't want to answer. You think this is weird? Even the most seasoned trial lawyers do this before opening and closing summations. You aren't too good for it and while potentially embarrassing, it's better than screwing up the real interview and feeling worse.

Follow up on an interview with a thank you note or email. Handwritten if you want to make a big impact and differentiate yourself. Cite something specific from the interview that you found interesting or helpful.

Networking into Employers

If you have a network, use it to get this job. In fact, we'd exhaust all options. Your first job will have a big impact on the rest of your career, whereas your choice of law school will have almost none as you ascend the ranks to becoming a more experienced attorney. We'll dive deep into law school rankings in Chapter 18.

What if you don't have a good network? What if you go online, find the perfect job, and you have no connections to the employer? Then go out, be aggressive, and go for it. But be different. Don't just send the resume and cover letter. Send something else of value to the person who will take time to evaluate your communication. If it is a particular lawyer at firm, then research them. Find out what they like. Music? Include a QR code for a Spotify or Apple playlist you made. They are into food, sports, whatever? Send them *something* that shows you did your due diligence and you are a giving person. Give to them before you ask them for something. Even if you don't know exactly what to give them, the thought counts. Besides, who doesn't want a QR code for new music? Only psychopaths. And you don't want to work with them anyways.

If you are sending something to a generic email account, you can still give that person something. Maybe you've researched the area and know of a good restaurant recommendation. Or take a short video of yourself being confident and appreciative of the opportunity for this person to review your materials. Whatever you do, just don't do what everyone else is doing or you'll get the same result, which many times is not the result you are looking for.

Mindset

Speaking of being aggressive, you must have a success mindset when looking for a job. Your mindset must be that you will not fail. "Do. Or do not. There is no try." (Thanks Yoda.) This may sound like BS, but it's not. Employers will get the vibe emanating whether you have this mindset or not. It's totally okay to be insecure and fake it a bit, but try as best as you can to convince yourself as well. Jason learned this the hard way when trying to raise his first fund as a venture capitalist. He failed to raise money when he first tried. He succeeded when his mindset changed to that being the only outcome.

Career Placement Services

Each law school has its own center. Some are good. Some are bad. Some are overwhelmed. All of them struggle with which students to help the most and which to put on the back burner. Don't for a second think that everyone is treated equally. This doesn't make them bad people, rather it makes them human.

Use this to your advantage. Network into career service before you need them and it will feel less transactional to them. Get to know them early in your career, ask them for advice and maybe buy them some coffee or pastries one morning. That's the thing with career placement: no one wants to talk to them until they need something. Imagine being on the other end of the table and treat them how you'd want to be treated.

All right, let's assume you got the job. Next up, let's talk about everyone's favorite subject: the bar exam.

10

The Bar Exam

Don't fail it.

Whether you have a job at the time of the exam or not: pass it.

Seriously. If you fail it, your best-case scenario is feeling and looking terrible. Maybe you pass it the second time, but it takes you six months to recover and it's hell getting there.

Worst case is that you lose your job.

Finishing law school is a tremendous accomplishment. If you aren't tired at the end of it, maybe you didn't try hard enough or you are just as lot smarter than us. (It's a low bar. We know.)

Don't take the foot off the gas, join a rock band and start relaxing like Jason did. He almost didn't pass the bar exam according to his practice tests.

Alex was in a must-pass situation clerking for the Wisconsin Supreme Court. Of the 12 clerks on the court that year, only Alex and one other clerk had to take the Wisconsin Bar, having attended out-of-state law schools, so failure would have been very public. Plus, he had a kid on the way. Had to pass. And he did. Be like Alex.

Push yourself to pass the test. Take whatever bar review class is relevant. Then take some time off before work to recuperate.

Obviously, each state has a different hurdle for passing, but states like California and New York have really hard tests. Jason still has nightmares of showing up late to the California bar exam.

That is all. Wait? Didn't think a book could have a chapter this short? Think again. We didn't want this message to get lost in the weeds.

Again: don't fail the bar exam. Please.

(P.S. Statistically speaking, some of you will fail the bar exam. If you do, mourn for a short period of time, figure out what went wrong, and pass it on the second attempt. Also consider what state you are taking it in. Maybe there is an easier state?)

11

You Got the Job—There Is No Time for Rest

Hopefully you've been taking good care of your mental and physical self, because the good news is that you got the job you wanted. You also passed the bar exam. The bad news is that the hard work has just begun. One thing to keep in mind is that you ideally want to start your first job in the best shape of your life. Whatever you choose to do will be challenging and you'll need the best version of yourself going into the job.

In the next four chapters we will go deep into strategies that we think you should consider, actions that will likely damage your prospects at your employer, a section about dealing with different types of personalities, and, finally, some advice about technology proficiency for lawyers.

Whereas most of the early parts of this books talked about concepts, this next part of the book will focus on tangible things you can do (or not) that will greatly impact your job and career.

CHAPTER

12

The Fourteen Commandments for New Lawyers (Okay, How about "Strong Suggestions"?)

Okay you got the job. Yay! It's day one, however, and you are rightfully nervous. You wish you had a little cheat sheet like you used to ace your exams and take the bar exam. Well, we've got you covered. Here are our 14 ~~commandments~~ suggestions for starting out in the world of attorneydom. Consider these to be 14 active things to bridge the divide we talk about.

We must send a special thank you to Professor J. Brad Bernthal at the University of Colorado Law School for some of the thought leadership in this chapter. Brad and Jason taught a highly successful class together at the law school for over a decade and Jason misses those days greatly. Without further ado and drum roll please. . .

1: Have a Learning Mindset

The minute you start your job, no matter how much your employer invests in training you, it's not sufficient. *You* are responsible for your education, not them. You'll see in the guest chapters that each author talks about a book or two that were impactful to them as attorneys. Reading is power. The internet is awesome. Use it. You are there to learn and everyone knows it. In case you are curious, here are Alex and Jason's most suggested books to read as you are starting out.

Alex: *The Hard Thing About Hard Things* by Ben Horowitz.

Why: Early in your career, you will find you are managing people de facto. Perhaps it's a legal secretary, assistant, or paralegal. Maybe you start your own firm. Learn the keys to managing in the context of a small business startup, which most lawyers never do and so law firms are often awful. Plus, from this book you will learn many challenges your clients face and be better positioned to empathize and advise.

Jason: *The Entrepreneur's Guide to Law and Strategy* by Constance E. Bagley and Craig E. Dauchy.

Why: It's the *Cliff Notes* to almost every area of law that matters to entrepreneurs with simple and accurate descriptions. If it matters to entrepreneurs (clients), it should matter to you. If you are going into business law, it's a must-read. And yeah, we know it's expensive. It's worth every dollar. Jason says this is the biggest hack of all time to get ahead for business attorneys.

More than just reading books, however, your mindset really matters. You should crave, not tolerate, constructive criticism. You should own and remedy your mistakes. You will make plenty of errors. It's okay. It's part of the process. Lastly, while you are taking feedback, owning mistakes, and fixing them, remember not to lose confidence. You must always keep that "shooters confidence" that no matter how bad things are going, you keep shooting. Think about Michael Jordan or Steph Curry in basketball. They always assume the next shot is going in the bucket.

2: Rely On but Mistrust Forms

Lawyers rely on forms all the time. One, it saves time and two, it saves their clients' money. Why reinvent the wheel every time? So, clearly you want to use forms when possible. Models and precedent are indispensable.

But there is a "but" coming. How do you know your form is a good one? Even if it is from your employer, it may have mistakes in it. Or parts of it may not pertain to your client's situation. Using a form can make you look smart, or bad. In the worst cases, it makes you look lazy and stupid. The number of times we've seen lawyers use forms incorrectly makes our heads spin and we've made sure never to use those attorneys again. This is a one strike and you're out rule.

So, while lawyers use forms all the time, have a baseline mistrust of all of them and even more doubt as a junior lawyer, especially the first time you use a form. If you don't know what every paragraph in a form means and how it applies to your particular situation, do not use the form. Find a resource to explain what that form is trying to do. Find a senior associate, mentor, Google result, or anything to teach you what is going on before you commit a large legal sin.

3: Beware of the Foggy Project Trap

You are standing in the office of a partner who gives you a project. You listen intently, ask questions, and show some empathy toward the situation. You walk out of the office and the "fog" starts immediately. "What the heck am I supposed to do?" You are completely confused about what the project is and are at a loss about what to do next.

First of all, recognize there are two ways the brain fog starts: the first is that you are inexperienced, and you just don't have the background to parse everything being thrown at you. The second is that the person giving you the instructions isn't doing a good job. Maybe they are too busy and don't give you clear instructions. Maybe they assume you can read their mind. Or maybe they don't actually understand the project that well, or they'd do it themselves!

Three suggestions for when such a fog rolls in: (i) calm down as much as you can, (ii) research what you can to get as smart as you can quickly, and (iii) revert back to the project giver and try again. Don't get hung up thinking you have to figure out the whole thing yourself; rather, get up to speed on what you can and then reengage.

Also, be healthily skeptical of any prior work previously conducted on the project. Don't take anything for granted and review and assure yourself that prior work looks like quality work.

4: Never Consider Anything That Goes to a Senior Colleague or Client to Be a "Draft"

You will be judged on everything you send to senior lawyers and clients. When one of them says, "Hey, send me a draft of X in two days," they don't actually mean they want a draft. They want the complete document. Mistakes, omissions, and bracketed items are not looked upon well, unless they are business points that you have no way of knowing. If you must use brackets on a legal issue, put in all reasonable options so that it is easy for the reviewer to quickly pick one and move on. Take pride in everything you send to someone who could positively or negatively affect your career.

Looked upon another way, approach each assignment as a sole practitioner, with no one to review or criticize or correct your work. Assume the client will rely on this. Just because it's marked "Draft" does not give you the latitude to turn in crappy work. Don't make any senior person read anything you don't consider totally done, otherwise you are wasting their time. Only turn in things that are 100% done.

5: Be More Organized Than Others

This is seemingly an easy one. It just takes a little time, effort, and brute force, but rarely do junior attorneys take this attitude and it costs them. Organization can make you look much more experienced and smarter than you are currently.

When you take on a project, make sure to ask questions to define scope, schedule, and budget. As you will be working on multiple projects at the same time, if you know these three things about each of them, you'll be better at budgeting your time and meeting deadlines. Always ask questions to ascertain each at the outset.

You should also invest in models, research, and creating your own forms. As we spoke earlier about being responsible for your own education, having models (for instance a spreadsheet that calculates share price in a financing) or having your own forms and research at hand can make you much more efficient. Few people do this, of course, because it takes time up front, but for the few of you who do, it will separate you from the rest.

Lastly, consider cheat sheets on relevant projects that you've completed. Maybe you keep a list of all the major deal terms you got on a particular deal. Maybe you list all the judges you've appeared before with little notes about them. Whatever you might forget that could be relevant should be put onto a piece of paper and kept at your desk. When Jason was early in his career, he wrote down all the major deal points for merger and venture deals he did. When someone would ask him, "Do you remember what X was in Y situation?"

Jason would always have a quick answer. Everyone thought he had a great memory and it reflected well on him. This was not the case. It was just good organization.

Another hack to consider is using your contacts as a database. Every time Jason meets someone (even today), he writes down interesting personal facts in the notes section. It helps him with context later down the road and also makes sure he can always find a good topic to chit chat about the next time he interacts with that person.

6: Take Ownership Without Request

People are quick to give up responsibility, so a junior lawyer that willingly accepts it (or just takes it) is appreciated. Just because you are the low person on the project doesn't mean it isn't your project or client. Treat everything as if you are the ultimate owner of it. Especially at law firms, partners love seeing junior lawyers own things because it shows them they can get leverage off of you. And in the best of cases, maybe they'll see you as a future partner.

7: Invest in Your Management Skills

You might be the new person on the block, but that doesn't mean you don't have to be a good manager. Immediately in your career you will have to manage at least four separate parties:

1. Your clients.
2. Staff at your place of employment.
3. Senior lawyers.
4. Yourself.

All clients need managing. Don't ever think otherwise. No matter how sophisticated they are, they've likely never walked in your shoes and even the ones that have usually forget what it's like to be you. You'll have to manage them with a soft hand and make sure you don't get into a situation whereby they spiral out of control and take you with them. This can be emotionally or intellectually draining. Manage the client and manage the project. In Chapter 13, we talk about managing different types of personalities.

Wherever you work, you'll likely have staff that support attorneys. These people need to be managed as well. If you get in good with the staff at a firm, you will be a star. Come off as a brat and you'll be treated as such—your life will be much more difficult. You'll want to manage the relationships, but also manage their time and work product as well. We'll go into detail on this point in the next chapter.

Managing senior lawyers is also called "managing up." You'll want to manage their expectations and the relationships you have with them. Our advice is to develop personal relationships with senior people at your employer, but never forget you are junior. If you have the opportunity to spend out-of-work hours with your superiors, do so respectfully. No matter how nice they may seem, they are your boss. Be very careful when it comes to things like drinking and partying. Even if they are having a good time, make sure you are having less.

Finally, managing yourself is key. We'll discuss later how to be a happy lawyer, but realize that managing your time along with your physical and mental health is not always easy as a new lawyer. You will only be as good of a lawyer as you are a healthy human. You'll also feel like you are juggling a few more balls (or chainsaws) than you think is safe. Being able to manage yourself in a multitasking and multi-master environment is critical.

8: Have a Three- to Five-Year Horizon

Whatever job you take out of law school, we'd like you to consider this a paid post-doctorate program. Someone is paying you to continue your education. When you are frustrated, tired, anxious, mad, sad, or burned out, just tell yourself you have an opportunity to learn, and someone is paying you to do it. We find this mindset helps many junior lawyers get through tough days, as we've been giving this advice for the past decade with much success.

Take a three- to five-year look at your position. It doesn't mean you'll be there that long, but we find that people who take this mindset have a better chance of success in their job. If you plan for the mid- and long-term, you'll develop skills that senior people in your organization have.

One of the areas to constantly focus on is, how do you add value? Always ask yourself, "If I was my client, would I appreciate what I'm doing and think that it adds value?" If the answer is no, then,

Houston, we have a problem. That should be a red flag to either engage a senior attorney to see if your project is on course, on scope, and on budget, or could reflect the larger issue that your employer is not helping you build a career. It could also reflect that you've taken nothing away from this book and aren't taking responsibility for your own career.

You should also consider creating an "interesting" practice for yourself. This means doing things that you find interesting and are intellectually and emotionally uplifting. If you aren't getting it at work, consider *pro bono* or community opportunities. Even if these opportunities are in a different practice area, it will still build your experience level. Follow your interests and invest time in you becoming an expert in your interests. It's a lot easier than becoming an expert in what you don't care for, and these days, experts in niche areas are more valuable than ever.

9: Plan to Develop Near-Term and Long-Term Advantages

If you want to have a better chance of a successful career, start your strategic planning on day one. What can you give on day one that will set you apart? And what will you need to succeed long term?

Here is an outline of a plan of attack to think strategically in the early days of your career. Note these are things that people with little experience, but effort and gumption, can all do. This isn't about talent. This is about hard work and determination.

1. **Work Ethic and Effort.** Show you are serious about your new profession and don't have a sense of entitlement.
2. **Body Language and Attitude.** Attitude is everything. To clients and bosses, they want to work with people who are positive, not negative. Think about smiling when you are meeting with a partner or client.
3. **Energy, Passion, and Enthusiasm.** Similar to attitude, bring positivity to your work, colleagues, and clients.
4. **Be on Time.** In a profession that bills for it, treat everyone's time as valuable. Always be on time. As a junior person, being early is even better. Strive for perfection on this one.
5. **Look for Singles and Doubles.** Don't look to hit a home run out of the park early. Small wins lead to bigger ones. Look

for small ways to improve the lives of your bosses and clients. Just don't strike out.

6. **No-Mistake Drafting.** You don't need to go to law school to be a good proofreader and not make mistakes. Be that junior person who always has clean documents. At this point, feel free to laugh at us if you have found typos in our book.

7. **Research.** When you research, don't just look at the issue you are working on, but also the bigger picture and use it as a method to train yourself. You won't bill that time to the client, but it will help you see the bigger picture from a senior level view.

8. **Project Management.** Make sure you keep on top of all deadlines and deliverables. Let nothing fall through the cracks. Be prepared. Always.

9. **Technology.** You are probably younger than many of your coworkers and clients. Make sure you understand the latest technology in your field. You probably have a leg up because you were born in the digital age.

10. **Past Experiences.** Don't forget about your past. Whatever it is, leverage what you learned there in your new job.

11. **Energy and Hours.** For those of you at law firms, this might be the most important one. The easiest way to get ahead and distinguish yourself early on is to work harder, longer, and with a cheery attitude (even if you are faking it). You might not want to hear this, but it's true and can really get you in a good place with senior people at your firm. Do extra.

So, what should you be thinking about looking ahead? What advantages should you consider as you mature in your profession?

1. **Hit for Power.** Now you are looking for wins. You are looking to be the problem solver and come up with the solutions that work.

2. **Pattern Recognition.** At this point in your career, things should start looking similar. Pattern recognition should be one of your strengths, but don't fall into the lazy trap of only using this skill and assess each situation as new.

3. **Client Development.** You bring more work in from the same clients who now love you. You foster relationships with potential new clients and maybe you even bring them into the fold.

4. **Expertise.** You should start to become an expert in your field along with any other fields you find interesting. Other people inside your employer start asking you questions.

5. **Social Capital/Network.** You build a network of people who augment your professional life. Maybe these are other lawyers, civic leaders, etc. You might join the board of a local nonprofit.

6. **Beside Manner.** You are calm, reassuring, assertive when you need it and practice empathy.

7. **Professionalism.** People look at you as a true professional. You are respected in the ways you conduct yourself both professionally and personally.

10: Understand How to Best Use and Foster Mentor Relationships

No one gets by in life without mentors. Get the right ones and you are golden. Get the wrong ones, or none, then life gets lonely and learning substantially harder. Being coachable is a strategic advantage. As we've mentioned many times before, the learning curve is steep. The quickest way to flatten it is to find good mentors, foster the relationships, and come up to speed more quickly.

A mentor is someone you respect, has expertise in areas you would like to be an expert in, who is generous with her time, and wants to see you succeed. These aren't people you pay. They may or may not be altruistic. They may just do it "because it is the right thing to do" or they may have some expectations on return, but not direct monetary payment from you.

Whatever the case, seek out mentorship. It could a senior person at your employer, a friend, family member, business leader, senior lawyer at another firm, etc. The more you have, the better. We aren't going to tell you how to engage mentors and find them. That's your problem, but we do have a few opinions on how to best use them and keep them involved.

Do you know how to receive mentorship? The first rule of receiving is listening. Don't interrupt, don't change the pace of conversation you are having, and follow the lead of the mentor. Ask questions, role play with hypothetical situations, and be a "sponge." If you are fortunate enough, you'll have several mentors. We've heard many times that having multiple mentors is akin to drinking from a firehose. It's important to manage this overwhelming situation. Everyone has a different capacity for parsing information. Developing skills to manage large amounts of information is a key to being a good lawyer, so get used to it. Also, keep in mind that not all mentors are correct. We wish we had a magic solution to tell you how to evaluate this, but we don't. Our best advice is to always trust your gut. If something feels off, then it probably is.

What's often lost in a mentee/mentor relationship, however, is fostering and maintaining the relationship. How do you prevent mentor fatigue and burnout? After all, none of us like relationships that are solely one-sided. In other words, what can you give back to mentors so they continue to help you?

You must realize that no matter how senior, rich, busy, or famous your mentor is, you can always provide something of value to them. You just have to figure out what the thing of value may be. We've found that almost all mentors like to hear when their advice has been used and helped you in some way. If you had a meeting with your mentor and learned something valuable, remember to let your mentor know when you put it to actual practice. We love getting emails that say, "Hey, remember three years ago when you said X? Well, let me tell you how that really saved my bacon recently." It just makes us feel like we spent our time well. Additionally, find some way to engage your mentor on something outside of their professional world. We've found that things like sending Apple or Spotify playlists, a cool YouTube video, a fun article or book are well-received. Jason, in particular, loves the music gifts as most of his music discovery these days comes via online playlists from people he previously helped out.

In summary, mentors are key ingredients to your success. Few junior attorneys pay attention to this, so it can be a large competitive advantage for you.

11: Flatten Hierarchies

If you ever get the chance to write a book one day, you'll find some sections of the book tedious, some interesting, and a few really exciting to write. We are really excited about this section because we think this advice is particularly unique and helpful. It's something Jason learned early in his career and it had a massive impact on his career. The concept is called flattening hierarchies.

When you start off, unless you hang your own shingle, you'll be subject to a hierarchy at your employer. By definition, you'll be at, or near, the bottom. Everything we talk about in this book is to help you rise up the ladder, be successful, and hopefully be happy. If you are looking for a "cheat code" to use, here is one potential.

The idea is this: you are the junior person at work, but you are no less important a human than anyone, even the senior partner. And in some areas of life, you may be more experienced than the person you are trying to impress. Let's use a real-life example to illustrate.

Jason started his professional life as a musician. (Shameless plug; Jason goes by Jace Allen online as a musician. Check him out!) Besides being a classically trained percussionist, he plays a variety of instruments and has been a band leader for over 30 years. Whenever Jason would take a new job, Jason would engage his superiors about music. Invariably, people up the food chain would wax poetically about their high-school, college, or long-lost band. Jason would keep tabs on who played which instrument, make assumptions about musical ability, and build a hypothetical band in his head. Once that was completed, he'd offer to put a band together with everyone, run it, and create the music charts, all so that his bosses could reclaim their lost stage glory. The offer was always accepted, and Jason would arrange for a local gig or two. In the process of practicing and getting ready for the gig, Jason's bosses would all see Jason as the senior person in this group. They would defer to Jason, ask him questions, and solicit his help. This essentially flipped the hierarchy they were used to at work. Jason was the partner now. The bosses were the associates.

Without fail, it changed the work dynamic. Although he was no better as an employee or more experienced, the senior people treated Jason differently and on equal footing. This worked for Jason several times, over several companies, both law jobs and not.

The bottom line is to engage your bosses on something you are excellent at (or at least better than them) outside of law. You can't compete there. At least not yet. It doesn't have to be a band. It could be playing a particular sport, having a great debate on an interesting subject matter where the boss learns something from you. It could be food or wine related. Anything. Just get them to see you in a leadership position: flip the hierarchy and reap the benefits.

12: Own Your Mistakes

Just accept right now you are going to make mistakes. It happens. You will be inundated with information, in a new job, perhaps in a new city and making new relationships. It's a time of great change in your life. When you make a mistake, don't brush it off. You should reflect on it and live with it a bit. It should hurt. You need to forgive yourself, but don't forget.

Own it. Tell whoever found it that you recognize it and will learn from it. Move on, but not too quickly—you need to learn the lesson.

13: Know What a Junior Lawyer's Value Is

Know what you bring to the table. Know what value you bring as a new lawyer. It most likely won't be your legal knowledge, but rather your raw thinking power. Your availability and the time you can devote to projects should be substantial. You will have new perspectives and abilities for a person your age that can be useful in your practice and your employers'. In general, the value you add is making other people inside and outside of the organization look good.

14: Keep Your Own List

We suggest you keep your own list, which is essentially your business model to succeed. We are sure you'll figure out other commandments suggestions that are helpful to you. Maybe some of our 14 are irrelevant to you. Maybe you'll write us that we forgot 3 important ones that will make us have to write another version of this book. Whatever the case, have a strategic plan outside of just getting the job and going the regular route. You can do better than that.

Bonus Commandment for Those Working with Contracts!

Okay, so we have one more we didn't know where to put but wanted to highlight. It only applies to those of you who will work with contracts. It's easy and small, but here's the pro tip: when creating signature blocks, put one signature per page and always leave the dates blank. This way if you get a name wrong on a signature block, or one changes, you don't have to go get everyone's signature again. Leave dates open until the closing date, then fill in.

CHAPTER

13

Common Mistakes New Lawyers Make That Limit Careers and Anger Clients

In the previous chapter we gave you advice on what to do as a new attorney. In this chapter, we'll focus on common mistakes new lawyers routinely make. These are the mistakes that create a divide between new lawyers and the real world in which they now operate. Again, knowledge is power.

Forgetting You Are in the Services Industry

You may have a professional license and fancy diploma, but lawyers are in the services industry just like doctors, plumbers, restaurant workers, and car mechanics. Our goal, as lawyers, is to make our colleagues, bosses, and clients' lives easier. That really is it. Don't get your head in a place that you are part of the legal industry, and you are above providing services for other people. Just because you get paid more than a client, for instance, doesn't mean you don't work for them. As the old saying goes, if you are getting paid, you have a boss.

Getting Frustrated and Thinking People Are Idiots

We've previously discussed this when talking about empathy, but don't fall into the trap of thinking your client or boss is an idiot. Even if they are idiots, it's not going to help your demeanor, energy, or the level of service you provide them. Work the issue, but don't be judgmental about those around you. It will only lead to a negative reputation. Keep your spirits up and your attitude positive to those around you.

Having Loose Lips

You will inevitably get excited about a particular assignment, client, or issue. Just remember to keep your darn mouth shut at the bar with your friends. Don't even talk to people inside your own company about anything unless they are on the project team. Having a reputation for talking is a career-limiting move.

Assuming Each State Has the Same Laws

Just because the law of Michigan says X, doesn't mean that Oregon is the same. And just because Delaware says Y is legal, don't assume California agrees. And just because federal law says Z, please, dear lord, do not assume that Canada should be similar. You think this is obvious? Then why do so many junior lawyers screw this up? Also, don't be myopic just because you took the bar in one state. Learn the advantages of the laws in other states, as well as courts and local rules as you come across them. Think how the differences might help your clients.

Treating Administrative Staff Poorly

Treating support staff poorly is a fast ticket out of town. Having legal secretaries, paralegals, and other staff supporting and working well with you is essential to being a successful lawyer. Remember, most of these folks have seen people like you come and go over the years. They have long memories and are good at pattern recognition. You will pay for the sins of your predecessors who didn't behave properly. Some of them will have chips on their shoulders regarding new lawyers with shiny new degrees. Many will rightfully deserve to have these chips given how they've been treated in the past.

What do you do to work effectively with support staff? Communicate with them. These are smart and professional people who want to feel like they are part of the team. They don't like surprises any more than you do. Communicate. We would suggest giving more details than you might think necessary, as you might be surprised that they know a lot more than you and can make you look great on an assignment.

You should also support and defend your support staff. If something goes wrong, never call them out in public. Take them behind closed doors and provide constructive criticism. If they do something great, feel free to praise in public.

Remember, these people work for multiple attorneys, so being organized, friendly, and inclusive will make them want to work for you as opposed to others who don't treat them this way. In short, by treating these staff positions as partners you will work effectively and buy some good karma for down the road when you need it.

Having a Sexual Relationship at Work

This rarely turns out well. Do your best to avoid it.

Being Inconsiderate of Others' Calendars

Consider when you are delivering work to senior people. If something needs to be done Monday, don't send to them Friday afternoon for their review. You just blew up their weekend. Deliver things early. If someone's weekend is getting blown up, it should be yours, not theirs.

Forgetting You Are the Leverage

Adding onto the last point, remember you are the leverage for your employer. If you aren't adding value, you aren't doing a good job. At a big firm, this means you are adding dollars to partner pockets. If you are a public defender, you are giving time back to senior colleagues. As one person said to us, "You can make yourself valuable or irrelevant every time you complete a project." While you are going to need to learn from senior people, you should not rely on them. They should rely on you. Don't assume they've done anything and be responsible.

Forgetting Who the Client Is

We touched on this scenario in Chapter 1, but let's dig in deeper. This is the case where you represent an entity by law but take direction from a human whose interests are misaligned with the entity. For instance, you represent Swearjar.com, a company that created a smartphone application that listens to everything you say and every time you swear debits your bank account and gives the money to charity. The CEO is your main contact who gives you direction, as any good CEO would.

Note, however, that the client is the company, not the CEO. After a successful few months of business, an investor and the CEO come to an agreement on investment terms for the investor to buy stock in the company. As part of this, the CEO wants an employment agreement. She asks you to draft it. She tells you she wants certain terms that heavily favor her. Should you do it?

The answer is no. It's in the company's best interests for either standard terms or no employment agreement at all. It's hard to argue that a biased employment agreement for the CEO is in the best interests of the company, but it is in the best interests of the CEO. You really should advise the CEO to seek outside employment law counsel.

You might get away with this if the CEO is the sole employee and founder of the company. It's hard to justify when there are a dozen employees and an outside investor. In fact, as a venture capitalist, Jason saw this many times where company counsel would suddenly turn course and represent the CEO over the interests of the company. Typically when this would happen, Jason would make sure that new company counsel would soon be hired. Oooops.

Note: Swearjar.com is a fictitious company that someone should start. The authors would be great early adopters.

Assuming Other Lawyers Are Good People

Law school teaches about ethics and proper lawyerly conduct. However, they don't talk much about the real world once everyone is "out in the wild." Let's face it, the level of egregiousness that conduct must rise to for a court to get involved is massively high. Don't assume that everyone is playing by the rules and doing the right thing. You or your client could be the ones hurt by this naivety. Never assume, until you get to know someone, that they are playing by the rules you learned in class.

Shortchanging Research

Don't shortchange your research. Read each case. Read them all the way through. Shepardize your cases. Don't rush, don't skip. Make sure the facts line up. Make sure the court is relevant. You screw this up once and you'll have a long road back to getting people to trust you. This part isn't talent, it's just due care and effort.

Failing to Understand Basic Intellectual Property Law

Regardless of what type of lawyer you are (litigation, business, or whatever), if you deal with the technology ecosystem, you must have a basic understanding of patent, copyright, trademark, and trade secret law. Go buy a book, talk to a friend, or search the internet to have at least a basic sense of the differences between these four areas. Your clients will know a lot about this subject matter. Don't make them teach you. It doesn't look very good.

Talking to Another Attorney's Client Without the Attorney

Often in less contentious situations like business, one may find themselves alone with a non-client. When someone is represented by counsel, make sure their counsel is present when you speak to them about a matter at issue. Otherwise just make polite small talk about the weather. The less said the better.

Screwing Up Billing (If You Bill Clients by the Hour)

New lawyers have found many ways to screw up billing over the years. Here are some quick tips to get you ahead of your peers and help you become a better biller.

1. Keep your time contemporaneously. If you have to go back and remember what you did, you'll never do so correctly.
2. Proofread your time entries before you submit them. Spelling the client's name wrong is not good for getting reimbursed.
3. NEVER FUDGE YOUR TIME. THIS SECTION IS IN ALL CAPS NOT ONLY BECAUSE IT'S THE WRONG THING

TO DO BUT ALSO ILLEGAL AND CAN LEAD TO DISBAR-
MENT OR IMPRISONMENT.

4. Take your descriptions seriously. Imagine you are both your senior colleague and the client when you proofread the bills. Would you pay this bill if you were the client? Does it look like you added value? Does the billing subscription properly and clearly explain what work was done? You should not expect senior lawyers to redraft your vague and worthless descriptions. Use active verbs and show value.

5. Don't bill everything. Give away hours as a junior associate and don't tell anyone. Make your work look better than it actually is. You won't have to do this your entire career, just when you are getting started.

6. Be efficient. Think of the expenditure of your own time as your own money. Always try to find more economical ways to undertake the same endeavor.

14

Relationships, Difficult Personalities, and Being the Calmest Person in the Room

As we've said before, being a lawyer is a people business. There are many people you will interact with whom you will need to influence, cajole, win over, convince, and otherwise get along with. It may be a client, a potential client, a senior partner, opposing counsel, or a colleague. And each will have a range of different personalities, some more difficult than others. This of course all depends on your own personality as well.

Keep in mind that even if we look to one "client," it may involve many different people at the client with different personalities and agendas. For example, lawyers working in the nonprofit world have many stakeholders who may not be an official client but still look to the lawyer in the room for the answers, regardless of her subject matter of expertise. Such stakeholders include donors, staff members, community-based partners, or those receiving services from the underlying organization.

Lawyers are trustworthy and should bring a levelheadedness that makes most involved believe everything is going to be okay. Are those stakeholders necessarily just looking for answers to legal questions? Absolutely not. But as in most instances involving lawyers, people typically seek calm guidance and reassurance that things will work out or at least become untangled in a manageable fashion. Being a lawyer means bringing armchair psychology to your practice. If you don't know what that means, then just remember to stay calm and always look to take anxiety out of a situation, not add to it.

There are two schools of thought when it comes to these dynamics, and they are well summed up by two of the better-known songwriters of the twentieth century: Bob Dylan and John Lennon. One mused that "everyone has to serve somebody" while the other retorted with "you gotta serve yourself." So which notion is the right one? As any good lawyer would answer when asked, "It depends." You've got to figure out a way to do both, however, if you'd like to ensure both short-term and long-term success. In the short term, it's all about the client. But while that sprint is important, the longer-term marathon will make your self-focus more vital. We'll dive into this in Chapter 19, "How to be a Happy Lawyer."

When we were thinking of writing this chapter, we went out to our network to solicit advice and feedback. One friend, Dave Beran, told us he had always wanted to write a book on this subject. So, we did what any good authors would do: we asked him to guest write this chapter. Dave is a multi-time general counsel and has always been the calmest person in the room from what we've seen. In fact, we wish we had more of his demeanor and less of ours when it comes to some situations. Dave came back with incredible advice that we adapted to the flow of the book. Thank you, Dave.

Challenging Personalities

Let's face it. A lot of people are challenging. Heck, you might be one of them. Regardless, being a lawyer seems to attract this crowd. Or maybe being a lawyer means that conflict is a part of life and people in conflict behave less mellow than they normally would. Whatever the case, prepare yourself to see the more challenging sides of peoples' personalities.

What makes a personality challenging or a client difficult or a third-party unmanageable? To quote Justice Potter Stewart, "I know it when I see it." And while Justice Stewart was referring to obscenity, difficult personalities can be similar in that there is a subjective nature to their identification. Here are a few traits that may be potential giveaways:

- **Lack of empathy.** If someone can't look past themselves, they might be challenging. Think of an only child who has been the center or attention for 18 years and refuses to consider their impact on others. We, of course, know that all only children reading this book would never fall into this category.

- **Manipulative.** Deservingly or not, the term "manipulate" has a negative connotation, because most folks equate it with someone controlling another person. It should go without saying that a person who is manipulative can be difficult, mainly because you can never be quite sure as to their intentions. What makes some personalities more difficult than others is the fact that some folks are not knowingly manipulative. These unaware influencers are really hard to deal with.
- **Bends the truth.** Note that we did not say someone who lies. Those who qualify as full-blown liars are not only difficult, but are to be avoided in life generally, whether in a professional or personal capacity. Here we are talking about the habitual braggart, exaggerator, or fibber.
- **Lack of self-control.** If someone cannot exert self-control then you need to understand that such a person is quite likely to ignore your advice, guidance, or instructions. This makes for a terrible client and a difficult counterparty. Many times, these folks have an acute inability to listen.
- **Refusal or Inability to Focus.** As a lawyer you need to spot issues, provide advice and execute upon the client's directions. If you have a client who is unwilling to focus, then it can be a challenging relationship, to say the least. We've seen a few entrepreneurs who fit this description quite well.
- **Refusal or Inability to Accept Reality.** While this trait may be challenging, it doesn't mean that the body housing this personality isn't fun, endearing, or can't be wildly successful. Steve Jobs is a great example of someone who refused to accept reality and a great example of someone known as a challenging personality. See also, Elon Musk. In any event, refusing to accept reality makes things particularly difficult for a lawyer trying to convince their client to settle a lawsuit or accept certain concessions in a negotiation.
- **Shifts Responsibility or Blame.** The best people to work with have a sense of personal responsibility and the ability to shoulder blame when necessary. Think about the opposite here. It's not fun. Especially when that person not only doesn't shoulder the blame but continually passes it around.
- **Incompetence.** Hanlon's Razor provides that "one should never attribute to malice that which is adequately explained by stupidity." And while it's nice to think that maybe not everyone is out to get you, it certainly does not make incompetent people any less difficult to work with.

- **Treats Some People Worse than Others.** This is the adage about how you can tell the character of someone by how they treat others who can do nothing for them. Always assume you are treated poorly behind your back with this type of personality characteristic.
- **Inconsistent Behavior.** Not necessarily bad or toxic, just difficult. The word chaotic comes to mind. More experienced people generally develop consistent routines and anticipated behavior and are thus easier to work with. There's a reason behind the saying, "Professionals are predictable, amateurs are dangerous."
- **Always Angry.** Think "Angry Again" by Megadeth (or really any heavy or speed metal from the 1990s on). While raw unbridled anger and seething may work well for moshing and breaking things, it doesn't necessarily play well in the professional world. We, unfortunately, know a few people who are always angry. It's not just challenging but tiring as well.
- **Acts Like a Jerk.** Unpleasant people aren't necessarily challenging, but they certainly aren't who you want to spend a lot of time with. In any event, so long as their offensiveness does not impede on your legal rights or stray into harassment, they are personalities that you will encounter and will have to at the least tolerate and, at the most, manage and handle with ease. Just don't let them rile you up.

The Lawyer's Job When It Comes to Challenging Personalities

"Why did you go to law school?" is a common question asked of most law students. There are common answers to this question, too: (i) "I've always liked to argue"; (ii) "I want to help people"; (iii) "I didn't know what else to do"; (iv) "I lost a bet"; or (v) "It's a better degree than an M.B.A." While we have never heard someone respond with, "I want to manage challenging personalities so that those people, their companies, their causes, and their dreams might be saved," it is indeed the reality.

As a lawyer, you are the fire extinguisher (or fire truck, as the case may be) positioned perfectly to help save someone from themselves and best guide such a person to the best outcome, professionally and, in some cases, personally.

Your job is not to be another difficult personality. Your job is to be the person who people loop in when the going gets tough, whatever the facts, no matter how serious or embarrassing it might be. If you do your job correctly, then you will have clients and others seeking your advice and counsel on things having nothing to do with the original problem you may have helped them with. There is no bigger compliment than someone returning for your advice. As a mentor of Jason's once said: "Strive to become someone's consiglieri, not just lawyer."

A good lawyer is the calmest person in the room, measured in their approach, and intentional in their execution once a path forward has been determined. We've all been asked questions over our careers that have made our heads explode in confusion. After we take an internal millisecond to recover, we are left feeling humbled and flattered that people would share their deepest insecurities with us.

More specifically, as a lawyer you need to (i) quickly identify the endgame for your client or other stakeholders whose interests you have been charged with advancing; (ii) assess where your client or stakeholder is now on the issues at hand; and (iii) figure out how best to get them to a reasonable conclusion, with a mindset of the ends justifying the means. Since we, too, are lawyers, we'll tell you that last sentence is subject to the following.

General Approaches to Managing Challenging Personalities

One caveat to this section on general approaches: if a challenging personality asks or tries to steer you to do or agree to something that is (i) illegal, (ii) wildly unethical, or (iii) completely against your core values as a human, do not do that thing and immediately put down the pencil and walk away from that person, task, or matter. Find someone more senior at your employer or whomever manages that relationship and talk to them.[1] By doing so you will rid yourself of guilt, keep your integrity, and, perhaps most importantly, exculpate yourself from such nefarious activity and the inevitable

---

[1] If a senior colleague is unavailable, seek other expert assistance and guidance as to how to best navigate this set of circumstances. This is likely a sticky professional responsibility issue requiring specific expertise.

consequences thereof. In our future chapter on happiness, we reiterate this guidance as a core point of remaining a happy lawyer.

Here's the good news. The best approaches to managing challenging personalities also happen to primarily be the core concepts of lawyering as described in Chapter 2 of this book. Sure, there are novel concepts around the edges and strategies to deploy that we will explore below, but the bottom line is that lawyers aren't typically called in to deal with easy-going, pleasant-to-deal-with, and predictable personalities. While the core concepts apply to all aspects of executing your job as a lawyer, they are particularly applicable to dealing with difficult and challenging personalities, not just in the practice of law but in all aspects of life.

1. **Be an Incredible and Attentive Listener.** A misconception, particularly prevalent among junior lawyers, is that they must contribute or "add value" in a highly visible or noticeable way. Nonsense. Some of the best and priciest lawyers employed by the top law firms on this planet contribute and add a ton of value but are quiet, nuanced, and most of the time fly so low under the radar that the client and even their colleagues forget that they are even there. How does this work? For starters, they listen much more than they speak. Second, when they do speak, it is typically to either draw out more information or steer people into a certain direction in seeking truth or to influence them to think a certain way. When dealing with challenging personalities, getting them to talk in more detail is a great strategy to disarm and understand their motivations and needs. Many times, this strategy entices a person to say things they were not prepared to tell you or even things they've not consciously thought themselves.

2. **Live and Breathe Empathy.** Current times (and quite likely throughout all human history, really) society does not necessarily encourage us to look beyond ourselves. As such, those who can do so are important because innovation and success on a broad scale typically come from collaboration or work amongst and with a community, not just one individual toiling away in isolation. There are outliers to be sure, but that is not the focus here.

Pope Francis coined the phrase "globalization of indifference," but you don't have to be Catholic to agree that there is a dearth of empathy among the general population these days. Pope Francis was generally referring to the indifference of groups of people, those standing by silently, not paying attention to the suffering of others, the results of which disproportionately affect marginalized or vulnerable populations. This indifference, however, on a smaller scale affects just how individuals face, manage, and interact with people on a one-on-one basis. That's intense and perhaps a bit heavier than what a junior M&A lawyer typically deals with on a day-to-day basis, but it's no less relevant or accurate.

There is a misconception that to be empathetic is to be soft, gentle, or caring. If you can be empathetic and transplant yourself to another person's worldview or emotions, then you have just attached a turbocharged jet pack to your ability to serve that client, boss, or person. Or maybe more importantly it gives you great insight into an opponent. Harnessing empathy will likely bring out kindness, at least as third-party observers can tell. The secret is that empathy doesn't just make you more effective but also more powerful. Put another way, if you are truly empathetic, you'll know which buttons to push should you need to.

Keep in mind that the person across the table, on the phone, or in the Zoom meeting most likely will not be Peter Frampton and close each conversation with "Do You Feel Like I Do?" [Editor's note: Dave is a music superfan. He is also old and therefore makes references to folks like Peter Frampton. We are sorry that almost none of you will understand this reference and ask for your forgiveness.] No, this will require work on your part to consider the person's past experiences, their future desires, and present intentions. This will require you to think, be curious, and remain open minded.

3. **Employ Apathy.** Yes. Apathy. You may be thinking to yourself, "Self, didn't they just say that empathy is the most important approach to managing or dealing with a challenging personality? And doesn't apathy fly in the face of that suggestion? Is this a typo or just a sneaky lawyer trick?"

These are all great points, and we certainly do not fault you for scratching your head here. Apathy is a tool that may come in handy when managing your own feelings and emotions. You will most certainly be attacked, belittled, taken for granted or worse by certain challenging personalities and it is important to remember that your personal emotions and feelings are not that important to people paying your bill. They want their problem solved. As much as they may like you, that is really their only goal.

Whatever comes your way, your reactions and ability to execute are in your control. Take an apathetic approach when it comes to yourself and do your best to be indifferent and remove emotion from how you handle your words and course of action. There are healthy ways to process the aggravation, frustration, and stress of dealing with these unsavory or difficult personalities. Your feelings should be tucked away in the backseat and have zero impact on your work. This does not mean to ignore your feelings. That comes after the work is done, and we will explore that later in the book. Just don't let your feelings affect your work. It's not only bad for your clients but also for your reputation.

4. **Espouse Understanding.** This is being empathetic, but on steroids. It's one thing to put yourself into someone else's shoes, but this strategy involves talking and asking questions that show you have thought deeply about an issue and what someone has told you. If you can supply evidence of deep understanding, not just empathy, you will likely be able to get to the heart of the matter easier and, even better, morph that challenging personality to a manageable client or trusted colleague.

5. **Commit to a Plan and Act.** Our two favorite lines in the *True Detective* TV series both come from season 1 and are both uttered by Detective Rust Cohle, the haunted detective portrayed by Texas's favorite son, Matthew McConaughey:
   1. To his partner in episode 5, "Good to see you commit to something."
   2. To an adversary in episode 8, "I strike you as more of a talker or a doer, Steve?"

Like many things in life, when dealing with challenging personalities, it's best to commit to an approach and then act accordingly. To do otherwise would cause you to spin your wheels and waste time, resources, and energy on thinking rather than simply acting and moving on. So, make Detective Cohle proud. Formulate a decision, commit to it, and act. Simply making a decision is one of the best-known productivity "hacks."

6. **Be the Calmest Person in the Room.** Combine items 1 through 5 above: listen, practice empathy, put aside your personal feelings, do your best to understand the nuances of the situation, the people, and their intentions, commit to a plan, and take action. Do all while neither raising nor lowering your heart rate. Be the calmest person in the room. If you take away only one thing from this chapter, let it be the immediately preceding sentence.

Sampling of Challenging Personalities and Tips for Dealing with Them

As in other parts of this book, we try to not only teach you theory, but pragmatic and actionable advice. Figure 14.1 shows 10 archetypes of challenging personalities you may come across, each embodying many (or in some cases, all!) of the traits described above. Some archetypes may be clients, some may be third parties, some may be colleagues, but in effect all are bosses and all are somebody you may have to serve or at least have a collegial and functional working relationship with.

In this section we attempt to (i) accurately describe certain challenging personalities with a moniker; (ii) describe how to identify such individual; (iii) provide a few specific tips on how best to manage each of them; and (iv) score each on a numbered scale of 1 to 10 based on level of difficulty: 1 being yourself, because we all know that we are easy to deal with, and 10 being a wicked combination of Carrot Top, Logan Roy, Bobby Axelrod, Sideshow Bob, and the advisor wherever you take your car in for service.

	Lack of Empathy	Manipulative	Bends the Truth	Lack of Self-Control	Refusal or Inability to Focus	Refusal or Inability to Accept Reality	Shifts Responsibility or Blame	Incompetence	Treats Some People Worse than Others	Inconsistent Behavior	Always Angry	Acts Like a Jerk
Self-Proclaimed Smartest in the Room	●	●	●			●	●					●
The "It's Not a Good Idea Unless It's My Idea" Guy	●		●			●	●	●	●			●
The Biggest Small Business Owner	●		●	●				●		●		●
Mr. Something to Prove	●	●										
The All-Powerful Government Lawyer	●										●	●
Mr. I've Never Been Told "No"	●	●	●	●		●	●		●	●		●
High-Performing Senior Associate/Junior Partner		●			●		●					
Unresponsive But Super Important Third Party	●		●				●	●		●		
The Abrasive Adversary	●	●	●	●		●	●	●	●	●	●	●
The Turf-Protecting Academic or Nonprofit Director	●		●	●		●	●	●	●		●	●

FIGURE 14.1   Challenging Personality Traits Belonging to Each Challenging Personality Archetype

Note that these archetypes are presented in no particular order:

1. **Self-Proclaimed Smartest Person in the Room**
   How to Identify:
   o Proclaims him or herself to be the smartest person in the room.
   o Classic "know it all" personality who responds to everything with "I know" and then adds something showing he knows it better than you.
   o Most likely talks over you.
   o Has impeccable credentials but struggles to name personal references that aren't a classmate or former professor.
   Tips to Manage:
   o Be super smart on those topics you will engage with this person on. Be proactive on performing recon, diligence on the latest developments in the area, and do deep dives on the details.
   o Show that you are just as smart, quietly and discreetly.
   o Know that the people who are actually the smartest in the room never act this way.
   o Make them look even smarter by supporting where necessary and correcting where appropriate but always with, "Yes, I hear you but also you were probably going to say. . ."
   o When you are wrong and this individual corrects you in front of others, respond with humor. Our preferred line when this occurs is to simply say, "Thank you. You passed my test." Humor disarms most of the population.
   o Employing apathy is key here; do not let their behavior get under your skin.
   o Consider whether you can connect with this person on a topic outside of your current engagement so that they feel like you are on their team.
   Level of Difficulty:
   o 6. Many hard charging clients and mid-level lawyers act this way. Get used to it, as they can be valuable clients and helpful colleagues once you understand how they operate.

2. **The "It's Not a Good Idea Unless It's My Idea" Guy**

How to Identify:

- o Makes you sing the opening stanza of "Emotional Rescue" by The Rolling Stones in your head, "Is there nothing I can say, nothing I can do, to change your mind?"
- o Speaks first, always. Interrupts others, often.
- o Demands attention and immediate responsiveness to their own thoughts or suggestions but seldom provides feedback on other colleague's ideas.
- o Is a "no person" to everyone else's ideas.

Tips to Manage:

- o You'll need to not only lead this horse to water, but you'll also need to get that horse to drink. Get in their head and start speaking in their language. Use phrases like, "That idea you had was incredible! Imagine if you slightly modified it so that it was legal!?"
- o Managing this type of personality can be useful not only as a junior lawyer but also as a business partner, parent, spouse, friend, or just when trying to pick a place for lunch among colleagues. Whenever you are trying to get someone else to embrace your idea as their own.
- o Give it a little less gas on the empathy pedal and a little more on being an active listener to understand exactly how this person operates and speaks. Start to speak this way and try to predict the way this person thinks.

Level of Difficulty:

- o 3. Once you get the hang of being a chameleon, you'll be able to crack this nut regularly.

3. **The Biggest Small Business Owner**

How to Identify:

- o Walks into a professional meeting with various counterparties, throws their keys on the table and says, "That's right. New Jaguar. Just picked up next year's model. Got the convertible." Seriously, we've seen this happen.
- o Built a business from the ground up, likely struggled initially and then absolutely killed it. Executed perfectly and now has vendors, banks, competitors, and job seekers clamoring to team up or get their business.
- o Considers lawyers to be a waste of money.
- o Risk taker and incredible businessperson.

Tips to Manage:

o Find out how they built their business. Be genuinely interested. There's a very good chance that they view lawyers as risk averse and, therefore, inferior. You need to show how you can be a helpful resource and a trusted compatriot (if a client) and a respectful admirer (if a counterparty or other third party).

o Show them respect that they've built something from the ground up. Empathize that it is hard to do and rare to achieve.

o Dive deep on long-term goals and always ask how you can be helpful, be it in terms of legal work, introductions, or other. Junior lawyers should consider themselves incredibly fortunate should they find themselves dealing directly with clients like this or even their lieutenants.

Level of Difficulty:

o 4. These are incredibly enjoyable and fulfilling clients to have. However, they can be a complete pain in the keister as counterparties on a transaction.

4. **Mr. Something to Prove**

How to Identify:

o Quietly doubts their own decision-making. Asks for reassurance on big-ticket items, even those that may not be primarily legal issues.

o Hesitant to talk about credentials or themselves.

o Takes pleasure in outperforming or otherwise destroying competitors or other adversaries (real or imagined).

o Dominating feels good to them.

Tips to Manage:

o Figure out the source of insecurity. Is it due to how they grew up? Did they go to school somewhere that isn't a brand name college or university? Are they short? If you can relate to any of these sources of insecurity, identify them and bring it up. Everyone wants to be heard.

o Build trust and figure out the best method of communication. Try to get into a rotation of communication with this client so they anticipate speaking with you often and begin to look forward to it.

Level of Difficulty:

o 6. This is above a 5 simply due to the amount of trust one needs to build to manage this personality.

5. **The All-Powerful Government Lawyer**

How to Identify:

o Works for the government.

o Has unlimited discovery power and resources.

o Denies he or she has unlimited discovery power and resources.

o May have a chip on their shoulder if you have a more prestigious or wealthy pedigree.

Tips to Manage:

o Good luck.

o Try to win with flattery. Subordinate yourself as you have no chance of out muscling them.

Level of Difficulty:

o 9 to 10.

6. **Mr. I've Never Been Told "No"**

How to Identify:

o Filthy rich, typically due to an inheritance or a one-time highly unusual windfall.

o Or parents were this way and they've never had to work for anything.

o Has literally not been told "no" in the preceding 10 to 20 years.

o Admires Kim Jong-un's negotiation style (i.e., what's mine is mine, what's yours is negotiable).

Tips to Manage:

o When negotiating, be prepared to bring the cake *and* the hammer but be mindful that unfortunately the hammer won't do much good if your client is on the receiving end of this person's wrath (and if Mr. INBTN has a bigger hammer (which is likely)).

o If this is your client, your job is to keep them rich, out of the papers, and above the fray. If this is your client's counterparty, then it is your job to suggest to your client they find another counterparty. If that's not an option, you must, under all circumstances, stay on this challenging personality's good side until they no longer have the resources to live a life of never being told no.

Level of Difficulty:

o 8.5. Second only to the All-Powerful Government Lawyer, solely since the APGL can unilaterally shut down a business, impose large fines, or put someone in jail.

7. **High-Performing Senior Associate/Junior Partner**

How to Identify:

o Stressed, hurried, and receives 10 calls a week from headhunters.

o Weighs 15 to 20 pounds heavier than a few years earlier.

o Responds to requests for time off due to a family emergency or other significant life event such as a wedding with "Ok. You have to live your life, I guess," or "That's fine but make sure you are available for anything that comes up," or "Did you know I closed a deal in the delivery room as my wife was giving birth? There's a picture of me with the kid in one arm and my phone up against my ear with the other!" Fun fact: we have heard one lawyer give two of these responses.

Tips to Manage:

o Make a great, no, incredible first impression.

o Listen, listen, listen. And follow up the listening with thoughtful clarifying questions.

o As you would with anyone, do great work, be a great communicator, and do exactly what you say you will do.

o Anticipate their needs and deadlines, and tackle anything you can that will make their life easier.

o Do not hesitate to push back when you know something they do not or spot something they have missed. Your job is to make them look great in front of everyone else.

o You may have to outwork them on a project to prove your value. Hopefully it's just one project.

Level of Difficulty:

o Somewhere between a 1 and a 10. If you are at a law firm, a high-performing senior associate or junior partner can make or break you in the early stages of your career. If you earn the trust of this person, then you will be given opportunities, responsibilities, and obligations that most junior lawyers only dream of. If you meet expectations, then the level of difficulty is closer to a 1. But if you cannot commit and execute, you will find yourself miserable working with a high performer.

8. **Unresponsive But Super Important Third Party** (think vendor, expert witness, opposing counsel's assistant, graphic designer, etc.)

   How to Identify:
   o Misses deadlines, cancels calls at the last minute, and requires constant attention up until a task is complete.
   o Work product or participation is vital to whatever project, case, or deal you are working on.

   Tips to Manage:
   o You typically realize that your super important third party is unresponsive when it is too late, i.e., after you engage them, and they begin the work. All is not lost, however, and you can still work to salvage the efforts, but you must be quick and attentive to this personality in the beginning to make sure there will be no surprises later.
   o Provide fake deadlines. Seriously. Like how you would set a sixth-grade child's alarm clock 15 minutes earlier than the true time to ensure they don't run late in the morning. You can provide deadlines to a third-party vendor that gives you a cushion in the event they blow it.
   o Heavy on the communication and employ more than one method (emails, follow up texts, biweekly check-in calls).
   o Here is where you need to really focus on empathy. In many instances, these third-party service providers or vendors are very likely treated poorly by other lawyers who haven't read this book. Treat each vendor how you would like to be treated and there is a great chance that your project will go to the top of their pile.
   o If you don't want to or can't provide empathy, buy them something like a nice bottle of wine. Sometimes you can buy loyalty.

   Level of Difficulty:
   o 7. A lot depends on just how super important the work product is that the third party is involved in producing. If its importance is extremely high, then you may do yourself a favor and have a backup vendor or plan in place as well.

9. **The Abrasive Adversary**

   How to Identify:
   o Fallback position is intimidation tactics, whether it's cursing, yelling, or calling others mean names. Asks questions

without waiting for an answer (e.g., "You think you're pretty smart, huh? Well, you're not!")

o Spits a lot when speaking. Listens to Five Finger Death Punch to calm down for bed.

o Believes that Johnny Lawrence (*The Karate Kid* version, not *Cobra Kai*) was misunderstood.

o Acts hostile even when responding to a yes-or-no question (e.g., Q: "Sir, do you want chicken on your salad?" A: "What the hell do you think!?").

Tips to Manage:

o Let them talk. A lot and often. Eventually they will wear themselves out, and if it's in front of a judge or jury, don't worry; those folks will see right through it. If it's in front of clients, even better. The only clients who like their lawyers to be loud, angry, and abrasive are those on TV or those who have a bad set of facts on their side.

o They may test your mettle in terms of trying to stay out of the muck. Remember to employ apathy when it comes to your own feelings. Don't let them ruffle you and simply stay the course.

o Keep them in check. If their behavior crosses the line and goes from unprofessional to harassing, consider filing a complaint with the state bar or their own law firm or company, but do so coming from a place of calm, measured contemplation and not anger or retaliatory thinking.

o Employ apathy and be the calmest person in the room.

Level of Difficulty:

o 2.5. Surprised by this? Don't be—typically the angry bluster is thrown your way as a cover for lack of good facts, lack of good lawyering, or lack of adequate resources. A point or two subtracted here, too, because this challenging personality's behavior will likely give you great tales to tell at your next dinner party.

10. **The Turf-Protecting Academic or Nonprofit Director**

How to Identify:

o Self-righteous and self-important.

o Resources are typically scarce so there is a heightened sensitivity to others who may encroach on such resources.

o So entrenched in their space that they no longer focus on the population they set out to serve and instead focus on themselves and their public relevancy.

o This is their work, their space, their kingdom, and their turf. They have no other identity outside of their job.
o Unwillingness to allow new participants into the space without first "kissing the ring" and asking the "right" people for blessing simply to help others.

How to Manage:
o Deploy your network and figure out whether there is common ground between you, your organization, and the challenging personality with which you will have to work or otherwise interact.
o Build trust slowly via sincere and substantial communications and ask what favors you may be able to do for this person.
o Determine early on whether there is a workaround, i.e., another person at the organization you can deal with who may not be as challenging.

Level of Difficulty:
o 8. Different from a typical client that values money or prestige. Like a politician in that power and turf are most important. Incentives may be difficult to identify initially; therefore, choosing which levers to pull may be a challenge.

Parting Thoughts

Identifying challenging personalities quickly and maintaining a consistent approach to managing such people is key to two things: (i) if it is a client, saving them from themselves in certain circumstances, and if it is another stakeholder, simply managing that personality in the best possible way and (ii) keeping your own mental, professional, and personal well-being intact. There are some who may claim that all people and all personalities are challenging. Those people are wrong and are likely to be the same people who walk into a room full of poop and say, "Hey, there's a lot of poop in here!" We prefer the people who walk into that room and say, "Hey, there must be a really neat and large animal somewhere in this stinky room! Watch your step!"

Be that person looking for the pony but do it in a way that is eyes wide open and armed with a good lawyer's brain full of thoughtfulness, healthy skepticism, and a deliberate working ability to deploy the core concepts of lawyering discussed above and elsewhere in this book. Godspeed.

This chapter could not have been written without the existence of certain individuals we've come across in our professional lives and their relentless efforts to be as difficult, abrasive, and all-around challenging as possible. Thank you. You've made us appreciate kind, thoughtful, and helpful people that much more.

15

Understanding Current Technology

Back in the day, lawyers didn't have to be proficient with technology because there wasn't any. Okay that is a little glib, but as recent as 20ish years ago, many lawyers didn't have computers on desks. Cell phones were more of a novelty than a necessity. Law firms devoted large parts of their office to word processing departments and couriers who would hand deliver documents both locally and afar.

We know this because we lived this. Today, the practice of law could not be more different from a technological standpoint. While few lawyers are tech geeks (we see you, future IP lawyers), it doesn't mean you don't have to be proficient in a variety of technologies to make your path as successful as possible.

In more blunt terms: don't be the technology luddite that is always struggling to keep up. Technology has two main uses in the law. First, it's used as a communications platform enabling you to provide better customer service. Second, it's an efficiency platform that allows your service to be delivered in the most cost-effective manner to your clients or save you and your organization time in completing your tasks.

This book isn't about teaching you how to use technology. That would be a very helpful, but immensely boring book to write, so we aren't the people to do it. Rather, we are going to clue you in on key technologies you should be comfortable with and the reasons for it.

We won't insult your intelligence and assume you can work a smartphone, text, and email like the best of them. What you might not know a ton about is cloud computing and storage. Services like

Dropbox, Box.net, Azure, iCloud, and Amazon Web Services allow for secure online storage of documents. If you haven't used these services, you should check them out.

You'll also want to know how you use your employer's particular document management system, eDiscovery platform, LexisNexis, Westlaw, and other bespoke software platforms.

Tread lightly when a client requests to communicate in a way you don't normally utilize. Communication channels like Slack or even Facebook Messenger are more and more popular with younger clients all the time. Our word of advice: only communicate on secure platforms that are approved by your employer. And try to minimize the number of channels so you don't miss anything. As discussed often in this book, however the practice of law is a service business, so you may ultimately need to defer to the client.

As for social media, keep in mind a few things. First, if you are on social media channels, consider what you have on those channels. Old tweets and pictures of beer party days may not be appropriate in your new profession. Before you start work (and ideally before you even interview for a job), review all of your social media content and make sure it is appropriate. If not, remove it immediately. You should assume that clients and colleagues will want to connect on social media, and you will be hard pressed to say no to them.

If you aren't on social media, make sure you at least understand what each major platform does. Depending on your position, you may have client social accounts you'll want to monitor to ensure they don't get into trouble.

CHAPTER

Words from the Wise

hile we did a lot of research and interviews to come up with our theses and support for this book, we also both hated being lectured at in school. We always liked guest teachers who would impart their real-world experience and knowledge upon us.

When we began this project, we knew from the beginning that our knowledge would never be sufficient to fully teach our dear readers and thus we decided to take a "village approach" to learning. In the following pages, we've assembled an extremely diverse set of lawyers who share their experiences in making the jump from school to employment. They detail their best advice, worst mistakes, and what roadblocks they overcame on their way to becoming successful attorneys.

In creating these guest chapters, we asked our writers to discuss anything they wanted in any format they chose, although we did provide a sample chapter that some chose to follow. We encouraged them to disagree with us. We told them that we would leave their words as-is, except for obvious typos. We didn't want to filter. In that vein, please don't miss Will Foster's parting advice about life and sandwiches in the footnote of his chapter.

We are especially proud of the cross-section of people who contributed. We wanted to represent a wide variety of experiences and backgrounds. Go take a look at the book cover if you want to see their (mostly) smiling faces.

Some statistics on our guest authors:

1. Number: 25 (for 24 guest chapters)
2. Age range: early 30s to late 50s
3. Male: 52%; Female: 48%
4. Race inclusion: Asian, Black, Hispanic, White
5. Diverse backgrounds: 66%

This is the best part of the book. We hope you enjoy these chapters as much as we enjoyed reading them. In case you want to jump around, here is a table-of-contents, by professional field and author, to help guide your journey. Maybe you'll feel some kinship with some of the paths these lawyers have chosen. Also, please recognize that many of these people have had several post-law school experiences and will speak from a variety of experiences, not just their current position.

1. Employment Lawyer – Lynne Davis
2. Colorado Attorney General – Phil Weiser
3. Litigation Partner – Kenzo Kawanabe
4. Corporate Partner – Rachel Proffitt
5. Director of Community Engagement, Colorado Department of Law – Matt Baca
6. Family Law – Kim Willoughby
7. Associate Professor of Law – Brad Bernthal
8. General Counsel in the beverage industry – Jolene Yee
9. Associate Chief Counsel with the California Department of Fair Employment and Housing – Greg Mann
10. Associate Director and Legal Counsel of Product at Twitter – Nicole Day
11. Assistant United States Attorney – Lindsey Beran
12. Trademark Practice Group Co-Chair – Robyn T. Williams
13. Chief Executive Officer and General Counsel – Alfred Levitt
14. "Hang the Shingle out Post-Law School" – Nicholas Troxel and Josh Fitch
15. Founder and Executive Director, Partners for Justice – Emily Galvin Almanza
16. Criminal Defense Lawyer/Wine Store Owner – Jennifer Zimmerman

17. Wealth Management, Trusts and Estates – Margot Edwards
18. General Counsel and COO at a venture fund – Jason Lynch
19. Bankruptcy Partner – Randall Klein
20. General Counsel at a startup – Stacy Carter
21. Director and Associate General – Nikki Stitt Sokol
22. Senior Deputy District Attorney – Ryan Day
23. Civil Rights – Tyrone Glover
24. Tax Lawyer and Professor – Will Foster

Guest Chapter 1

Name: Lynne Davis

Current Position: President of IMC, Inc., a law firm focused exclusively on employment law and specializing in independent investigations and mediations of employment claims and counseling companies and executives

Former Post-Law School Positions: I formerly worked as a partner at Employment Matters Counseling & Consulting, counsel at O'Melveny & Myers LLP and an associate at Cooley LLP

Legal Practice Area: Employment Law

Law School and Graduation Year: University of Michigan Law School, 1998

Time between undergraduate and law school: 1 year (paralegal)

One or two books I recommend: Two books I recommend are by the same author, Laura Vanderkam: *I Know How She Does It* and *168 Hours: You Have More Time Than You Think*. Each of these books explore work-life balance and pragmatic approaches to achieving that balance.

Short background on why I went to law school

My interest in law really grew out of my college major, Political Science, and the Women's Studies courses I took as an undergraduate. The human element of discrimination and harassment at a place of work based merely on personal characteristics—a person's skin color or their gender—incensed me. I wanted to fight the good fight.

What frustrated me most about coming out of law school and/or what frustrates me with regards to people I work with or hire who are newly out of law school

The most frustrating part for me coming out of law school was that I knew absolutely nothing about being a lawyer from a practical standpoint. I recall a mid-level Associate telling me during my first year out of law school that, when she was a first-year lawyer, a Partner told her to file a document, and she filed the document in the client file. The Partner, however, meant to file the document in court before a deadline. That about sums it up for me. I, too, did not know the important difference between "file" and "file."

In terms of what frustrates me with junior lawyers, it is really about accountability. Accountability to different people and on multiple fronts. Accountability to your biggest client as a junior lawyer—the Partner you are working under on a particular project—is being there when you need to be there, early and ready to work. Accountability is also attention to detail. When you hand something in for review, it should be thoroughly vetted. If someone hands something in to me that was not carefully reviewed, I wonder what else that person may be missing.

How have you used (or not) the core concepts of lawyering as this book proposes: Empathy, Listening First, Asking Questioning, and Giving Advice?

I use the core concepts of empathy, listening first, asking questions, and giving advice on every matter. Employment law is very personal, and it is imperative that I am empathetic. For much of my practice, I am in the role of a neutral, either as an independent investigator of employment claims or mediator of disputes, and I deal with sensitive subject matter, ranging from bullying to race discrimination to sexual assault on college campuses. I must be empathetic, and I must listen first in order to do my job effectively. It starts with a story, and regardless of whether that story can ultimately be corroborated or not, I need to approach each matter with empathy and an open mind.

Listening first has helped me to read a situation and adapt my approach accordingly. I need to meet people where they are, and employees who come in to meet with me run the gamut from incensed to tearfully devastated. I like to hear the uncut version of the story, and then I like to ask questions afterward. I need to understand the facts and I am often asking questions designed to obtain the factual basis for claims so that I can piece the puzzle together.

Advice for my counseling and executive clients is MY role as their attorney. I never lose sight of the fact that they are contacting me for legal advice. There may be business or personal matters that factor in to their ultimate decision, but it is my job to give them the legal perspective.

As a neutral, I am not providing "advice" in the traditional sense, but I do need to provide factual conclusions. I need to make tough decisions on credibility and review the totality of the evidence to determine whether the weight of the evidence indicates that something did or did not occur. I cannot wiggle out of making a determination or I am simply of no value to my clients.

Biggest mistake(s) you made while in law school

Not asking for clarification. My Contracts professor taught the subject backward. I was a Political Science major and had never heard of "offer" and "acceptance." I was lost. It was not until I bought one of those study guide books that acceptance made sense AFTER I figured out what constituted an offer. I should have asked for help (and I should have learned about those study guide books earlier!). I now deal in contracts a fair amount, so it is important to understand the basics.

What class(es) did you wish you had taken while in law school? In or outside the school? What about today?

I wish I had sought out some practical business classes. My focus was employment law and litigation, which has served me well, but at the end of the day, my clients are businesses and business acumen helps. I did not need to get into the weeds, but I am sure there were some beneficial classes I could have taken at the business school. I did take a class in the graduate program in English on my favorite author,

Toni Morrison, which was a wonderful experience. I highly recommend taking advantage of what a university has to offer outside of the law school.

Most useful classes in law school

The most useful classes were those that were tied to employment law and those that were taught by inspiring professors. The subject matter itself was important to my knowledge base and inspiring Professors truly do make a class impactful. My Fourteenth Amendment professor was the head of the ACLU in Los Angeles and flew into Ann Arbor each week for a Thursday evening class. He had a passion for the subject and for teaching that would have made any class interesting. One of my favorite classes in law school—and one of the most popular classes—was Blood Feuds. The course was on the community, culture, and formation of legal and societal norms for Vikings. What kind of course is that for a top 10 law school one might wonder? It was interesting, explored the history and basis of setting up laws and it was taught by a teacher who made it great day in and day out. Seek out classes that are tied to your area of interest and classes with professors who have reputations for inspiring students.

How did you decide what to do post-law school? With hindsight, how good of a job did you do?

Silicon Valley was hot when I graduated from law school. It was, and is, innovative, business-minded, and filled with the smartest people around. I wanted a big law firm in that environment, and that is where I went. I am so grateful I did. The employment group at my firm in Silicon Valley was much different than employment groups at other firms around the country. We specialized in solving issues hand-in-hand with business attorneys and companies. We were not nearly as focused on motions and court hearings as similar departments in other locations, though we did those as well, than we were focused on solving issues from a pragmatic point of view. That mindset fits well in my current practice and area of expertise.

Biggest mistake you made at your first job

The biggest mistake I made at my first job is really the same as the biggest mistake I made in law school—not asking for clarification. Reflecting back now, I think I was intimidated by the superiorly talented people I worked with and the impressive caliber of clients we worked for, and I was afraid people would start to think that I was not as smart as they thought when they hired me. Some days I felt like a fraud because I really had no idea when I first started how to actually be a lawyer. I can see that clearly now, and asking questions would have saved me a lot of lost time going down rabbit holes, subpar work product and stress.

Best advice you received or have given for those coming out of law school

The best advice I received was as a paralegal, and that was to keep my clients updated and in the loop. The Partner who gave me that advice reminded me that the client will not know what I had done to move things forward on their matter without telling them, and he told me to inform the client as to status before they feel the need to ask. It was a reminder that at the end of the day, we are in a client-driven business.

One of the most important things I learned in my early years as a lawyer was something I observed. The head of my employment group at my first law firm has an important and big job, and many of his days were going from call to call to call with clients on vastly different matters. I watched him give his full time and attention to each call he was on. He could have easily been distracted on a call, thinking about a call he just had or a matter he needed to discuss on a call later in the day. But he wasn't. He was present, "on," and brilliant in each call with each client. To me, it was a lesson on being present and engaged exactly where you are and learning how to compartmentalize in the face of a daunting schedule and responsibilities.

Worst advice you received or have given for those coming out of law school

I think a big pitfall for junior lawyers is advice regarding the number of billable hours they should reach each year. Do not get me wrong, it is an important metric for law firms, but I think there is a tendency to stockpile hours. As a junior lawyer, I was not privy to the ramifications of over-billing a client. As a firm owner, I am. Clients do not like to work with law firms that charge too much time to get things done, and while Partners are willing to write off time for junior lawyers who are learning, they are seasoned professionals who know about how much time things should take even for junior lawyers. The mindset that my purpose and goal is to bill as much as I can to a particular matter so I look like a superstar is not a client-driven mindset and we are in a client-driven business. Working meticulously, yet efficiently, is a valued trait.

How have you remained happy in your profession? Have there been times when you were not? If so, what did you do to improve your situation?

Flexibility has helped me remain happy as a lawyer. I put in my time, learning from the best and working long hours. I ordered many dinners at the office and worked lots of weekends. The experience I gained, though, gave me flexibility down the road to start my own law practice and to work with clients and on matters of my choice. I did not love to litigate and I was able to leave big firm life, stay within my area of expertise, and find a niche in non-litigation matters. I am not entrepreneurial AT ALL, so this was a big leap, and one I have never regretted. I tell everyone that I will never truly retire. The business is mine, and I have a choice as to what matters I take on and when.

If you could go back in time and tell your younger self something about making the transition from law school to the real world, what would it be?

I would tell my younger self to soak it all in—the positive and the negative—and see beyond where you are currently. I worked for two large firms and there were a lot of expectations. One of the Partners I worked with left letters on my chair that I had already sent out to the client or opposing counsel, which he knew, completely marked up with red pen. Finding those mark-ups on my chair some mornings was not easy, but I can write a hell of a letter now. Give yourself a break and take all you can out of your experience and make a true decision about your future in the law—what you want it to be—once you have that experience under your belt.

Guest Chapter 2

Name: Phil Weiser

Current Position: Colorado Attorney General

Former Post-Law School Positions: Dean and Professor University of Colorado Law School; Founder and Executive Director Silicon Flatirons; Senior Advisor, National Economic Council; Deputy Assistant Attorney General, US DOJ; Senior Counsel for Telecom Policy, US DOJ; and law clerk, U.S. Supreme Court.

Legal Practice Area: Telecommunication and Innovation Policy

Law School and Year: New York University School of Law, 1994

Time between undergrad and law school: One year between, working on political campaigns and in New York City government

One or two books I recommend: *Mindset* by Carol Dweck and *Getting to Yes* by Roger Fisher and William Ury are great to expand the brain in a useful way for the profession of law. And just for fun, *Big Fish* by Daniel Wallace.

Short background on why I went to law school

I was really focused on how to prepare for public service. Service was always top of mind, and I believed, with the help of a mentor, that law school would prepare me for public service. It was absolutely the case.

What frustrated me most about coming out of law school and/or what frustrates me with regards to people I work with or hire who are newly out of law school

My overall critique of legal education is that it doesn't develop enough soft skills, including emotional intelligence, which are important for lawyers. Ideally, every student would take courses like negotiations to develop a problem-solving mindset. The idea that problems are solved in the courtroom (as law school repeatedly teaches) gives students a warped perspective on interpersonal dynamics.

How have you used (or not) the core concepts of lawyering as this book proposes: Empathy, Listening First, Asking Questions, and Giving Advice?

Listening first is an important concept. Included in this is humility. My first boss told me, "I'm not afraid of what I don't know; I'm afraid of what I think I know." Listening first is part of a broader competency that I would call humility. The question you don't ask will get you in trouble. Be humble and honest about what you don't know.

Empathy determines whether people believe you care about them or not. If they think you don't care about them, it undermines the relationship. Law is a relationship business. Empathy can be practiced and honed. Ken Sharpe and Barry Schwartz wrote a book called *Practical Wisdom,* which talks about a lot of these soft skills. I think they are correct when they say, "While it's debatable whether it (empathy) can be taught, it can be learned." Part of how you learn is working in a group setting and getting feedback about how you listen and empathize.

As for asking questions, I call that intellectual curiosity. If you are enthusiastic and have a learning mindset, it will serve you very well.

In the context of giving advice, this falls under the idea of problem solving. For any lawyer, you must be willing and eager to solve problems early on in your career. At our best, we are creative problem solvers.

Biggest mistake(s) you made while in law school

I worked my first summer for a civil rights lawyer and I didn't ask for guidance on an important project. I turned in some work that was incomplete and he had to spend his entire weekend fixing my mistakes and compensating for the research I failed to do. It was a lesson that has stayed with me.

A frustration involving students or people that I hire is when people don't ask enough questions. They might assume they know things because they don't want to appear dumb. Or they spend too much time on doing things that aren't useful because they are afraid to ask for guidance.

Most useful classes in law school

Negotiations, seminars, and clinics.

How did you decide what to do post-law school? With hindsight, how good of a job did you do?

I clerked for Judge David Ebel on the Tenth Circuit Court of Appeals. While in law school, a trusted mentor told me that clerking would be a great experience. I knew nothing about the experience and it was not on my radar screen. He was right.

Biggest mistake you made while at your first job

The first memo I wrote contained way too much extraneous information. I got a lot of feedback and adapted. Ultimately, I learned how to follow Justice Ginsburg's counsel: "Get it right and keep it tight."

As a person who works with junior lawyers, I think many people don't appreciate the value of looking for a job that gives them the best experience and best mentors, versus going for money. I realize that law school isn't cheap, but I advise students to play the long game by developing valuable experience and mentors early in their careers.

Best advice you received or have given for those coming out of law school

Take the job with the best experience. Invest in the franchise of you. It's your most important investment.

Worst advice you received or have given for those coming out of law school

Besides not going for the money, people need to focus on what they are called to do. I have seen people psych themselves out because they think they should be doing something else. Listen to your calling.

How have remained happy in your profession? Have there been times when you were not? If so, what did you do to improve your situation?

I've been fortunate to keep myself in positions where I'm continually learning. This makes me happy. I need to feel purpose and meaning in my work to be happy and fulfilled. When I'm less happy, I always ask myself, "Is this the right thing for me to be doing?"

If you could go back in time and tell your younger self something about making the transition from law school to the real world, what would it be?

Trust the process and enjoy the journey.

SUCCESS in the legal profession

If you are reading this book, you are likely in (or thinking about attending) law school. The authors of this book have mountains of advice for you, which may conflict because each of us has our own experiences and perspectives. So as you read this book, be introspective. There are many paths to success, and ultimately, you will chart your own course. I hope that some of our suggestions assist you in your journey.

Guest Chapter 3

Name: Kenzo Kawanabe

Current Position: Partner at Davis Graham & Stubbs LLP

Legal Practice Area: Litigation and trial. Fellow in the American College of Trial Lawyers and instructor at the National Institute for Trial Advocacy

Law School and Year: Georgetown University Law Center, 1997

My Background

I am a fourth generation Coloradan from the rural San Luis Valley in southern Colorado. My great-grandparents on my father's side of the family immigrated from Japan to California and then to southern Colorado to farm the land. Because they came to Colorado in the 1920s, they did not suffer the injustice of the internment camps during World War II. My grandparents on my mother's side, however, were not so fortunate. They were Japanese American citizens living in California who were forced to leave everything to live in an internment camp in Arizona, simply because of their race. My family's story is a horrific example of the failure of the Rule of Law, which motivates me to uphold the Rule of Law in my practice and *pro bono* work.

The Legal Profession Needs You

The Rule of Law is a cornerstone of American society, and is designed to apply equally to each of us, ensuring fairness and justice. But "Rule of Law" are simply words, only meaningful if people uphold them. Lawyers are responsible for upholding and enforcing the Rule of Law, and American society needs you now more than ever.

We have a global access to justice crisis. The Rule of Law only works when everyone has access to a fair and just system, otherwise, the system risks failure. Recently, the Institute for the Advancement of the American Legal System and the Hague Institute for Innovation of Law (HiiL) conducted a study that shows that this civil justice crisis exists in the United States.[1] Lawyers improve access to our system of justice. In my *pro bono* work, I have represented refugees seeking asylum, poor school districts in desperate need of equitable funding, and blind tenants in their landlord/tenant dispute. I know that my legal representation made a positive difference in these cases. Whether you enter public service or private practice, make it a point to help people access our justice system.

Additionally, the legal profession struggles with diversity, equity, and inclusion.[2] Having lawyers from, and working in, our various and diverse communities betters our justice system and promotes the Rule of Law. I encourage you to get out of your comfort zone. Work to understand and build bridges with communities different from your own.[3] You and our legal profession will be better for it.

Lawyer Skills

There are certain fundamental skills[4] that allow newer lawyers to succeed regardless of legal practice. Based on my experience, **character** is at the top of this list. To be a good lawyer, you must have integrity and a high level of trustworthiness. This comes in various shapes and

---

[1] Hague Institute for Innovation of Law and Institute for the Advancement of the American Legal System. (2021). *Justice Needs and Satisfaction in the United States of America.* https://iaals.du.edu/projects/us-justice-needs.

[2] American Bar Association. (2021). *Profile of the Legal Profession.* "Growth of the Legal Profession." https://www.abalegalprofile.com/demographics.

[3] During World War II, Japanese Americans were falsely regarded as untrustworthy, which allowed for their internment. Coloradans are proud that our governor (and lawyer) Ralph L. Carr took a principled position against the internment camps. *See* Schrager, Adam. (2008). *The Principled Politician: The Ralph Carr Story.* Golden, CO: Fulcrum Publishing.

[4] I serve on the Board of Advisors for the Institute for the Advancement of the American Legal System. IALLS Foundations for Practice is ground-breaking work that seeks to identify the foundations that entry-level lawyers need to succeed in the practice of law. *See* IAALS. (2021). *Foundations for Practice.* https://iaals.du.edu/projects/foundations-practice.

sizes, but ultimately, it is about honoring your commitments including to our professional ethics. Discussing character and integrity in
platitudes is easy, but what do you do when you believe your client
is not being truthful? Or when you find that harmful document or
adverse case? Let your moral compass and our profession's oath[5] and
ethics rules be your guide. And remember, your **reputation** is critical
to your career.

In addition to character, other skills include **work ethic, empathy,**
and the **ability to juggle** (e.g., handling numerous cases and responsibilities at the same time). Obtaining work experiences prior to and
during law school help you establish these foundations. **Teamwork**
is a must as I do not handle cases or go to trial alone. Having experience on teams (e.g., athletics, nonprofit board, or committee work,
etc.) helps establish this skill.

Litigation and Trial Skills

In litigation and trial, regardless of type of law, there will be numerous skills that you need to develop and master. Find mentors who will
help you prepare and then evaluate you before, during, and after
each task. **Mentorship** is key to your success in any organization, as
mentors teach you the necessary skills while guiding you through the
politics of your particular organization. Work to find and cultivate
relationships with these mentors. There are also various organizations (e.g., National Institute for Trial Advocacy), which teach many
of these skills through repeat performance and evaluation. Learning
new skills is a difficult and challenging process. Have a **growth mindset,** and analyze your performance with the help of your colleagues.
Have the **humility** to understand that you can always be better.

---

[5] You will take an Oath of Admission that is (or will be similar to) the following Colorado Attorney Oath of Admission, which states in part:

   I will treat all persons whom I encounter through my practice of law with fairness, courtesy, respect, and honesty;

   I will use my knowledge of the law for the betterment of society and the improvement of the legal system;

   I will never reject, from any consideration personal to myself, the cause of the
   defenseless or oppressed;

In litigation, you will need to gain experience and training in a variety of tasks. At the end of this guest chapter is a checklist of experiences that you should eventually obtain over several years. There are also a few key skills that are worth emphasizing.

Write, Write, Write

One of the most important skills in litigation is writing, which can also be one of the major inconsistencies in new lawyers. You become a better writer through practice and mentorship. While in law school, join a journal or obtain externships which involve writing (e.g., working for a judge, appellate lawyer, etc.). Apply for a judicial law clerk position after law school. I was fortunate to have clerked for the Honorable Chief Justice Mary J. Mullarkey of the Colorado Supreme Court, who was the first female in that role. During my clerkship, Chief Justice Mullarkey explained her legal reasoning and made me a better writer. She helped me to understand that her writing should be clear so that the parties and practitioners understood the legal reasoning in the Court's opinions, which serve as binding guidance to lower courts on how to apply the law. Your goal is to ensure that your legal brief is well-researched,[6] organized, clear, and persuasive.

Be a Storyteller

Regardless of the complexity of the case, human beings are wired to communicate through stories. When you are in trial, your job is to tell your client's story in the most persuasive way possible. You know

---

. . . .

Colorado Supreme Court Office of Attorney Regulation Counsel, *Oath of Admission.* https://coloradosupremecourt.com/Current%20Lawyers/Oath.asp. Always remember your Oath.

[6] Extensively research the relevant issues. One of my early mentors analogized legal research to a tree. The issue is the tree trunk, but you must also follow the branches to fully understand the issue. And when you present the issue in your legal briefs, fairly present relevant cases (favorable and unfavorable) and the other side's arguments.

the facts and the law, and you must present them in a story that is relatable for the jurors. Too often, new attorneys "think like a lawyer" to the exclusion of their common sense and their own experiences including notions of fairness. Do not underestimate the power of your own life experiences. Be **genuine**. Jurors will relate to who you are, not someone you are pretending to be.

Additionally, a lawyer must develop empathy—not only sympathy—for the client's circumstances. If lawyers do so, they are better able to solve their clients' problems. Push yourself to leave your comfort zone and obtain new experiences. This includes learning about and assisting communities with which you are unfamiliar. These experiences empower you with empathy (in addition to becoming a better person), and you will be better able to relate to clients and jurors who often come from backgrounds very different from your own.

The best way to obtain trial skills is through experience in the courtroom. For newer attorneys, courtroom experiences may be hard to obtain. Perform *pro bono* work, which allows you to obtain trial skills in addition to helping the indigent and improving access to justice.[7] I handled my first court argument in a *pro bono* criminal case, and obtained invaluable experience working on refugee and asylum matters.[8]

Be Happy

Finally, check in with yourself as to your happiness. Litigation and trial are hard. The struggle will make you better, but evaluate—and consistently reevaluate—whether your job brings you happiness. A law degree presents so many different opportunities, and life is too short to be miserable. I am fortunate to have had a fulfilling career to this point. I wish you the same.

---

[7] Hoagland, D.W. 1995. "Community Service Makes Better Lawyers." Katzmann, R. (ed.). *The Law Firm and the Public Good.* Washington, DC: The Brookings Institution.
[8] Kawanabe, K. (November 2005). "One Refugee: A Commercial Litigator's Pro Bono Experience with Immigration Law." *The Colorado Lawyer* 34 (85).

LITIGATION/Trial Skills[9]

- Client Relations
  - Communicate with clients regarding:
    - Goals and strategy
    - Budget
    - Case status
    - Discovery and trial preparation needs
    - Settlement
- Investigation and Discovery
  - Litigation hold
  - Collect relevant client documents, witnesses and case facts for strategic presentation
  - Supervise document review and prepare privilege log
  - Draft initial disclosures
  - Draft written discovery requests
  - Draft responses to written discovery requests
    - Gather and prepare documents in response to written requests for production
- Case Analysis and Management
  - Develop case strategy
  - Handle day-to-day management of small and medium-sized case
  - Supervise junior attorney on a case team
  - Handle day-to-day management of large-sized/complex case
  - Prepare case plan and budget
    - Oversee compliance with budget
  - Prepare research memoranda
  - Develop proficiency with electronic litigation tools (i.e., document databases)
  - Draft a scheduling or case management order
    - Negotiate resolution of case management issues with opposing counsel
  - Prepare for and handle mediation
    - Act as lead counsel in negotiating a settlement in simple case

[9] Note that all of these skills are obtained over several years, with increasing degrees of difficulty in each of these categories.

- Act as lead counsel in negotiating a settlement in complex case
- Draft settlement agreement
- Drafting Litigation Documents
  - Draft demand letter / response
  - Draft a complaint
  - Draft an answer
  - Draft a removal petition
  - Draft discovery motion
  - Draft simple motions/response to simple motions
  - Draft a motion to dismiss/response to motion to dismiss
  - Draft a summary judgment motion and supporting brief/ response to MSJ motion
  - Draft complex motion/response to complex motion
  - Draft appellate briefs
    - Present appellate oral argument
  - Prepare key pleadings, depending on your practice (e.g., class certification, patent infringement contentions, etc.)
- Depositions
  - Prepare for and take deposition of peripheral fact or client witness
  - Prepare for and take deposition of pivotal fact witness (e.g., 30(b)(6) witness)
  - Prepare for and defend deposition of client witness
  - Prepare for and defend 30(b)(6) deposition
- Experts
  - Locate, interview, and retain expert witness
    - Work with expert witness
  - Prepare for and defend an expert for deposition
  - Prepare for and take an expert deposition
- Courtroom
  - Prepare for and handle scheduling conference
  - Prepare and present argument at hearing for a simple motion
  - Prepare and present argument at hearing on a complex/ pivotal issue
  - Conduct direct and cross examinations of peripheral witness in a hearing or trial
  - Conduct direct and cross examinations of pivotal witness in a hearing or trial

o Conduct direct and cross examinations of expert witness in a hearing or trial
o Assist in trial preparation and second chair trial or arbitration in simple case
o Prepare for and act as lead counsel at a bench trial or arbitration in simple case
o Prepare for and act as lead counsel at a jury trial in a simple case
o Assist in trial preparation and second chair complex trial or arbitration
o Prepare for and act as lead counsel at a bench trial or arbitration in complex case
o Prepare for and act as lead counsel at a jury trial in complex case, including:
  ▪ Jury selection (*voir dire*)
  ▪ Opening statement
  ▪ Direct examinations
  ▪ Cross examinations
  ▪ Experts
  ▪ Dispositive motions (*e.g.*, Rule 50)
  ▪ Closing statement
o Experience the suspense of watching the jury enter the courtroom, as you await the verdict

Guest Chapter 4

Name: Rachel Proffitt

Current Position: Partner, Cooley LLP

Former Post-Law School Positions: Partner, Wilson, Sonsini, Goodrich & Rosati, P.C.

Legal Practice Area: Corporate Securities

Law School and Year: University of California Hastings College of the Law

Time between undergrad and law school: Time only for a road trip. . .

One or two books I recommend: *The Entrepreneur's Guide to Business Law* by Constance Bagley and *Venture Deals* by Brad Feld and Jason Mendelson.

Staring at a blank page with an impending deadline to share my thoughts with you offers a vivid glimpse into the life I could have led had I pursued one of my early-in-life career ambitions in journalism. Not a source of profound regret it turns out. Of course, you didn't pick up this book, nor make it to this chapter, to be talked in to or out of any particular profession—you're about to embark on a very exciting career! So, I will just preface these thoughts with the truth that corporate partner in Big Law was never on my list. Yet, here I am, nearly 20 years out of school, doing most days what I really love. How did I get here, and what are some secrets of success? Trust no one that tells you there's a perfect script, but indulge me as I share some perspectives that may be helpful as you take the leap from the classroom into the professional world.

Don't Close Doors

Before you start to question whether you should have kept your class selection broader as you rounded out your law school career, pause. I am not suggesting that if your 12-year-old self decreed that you were going to be litigator like the generations before you and you've diligently followed that path, that now you should also spend time moonlighting in transactional assignments in your new job. My point is more a frame of mind. I spent at least the first 18 months of my legal career (probably closer to 24 if I'm being honest) terrified someone was going to walk into my office and realize they'd made a huge mistake in hiring me. Not only was I very fearful they'd realize this was all in error, I also regularly debated whether I had in fact made the right decision for me. I was the accidental lawyer, the English major not quite qualified for much, turned law student. In fact, my regular answer to "what are you doing these days" was that I was working at a law firm for a few years to get some experience. I actually kept business school applications in my bottom drawer for years as well, often flipping the high-gloss pages, daydreaming of my next chapter.

But, since I was there, I committed to doing my best with what was in front of me. I worked hard, I did good work, I took constructive feedback, I developed relationships, and I grew as a lawyer. Years passed. Each review cycle seemed to suggest I was doing something right, so I kept at those somethings. I tried new projects, I worked with new partners, and I accepted opportunities to contribute to the fabric of the firm through recruiting, training, and mentoring. A few more years passed and that put partnership on the horizon. Again, not on my bucket list, and my junior associate self would have scoffed if you'd asked me about the prospect of becoming a partner, anywhere. However, what became clear to me during those late nights and skipped holidays was that I would do everything I could to position myself for that promotion, leaving it up to the firm to make its decision—I wouldn't sabotage the possibility.

This perspective set me apart from others. I worked with one associate who literally had his last day of work in "big law" circled on his calendar, years in the future. It was no surprise to anyone that he wanted to pay off his debts and then be done, and that day couldn't come fast enough. He left on that red-circled day with little more fanfare than what I think was a goodbye wave as he walked out the door. His opportunities were different than mine, as his level of investment was discounted. Another associate was gunning for partnership the moment she walked in the door, and while to some that level of drive may be endearing, for others it read as a blind spot and demonstrated an off-putting lack of self-awareness. She was hyper-competitive, trying too hard to win affection and unwilling to accept what is a natural and very steep learning curve, nearly in denial she didn't know how to do this job already. Again, her opportunities were different than mine, often drawn from a smaller pool of people willing or choosing to work with that energy.

Simply put, I kept my mind open, so that opportunities continued to present themselves and decisions remained mine to make. Had I chosen to feebly apply myself, or taken to heart my "few years gig" sentiment, or failed to accept all I had to learn, I doubt I'd have been able to reach the gates of the partnership with any chance of passing through.

Remember, Reputations Are Sticky

Despite the fact that there may be more lawyer jokes than there are lawyers, most legal communities are quite small. Perhaps you attended a large university or opted into one of the bigger law schools, and enjoyed some degree of anonymity. In this industry, your reputation will follow you, forever, so do not underestimate the impression you can leave with someone no matter how brief the interaction. I still remember the first person to stick his head into my office on my first day of work, welcoming me to the firm, saying he was excited to work together. He was a mentor of mine for many years. I also remember the first person to bring me to tears in this job, fortunately an infrequent occurrence. She wasn't nice, she didn't respectfully interact with her associates, and she never seemed happy—with anything. I remember the day she left the firm, and the relief I felt to never have to cross paths with her again. Yes, I am certain I could still pick her out of crowd. Lastly, I remember being mentored by someone on the other side of the table in a transaction. I was a young lawyer, he may have only been a couple years ahead of me, but instead of taking advantage of our knowledge differential, he chose to help me learn. He would ask if, in fact, that was the approach my client wanted to take, when perhaps another alternative was available. He wasn't patronizing, he was just kind. Not only did I feel so grateful for his empathy in the moment, but his approach stuck with me, always. In fact, this was one of a few key experiences that helped me sort out what type of lawyer I was going to be in this ecosystem. To this day, I'm still happy when we have an opportunity to work together.

I'll talk more about this below, but this is probably one of the most critical pieces of the success puzzle in my mind—figuring out who you want to be in this career. Everyone will have their own style, their own approach—some will elect to be obstinate because they want this job to have some fight in it no matter what, some will elect to be collegial and collaborative because that feels like a more natural and sustainable way to practice, some will feel uncomfortable in the gray that lives between the black and white of law school and cling to rules for safety and may struggle to provide practical advice, and the list could go on for pages. What has consistently proven true for me is that having a reputation for doing right by my clients and those around me, my colleagues and those on the opposite side of a transaction, and for being human—owning mistakes, being kind— has never led me astray. Yes, this leaves it up to those interacting with me to rise to the occasion, but, if they don't, that's on them, and I can rest comfortably knowing I've done my best and haven't been pulled in a direction that doesn't resonate with me. Regardless of who you chose to be, just know it's a choice that is difficult to unmake, which makes early impressions, early interactions in your career, incredibly important. I think sometimes folks lose sight of the fact that all of it matters—the interactions with your colleagues, even in your first few weeks, the way you treat your assistant when no one else is around, the tone you take with opposing counsel—all of it makes a mark. I tend to find that inconsistency of approach through the various interactions doesn't end well, as some part of it isn't real. The associate that is a yes-person to their client no matter the ask, cares only about what senior attorneys think of them, argues to argue with opposing counsel, and is condescending to their assistant? I'll let you decide the character that underlies and the motivation that drives that person. Remember that when your name is offered as a resource on a project, comes up as a referral, or shows up on a working group list, people will react, and often those reactions are based on an early or one-time impression. Lawyers are a lot of things, but stubborn in their beliefs and proud of their long memories are among their most prized traits, and striving to reinvent yourself is not where you want to be spending your time.

Listen, a Lot

There's a balance to be struck here, as I don't want to send you into your new profession on mute. You just finished years of schooling and practical applications of your lessons, and I'm sure you're eager to deploy them. Hoping this isn't the first time you've heard this, law school doesn't prepare you to actually practice law. Practicing prepares you to practice law. At its core, most of this profession is still very much an apprentice model. You learn by seeing and then doing, and of course some good old fashion substantive training sprinkled in doesn't hurt, but that alone will not be enough. I can usually spot the new lawyers that ultimately will need some recalibration. They come in fearless, confident that they have answers to everything, and often a better way than what is described to them. While this persona may work in some settings, before deploying, please consider that it may not. There is something very endearing, and often self-fulfilling, about the associate who comes in eager to be trained, aware of what they don't know, who is both happy to contribute and also knows when to learn from those around them. That is not an instruction to cast off your sense of self, nor to refuse to share your opinions, but it is a reminder that every single person in the building you're about to walk into has been there longer. Every single one of them.

Having said all of that, let's take a quick page out of my lessons-learned playbook. Back to my first couple years as an associate, I was terrified. Apparently, that state of being didn't lend itself well to certain first impressions, at all. I certainly knew what I didn't know, but frankly that felt like every single thing, so I resorted to listening—nearly exclusively. Were you to meet me now that may feel like a tall tale, but it's the truth. Fortunately for me, I both outgrew that, and had some very forgiving mentors along the way. Naturally, one of my dearest friends today was one of the folks that I must have found most intimidating. Countless meetings we sat in where I probably should have said more, or anything, really. I kept my contributions to a minimum, and primarily relied on others to fill the space.

Over the years, as we continued to work together, and I gradually found my voice, he finally admitted to me his first impressions—no sugar coating—he was convinced I was just aloof! Aloof! I'm not sure someone could have found a more insulting word, but I share this so you have that perspective. I literally was anything but that. I cared about my job, and was intently focused on doing well. But people obviously had their own read on me, and at least one person thought I was very uninterested in what we were doing.

So, when you join your new team, be mindful of how you present, and even if you utter only enough words to ask some questions, engage. There's apparently too much to be misread into silence. And to not lose sight of the message, whether you trend to the "don't know when to stop talking" camp, or are a "happy audience member," make sure you're actively listening. There is something to be learned from everyone. Maybe it's the person you most want to be like, but maybe also it's the person you very much do not want to become—there is value in absorbing it all.

Be Authentic

I don't have a degree in psychology, although some days I may feel I need it, but that doesn't stop me from offering this word of advice in most parts of my life. Life is just too short to playact your way through it. So, notwithstanding these perspectives I just shared, I'm going to leave you with one parting thought—be yourself. This means you need to invest time getting to know who you are at your core, what makes you happy, what drives you to succeed, what makes your days feel rewarding when you close your eyes at night, and what gets you jumping out of bed in the morning. It's okay if you don't have succinct answers to that today, but if I could focus you on one thing, it would be that—get to know yourself no matter how long that takes and be true to that self. For me, it's been a journey, one that I am still on, but with each revelation, I try to finetune my path. As my late father said to me, the thing about yourself is that you can run all you want, but when you get to where you're going, you're still there. Nothing has proven truer. The more I can bring of myself into my daily existence, the happier I am. To be quite direct, if you get fired from this first job of yours for being you, trust me, it will ultimately be the best thing that happens to you. When we show up as ourselves, are appreciated for doing just that, and thrive not despite, but because of, who we are, there is nothing more gratifying. The best part of course is that it takes no effort, no memory of trained traits, to be you; you just need to allow yourself to present honestly, authentically, with those around you, and ultimately nothing will help you succeed more than that.

Guest Chapter 5

Name: Matt Baca

Current Position: Director, Community Engagement Division, Colorado Department of Law

Former Post-Law School Positions: Staff Attorney, Colorado Legal Services – Migrant Farm Worker Division; Associate Attorney, Earthjustice (Northwest Office); Judicial Law Clerk, U.S. District Court (E.D. Va.). Writer of short humor and fiction: http://www .mattbaca.org/.

Law School and Year: Joint JD/M.P.P. at New York University School of Law and the Harvard Kennedy School, 2011

Time between undergrad and law school: None (which I don't recommend)

One or two books I recommend:

1. *Just Mercy* by Bryan Stevenson – Below I talk about being grounded in your values as a lawyer and a human, and there is no better example than Stevenson's belief in and work toward the notion that we are all more than the worst thing we've done.
2. *To Kill a Mockingbird* by Harper Lee – I hesitate to include something so obvious, but for me, it still inspires as to how a lawyer's advocacy for an individual and for justice, even against long odds and even when ultimately unsuccessful, is sacred in our profession.

Prologue – An Anecdote

I woke up the other morning with a thought stuck my mind like a rock in my shoe: the year 2100. That year is not so far off, really. As of this writing, it is 79 years in the future, and there are of course many people alive today who remember 79 years in the past (1942). But yet, it occurred to me that by 2100 my four-year-old will be 83 and my two-year-old will be 81; if they have kids, those kids will probably be in their forties or fifties; if those kids have kids (my great grand-children), they could be in college in the year 2100. All that to say something very obvious: it all goes so, so fast.

A Few Ideas on How to Be a Lawyer that Only Halfway Correlates with How I Have Actually Behaved, as We Collectively March Toward the Year 2100

That's the main thing. If it were socially acceptable, I would end every sentence with every new lawyer: as we collectively march toward the year 2100. Because if you haven't yet, at some point soon, you will feel in your bones all these cliches about time that have survived for a reason. The only time we have is now. The days go slow, the years go fast. You will feel this as your kids grow from babies to school-aged in two seconds or your parents—who you remember as youngish—begin impressive decades, or friends' kids become your colleagues. When movies you loved as a kid look pixelated and old.

The worst I could offer would be to say life is short so do what you love, which I promise I won't do, at least not until the very end and not without an apology. But here's the thing I would tell myself if I could go back in time: now is when you examine what matters to you and to try with urgency to align those in your life and your career. I'll call these things that matter to you your values. The moment is now. The moment is now. The moment is now, as we collectively march toward the year 2100.

We can all scrap the idea that there is work and there is life and that these are two fully separate and sealed universes—it's all part of the one life you get. I don't mean to suggest that you shouldn't try very hard to protect non-work time from work—you absolutely should—but it's all life, all part of the same messy timespan you have between now and 2100. What I mean is: the values you have for life, those have to be the same ones you explore and interrogate and, ultimately, apply to your work.

Let's talk about these in two categories. The first is how you work. The second is what work you do.

How you work. Do you want to be a helpful, collaborative person? If you value kindness, don't expect to be happy in an unkind practice of law. Know yourself and know it before you spend eight or twenty years bobbing along in hostile waters. And if you don't instinctively value kindness and empathy and compassion, or even if you do, remember that we all stumble toward them and often fail; George Saunders said it persuasively:

"At the end of my life, I know I won't be wishing I'd held more back, been less effusive, more often stood on ceremony, forgiven less, spent more days oblivious to the secret wishes and fears of the people around me. So what is stopping me from stepping outside my habitual crap? My mind, my limited mind."

Working on that limited mind's capacity for generosity is always worth the effort.

Also, do you value time outside of work? If I hope anything for you and for me, it's that—finding the balance that most brings you joy. The right balance will change over different seasons of your career, and while balance is a difficult goal for lawyers to achieve, it couldn't be more important. It is. It is, as we march collectively toward the year 2100.

The second category is what you do for work.

Your practice area and you are going to be like one of those older couples who, over the course of decades, start to look like each other, speak with the same idiosyncratic turns of phrase, wear matching clothes unintentionally. And it is so, so easy for a decade to slip by and all of a sudden you realize you're now a lot more like your clients and colleagues than the kid who wrote your law school entrance essay and you wonder—Do I even like these people? Why do I still have to care what they think about me?—so my suggestion, humbly, is that you start asking today if you value the values of your type of practice.

This question—if not fully unique to lawyers—is probably rare. I don't imagine optometrists have to ask whether treating this or that person's eyes will make them feel morally bankrupt. But here we are, as lawyers, with something to say and do about the operation of lives and society.

So there are some values to stay away from. How about the things you want to go toward? It's important to have these—nothing perfect or idealized or entirely fanciful but some value or ambition that calls to you. The waves will push you this way and that, but if you aim toward something you like, you're more likely to get there. So if you want a relatively stress- and angst-free career and to live in the mountains, that's good to acknowledge and to go for, starting now. Or if you want to live in Spain or Wichita, or if you want to write novels or be a teacher, these are all plausibly consistent with a career as a lawyer, but you have to be deliberate and bold about declaring them your values and pursuing them, even as those around you may wonder why you want to take a step off the ordinary path. Inertia is as hard to overcome in a career as in nature—not impossible, but harder as your career gathers mass.

But we also need to interrogate the values and goals we think we hold, that destination where you want to aim the ship. You need to do so honestly and to find in yourself and your values those euphemisms and half-truths you are trying to foist on yourself.

Like you might say: I want to make an impact, make the world better. What you may mean, when you really stop and examine it, is that you want power over people's lives. The former requires and generates humility; the latter will never be satisfied, even if you someday are the Czar of Public Interest (or of America, or anything else). As Victor Hugo said, "How easily ambition calls itself vocation." I want you to want to make the world better—I want that for myself too—but my point is to please not let yourself get away with altruistic-seeming falsehoods in your own self-examination. Know what you really value, really want—even those things you wouldn't utter aloud, and then ask yourself hard questions about them.

Another you might say: I want the best legal training or to be in a practice with resources or to do cutting-edge, big cases. What you may mean: I want to be at a firm and the real reason is because I want money but I can't just say: "I want money." Again—be honest with yourself. Nobody but you gets to judge whether you need the money to pay off loans or support family or just because you want the security of it or something else. But I ask that you are honest and in so doing to please not accept without examination the law firm recruiting bromide that law firms are the only setting where good lawyers emerge or decent livings can be earned.

So that's my advice: work on a set of values in how you work and in what you do. And give them the same scrutiny you would an opposing witness with questionable motives.

Epilogue – Quicker, Unranked Observations, as We Collectively March Toward the Year 2100

1. Help your peers; this is intrinsically good. If you don't care about that, it's also cynically and instrumentally good (they may later help you).
2. Don't look at your phone all the time, at all hours of all days. To be more concrete and even controversial: don't sleep with your phone in your room—stress-reading an email at 3 a.m. accomplishes nothing for no one, and sending an email at that hour makes the world less like the one we all want to inhabit.
3. Some values and instincts you hold are bad. Knowing your values is a start, but what if you have bad values, with roots that run all the way down? We all do. Wanting to show Ricardo—or whomever—and all his colleagues that he's a real idiot asshole and a bad lawyer will sometimes call to you as a motivation, and it will never, ever be good. That's where your faith tradition or moral compass comes in, where training on things like implicit bias matters. Acknowledge bad instincts, see them, and resist.
4. You aren't the smartest or the most superlative anything, and you don't need to be. You just need to be smart enough. The tools that have gotten you here will continue to serve you. Hone them.
5. Abraham Lincoln's unimprovable guidance on how we should act as humans (and lawyers): "With malice toward none, with charity for all, with firmness in the right."
6. A project for a whole career: getting the dial calibrated so that you can hear criticism but not obsess about what others think—especially the unfair, petty stuff.
7. For when you don't have that dial set right, keep a kudos folder where you collect nice things people have told you so that you can, during the low times, give yourself a boost.
8. Everyone else is also trying and failing and blundering and eating and sleeping and crying and laughing, and if we can recognize we are all—your colleagues, opposing counsel, clients, bosses, paralegals—on this planet only briefly and only together, then I don't know what except that the world will be nicer. Better said by Bryan Stevenson: "We have a choice.

We can embrace our humanness, which means embracing our broken natures and the compassion that remains our best hope for healing. Or we can deny our brokenness, forswear compassion, and, as a result, deny our own humanity."

9. Life is short. The year 2100 is near. Do what you love. (Sorry.)

Guest Chapter 6

Name: Kimberly R. Willoughby

Current Position: Principal, Willoughby & Associates

Legal Practice Areas: Estate Planning and Administration; Matrimonial Law

Law School and Year: University of Virginia, 1994

Time between undergrad and law school: 1 year (went camping)

One or two books I recommend: *Never Split the Difference* by Chris Voss; *Tribes* by Seth Godin; *The Hidden Brain* by Shankar Vedantam

Short description of my law school experience

I went to law school because I loved philosophy, history, and politics, and while a Ph.D. in any of these areas guaranteed unemployment or academia, law school offered the ability to potentially put my interests here to actual use. While in law school, I took every theory class possible and entered a master's program in history. I studied a lot.

At the law school freshman orientation, they told us, "After you graduate UVA, you have the job. Don't worry about that. We have a B mean. Don't worry about your grades. Look to your right. Look to your left. One of those people will be a judge. Your job while you are here is to get to know your fellow UVA law students."

Almost 30 years later I can tell you this—no, we were not guaranteed the job. Most judicial positions are not coveted positions anymore. However, they were right about the grades: I did not break past the B mean, and grades were irrelevant to my career. They were also right to tell us that one of the most important things law school had to offer was lifelong connections. At the time, I did not understand that if you attend a law school filled with people you don't want to develop a lifetime connection with, you will miss out on one of the most important things law school has to offer. Law school offers community and a network that can serve as a springboard to the rest of your life, including (but not limited to) your career.

The Path of My Legal Career

When I graduated law school, I immediately moved back to Colorado and started at a traditional large firm. The associates were (at first) really excited to do rote, boring work and the partners trained us just enough to be useful to their billing needs. I traveled a lot with my supervising partner, but I felt I was there mainly to keep him company. I did not particularly care for the entire experience and the firm went under within a few years. I then did a clerkship at the Colorado Court of Appeals. That position fit me better, but it was pretty lonely. One thing I learned from reading trial transcripts, however, was that a lot of trial lawyers are, well, not exactly Perry Mason. I came away with the notion that if being in a big, fancy firm did not guarantee stability and my lack of trial experience did not ensure ridicule, I might as well open my own office.

So I did. I practiced "door law," meaning, if it came in the door, I took it. I worked practically for free. I represented all sorts of people—alleged child abusers, teenage mothers, prostitutes, general scammers. I had a client ask me to meet him at a bar so we could watch the news clip of him holding up a bank. "Should I turn myself in?" he asked his 26-year-old lawyer. I went to court a lot. A magistrate yelled at me in the courtroom one day when I told her the case had not settled because I needed trial experience. I very actively sought out mentors. I joined everything. I worked in areas without much law. I testified in front of the legislature. I took on cases that could make new law, and I did make new law in Colorado.

Eventually I gained leadership roles. I wrote a lot in the industry journals. I taught constantly at CLEs. Most people in the bar associations knew me or knew who I was. Eventually I charged more for my services.

As I write this, I am nearly thirty years into practice. I am nationally ranked as one of the best in my field. I am the only active attorney in the nation granted a Fellowship to two national, very selective organizations in my practice areas. While many of my colleagues are suffering burnout, I have never been happier in what I do for my vocation. I genuinely like my clients and my colleagues. I keep learning a tremendous amount every day.

My practice areas, however, require deep skill sets that are not in law school. My practice areas involve death and family legacies. They involve the moments in a life where people look closely at who they are, what they did with their lives, and how they want to be remembered. I should have taken classes on how to become a priest.

Law Is a Service Industry

Law schools and firms do not actively teach that law is a service industry. Those who go into law tend to be "type A" people who are largely driven by their need to be seen as smart and important. However, delivering a service is about the client. Whether the client is an individual or an entity, lawyers interact with people. The most successful lawyers are the ones who are able to put their egos aside and give the client the experience of being heard, empathized with and of being important.

What is frustrating about new graduates? How have you used the core concepts of lawyering this book proposes?

It takes graduates too long to realize it's not about them. Law is a service industry. Clients do not care about you anywhere near as much as they care about themselves (if they care about you at all). The faster you learn to "do unto others as they would have you do unto them," the faster you can be an excellent, sought-after lawyer with an amazing reputation.

What does the client want? Mainly, for the person serving them to treat them like it's all about *them*. The happiest client is the one who feels like he or she is your only client. The successful lawyer tries to get into the position of the client. What do they need? What do they think they need? What are they worried about? What is their stated goal? Is there another actual goal? What do they think you can do for them? What will make them feel attended to and important? What will give them an outcome to make them talk to other people about you? Little of that has to do with your credentials or how well you analyzed case law.

To determine what your client wants and needs, you need to ask lots of questions. Research them, their position, their company, and their story. My firm's intake process includes researching potential clients before they talk with a lawyer. When the client retains, we have a series of "dossier meetings." We talk about the client—What do they need now? How do they most effectively receive information? What frustrates them? What makes them happy? How to they best like to be attended to? What are their interests? What things in their worlds are stressors? What brings them joy?

Serving the client requires listening to the client and showing them that you are listening. Once you have asked lots of questions and listened, you can better put yourself in the client's position.

Find your tribe. When you do, service is a two-way street. You will feel, and you will be, the most successful when you serve those you feel good about giving your time and energy to. This is a very basic human reality. People want to feel that they are a part of something meaningful. Most attorneys join the legal profession to be helpful and to be part of something they believe is important. You will best be able to employ the core concepts in this book when you genuinely feel connected to those you serve. This is akin to the adage, "Do what you love and you will never work a day in your life." If you do **for** those you have a connection to, and **with** those you have a connection to, "work" becomes how you live.

Biggest mistake(s) you made while in law school

The two biggest mistakes I made were studying too much and not going to a law school that fit me. Likely, I studied too much because the school did not fit me. The people at my law school were not my tribe, and as a result I did not make the connections that would have enriched my experience there.

Looking back, I would have done better to choose a school in a state where I wanted to live, with students who were passionate about social causes, and that offered more ways of getting trial experience.

What to learn while in law school

Law school does not teach you how to be a successful lawyer. It teaches you how to think in a certain way. Remember in the first year of law school your brain just *hurt*? Everything was new and presented in a way that did not mesh with how you learned before. Law school mainly teaches you to think in a certain way, and how to find information about the law. Take the classes that interest you, as most non-required classes are not very helpful to your career. Take classes that will help you pass the bar. Do externships so you can assess who your tribe will be after law school.

The classes I loved in law school were about theory or history. I did not take them to get a job. As it turned out, they were fundamental to my success because they taught me how to think, how to understand, and kept my brain creatively working on big concepts.

If you want to be a successful practicing lawyer, you must know the law in your practice area, you must learn things that give you a creative edge, and you must understand how human brains and groups of people work. You need to learn anthropology, cognitive psychology, and some popular neuroscience. You need to understand social systems, and how small and larger groups of people function well together. You need to know what causes people to think a certain way and behave a certain way. To convince someone to do something (a judge, a client, opposing counsel), you need to get inside their head and their brain, which are often two completely different things.

Make this your mantra: Know yourself, accept yourself, be yourself. Know what you are good at and do that in law school and afterwards. "Law" is a very big tent. It encompasses what you are good at. Stop trying to be what your dad/mom/girlfriend/Netflix series told you to be. Be your very best self, every day, but accept who that is and be that person. You will never be successful trying to be what you are not.

Most useful classes in law school

Legal writing. You *must* learn how to write to be an effective lawyer.

How did you decide what to do post-law school? With hindsight, how good of a job did you do?

I applied for jobs and I was offered a prestigious firm position. In hindsight, I should have been more open to options other than a big firm. I never thought I would be interested in matrimonial law or estate planning. However, after starting at the very bottom and working my way up, it was clear that those were the exact areas in which I had strengths and something to offer.

What was the biggest mistake you made while at your first job?

Pretending I was interested in it. When I was laid off, the partner who sent me on my way suggested that I should look at positions in social advocacy. While my ego was bruised by the message, "You don't actually belong here," she was absolutely right.

What was the best advice you received or have given for those coming out of law school?

Find a mentor. However, a mentor is not someone who you call once a year with a legal question. A mentor is someone invested in you and who you are invested in. The only way to have an actual "mentor" is to spend time with that person, empathize with that person, listen to that person, and ask a lot of questions. Also, give him or her a reason to empathize with and listen to you.

What was the worst advice you received coming out of law school?

"Do not take payment in drugs." It's not bad advice per se, but I was sharing an office with this person, and he apparently thought this was advice I needed. I had not yet found my tribe.

How have you remained happy in your profession? Have there been times when you were not? If so, what did you do to improve your situation?

True happiness is something you realized you attained when you look back. Strive to be useful and connected and you will feel good in the present. When you look back, you will realize you were happy.

Unhappiness, however, is definitely a "now" thing. Whenever my practice was draining instead of sustaining, I made a list of all of the things I did not like about my practice, and all the things that I did like about my practice. Then I made a specific plan for getting rid of the things that I did not like and for increasing what I did like. This always works, but it is something that must be done every couple of years.

Guest Chapter 7

Name: Brad Bernthal

Current Position: Associate Professor at Colorado Law. Founder of Brain Cramp Camp, a mental training program for tennis players.

Former Post-Law School Positions: Associate Attorney in law firms, including work in a medium-sized law firm in Boulder, Colorado (Berg Hill Greenleaf & Ruscitti LLP), a large law firm's Denver office (firm is now Hogan Lovells), and an iconic San Francisco firm, Brobeck, Phleger & Harrison LLP, that unfortunately met its demise.

Legal Practice Area: Teaching and research specializing in startups, entrepreneurial law, and early stage finance (such as angel and venture capital investments)

Law School and Year: Colorado Law, 2001

Time between undergrad and law school: Four years. Played semi-professional tennis, taught English in Korea, and managed an undefeated softball team while interning for Senator Bob Kerrey (Nebraska) on Capitol Hill.

One or two books I recommend: *Peak: Secrets from the New Science of Expertise* (2017), by Anders Ericsson and Robert Pool. Another accessible, popular book distillation of deliberate practice research is Geoff Colvin, *Talent Is Overrated: What Really Separates World-Class Performers from Everybody Else* (2009).

Deliberate Practice and the Arc of a Legal Career

This is a section about expertise. Expertise is a concept that we often laud as desirable. But we seldom think deeply about what expertise actually is or, further, how to become an expert.

Your best bet for success in transactional law is to build a non-fungible, expert mental model, marked by specialized insight and excellent judgment. (Aside: it also would help you to be able to learn to effectively work with the machines, too.) Experts perceive more than nonexperts (yes, they "see" the same things differently), experts retrieve more than nonexperts (often because experts see one pattern while nonexperts see multiple, disconnected points), and experts process information better than nonexperts (they see the right moves, so to speak).

The question is how to become an expert.

Isn't this what law school is for? No. I am a law professor. I take my job seriously. But even in my good years, I do not produce specialized attorneys, let alone experts. Three years of law school may seem long. Yet research underscores that three years is not long enough to produce an expert. Moreover, law remains a profession—in the United States, at least—where graduate education training is generalist in nature. Law school teaches the fundamentals of thinking—and writing!—like a lawyer, and exposes students to a wide range of substantive areas. Every JD, like it or not, studies Constitutional Law, learns something about evidence, spends way too many hours navel gazing about contractual consideration, and dies a little bit inside while acquiescing to Bluebook citation exactitude.

You are expected to acquire a specialization, and ideally expertise, through post-graduation work experience. Large amounts of your development hinges on what you learn, train for, and acquire once you leave law school. Again, the question is how to become an expert.

My suggestion: Take a deliberate practice approach to your 7 to 10 years after law school.

What is deliberate practice?

Deliberate practice, a concept originally developed by cognitive psychology scholar Anders Ericsson, explains what separates experts from non-experts. It is a theory of expertise based on empirical examination across a range of domains: music, chess, sports, and other professional settings. Deliberate practice observes that, across disparate pursuits, experts actually train in very similar ways. And, notably, experts train differently from non-experts.

Training among individuals who become experts is marked by four elements.

- One, the training is well-designed, typically by an expert in the area.
- Two, the training involves practice—in the sense of preparing for a future performance—with exercises that can be frequently repeated. Exercises often focus upon areas of weakness.
- Three, expert feedback is continuously available. Training does not occur in the dark. Outside eyes provide critique and feedback.
- Four, training occurs at an unusual intensity. Activities may be deeply engrossing. But they are also exhausting and demanding. Many high-level performers can manage only 4 to 5 hours of deliberate practice-style training per day. And they often sleep a lot, too.

The good news: deliberate practice makes visible a repeatable methodology about how experts get made. You can follow it. Taking this approach naturally leads to what Carol Dweck calls the growth mindset, too, as you are aware of the importance of improvement. The tough news: the method involves a ton of hard work. Moreover, the default is that your legal workplace is unlikely to train you with principles of deliberate practice in mind.

Deliberate practice, as it relates to acquisition of expertise in business law, presents a problem: the practice of law is not practice at all. In common parlance, such as the classic Allen Iversonian usage of practice, practice is a low stakes environment of skill acquisition and preparation for future performance. In the legal world, practice is actual work. Real clients. Stakes on the line. Billable hours. People get angry and happy. You know—the real deal.

Most of you will take jobs in firms and companies that, understandably, prioritize the client and company work that needs attention at any particular moment in time. This may or may not track your developmental needs. Work comes to you in haphazard and ad hoc ways. As a training method, this is not what deliberate practice would suggest. Some employers might monitor and measure the development of your skill set. Most will not. Rarely will you work in situations that align with what deliberate practice literature would suggest is your most likely path to expertise.

Bottom line: you need to take ownership of your own path to business law expertise.

What are the elements of expertise for deal attorneys?

Deliberate practice provides a methodology—i.e., the how—about how to become an expert. This still leaves the question of the most crucial dimensions—i.e., the what—that legal deliberate practice training should isolate and focus upon.

The cop out to the "what" question is the same answer as you wrote on your torts exam: it depends. And it is true that different legal roles within the transactional legal universe require different capacities. Yet we can say something more about the what of legal training.

Mentors and senior members on your teams can help you identify the crucial elements which define expertise in your legal area. In particular, there are three categories to consider in developing a legal deliberate practice training regime.

- One, identify substantive legal areas that experts in your area know inside-out. Consider which doctrinal areas, and specific subareas, must be mastered. You might have completed coursework in the area. Consider how to go deeper in substantive expertise during your first 7 to 10 years after graduation. Read treatises. Pull law review articles. Write white papers. Co-author pieces with a respected senior attorney for the state bar publication. Find ways to go deep.
- Two, inventory the skills required for expertise in your legal area. Skills refers to methods, tools, and applied techniques used by expert attorneys. Negotiations, transactional drafting, and oral communication are obvious cross-cutting skills for trusted deal attorneys. Other crucial business law skills remain almost invisible to law schools, including process management, understanding innovation methodologies (e.g., design thinking), change management, and leadership. Look for jobs that you would like to be ready for in 7 to 10 years, isolate the skills involved, and practice them.
- Three, identify the crucial pockets of non-legal insight, which I call domain knowledge, for the type of job you'd like to have in the future. Domain knowledge refers to substantive non-law

areas that expert deal makers and businesspeople are familiar with. The domain knowledge in your legal role may include financial literacy, knowing an industry sector, understanding a type of technology, familiarity with economic principles, and insight about routes to market. Catalogue the domain expertise required for expertise in your legal area and craft a plan to acquire it.

Design a Deliberate Practice Training Regime

Now craft and execute a deliberate practice legal training regime. You will almost certainly need an expert—or experts—to help you craft this plan. This is where mentors and great supervisors are gold. You need someone to help you identify your current weaknesses, craft exercises and other opportunities to expand your abilities, and provide on-going feedback along the way.

Some aspects of legal work, with a little effort, lend themselves directly to a deliberate practice approach. For example, attorneys in areas with repeatable processes and tasks, such as merger and acquisition practice, get many repetitions on tasks, such as arranging disclosure schedules to working through asset purchase agreements. Layer on continuous and on-going feedback from an expert, and this type of work might lead naturally to M&A legal expertise.

Other aspects of business law expertise may be well outside your day-to-day work and require a much more concerted effort. For example, let's say you recognize that financial literacy—e.g., reading financial statements—is important to become a general counsel, but your day-to-day work today primarily involves licensing deals. You might start with a basic finance course on-line, such as through Coursera. Then you might begin analyzing financial statements, trying to see what story the numbers tell, and then get feedback from an expert about what they actually say.

If you'd like to look further into deliberate practice, a starting point is the book *Peak: Secrets from the New Science of Expertise* (2017), by Ericsson and Pool. Another accessible, popular book distillation of deliberate practice research is Geoff Colvin, *Talent Is Overrated: What Really Separates World-Class Performers from Everybody Else* (2009). And if you want to go to the root of the literature, start with Ericsson et. al., *The Role of Deliberate Practice in the Acquisition of Expert Performance* (1993).

A deliberate practice lens, fundamentally, gets you to think about your legal career on a 7 to 10 year horizon. That long-term view helps you see a larger perspective than the day-to-day. Deliberate practice highlights that expertise is not a "you either have it or you don't" natural skill. Rather, expertise is earned over time. Deliberate practice illuminates a viable path to get there.

Guest Chapter 8

Name: Jolene A. Yee

Current Position: General Counsel & Vice-President Government Affairs, Delicato Family Wines; Adjunct Professional Faculty, Sonoma State University – Global Wine Executive MBA Program; Advisory Board Member, Hamel Family Wines.

Former Post-Law School Positions: Associate General Counsel with E. & J. Gallo Winery; Associate with Cooley Godward (now Cooley LLP); Foreign Legal Consultant with Kim & Chang.

Legal Practice Area: General Counsel and Government Affairs (aka regulatory/legislative nerd). Started my legal life negotiating talent contracts for a small independent film that no one should ever see but starring some really cool actors, then migrated to acquisitions of financially distressed assets, did a short stint in the tech sector before finally finding my "work soulmate' in the alcohol beverage industry, advising two of the finest wine-making families in the business on everything from grape to shelf, with a significant amount of my earlier career spent on M&A and international collaborations. Along the way, I made it a priority to focus on "women's issues" in the workplace, which all of you should now know really means EVERYONE's ISSUES in the workplace, but doing my best to generate interest in programs focused on the development, retention, and promotion of women.

Law School and Year: Why does Jason need to know my age??? University of California Hastings College of the Law, 1996. Yes, technically I was senior to him at Cooley (where we met) but he knew a hell of a lot more than I did about how Silicon Valley law practice worked.

Time between undergrad and law school: 5 months. I graduated from UCLA a little early and decided to try my hand at "English Living";

I did a "pupil barristership" and took a class on the European Community and lived in London, and it was an absolutely amazing way to learn that I did not want to be a criminal defense lawyer.

Some books I recommend: I love books. I love the way they look on my bookshelf every which way, and we have LOTS of bookshelves all over the house. This is a tough question.

1. *The Alchemist* by Paolo Coelho. This is a fable that you can read in a snap. But whenever someone I know is "stuck" I give it to them to read. You can do it in one sitting. When I was floundering around not knowing what I was supposed to do next, a friend gave me this book and it changed my life.
2. *Getting to Yes* by Roger Fisher and William Ury. This is the gold standard of negotiating and many of the processes if used properly really do work. The authors have done a decent job updating the examples in the most recent edition.
3. *Difficult Conversations: How to Discuss what Matters Most* by Douglas Stone. This is a great handbook by some of the same folks who crafted *Getting to Yes* from the Harvard Negotiation Project on how to approach to tough conversations you really need to have.

The nontraditional reason that had a kinda-sorta traditional outcome— Why I went to law school and what happened when I got there

When I was growing up, I was a chatterbox and described as "bossy" (today we just call that practicing my leadership skills); I loved to watch *Perry Mason*, my favorite book was *To Kill a Mockingbird*, I loved to talk, and in junior high I successfully prosecuted the big bad wolf for terrorizing Little Red Riding Hood in Moot Court (or something like that) and everyone used to tell me I should go to law school. But I went to law school for none of those reasons. I went to Law School for EXPEDIENCY.

When I was a junior in college, I decided I wanted to be an academic, and I wanted to teach. And one of my favorite professors sat me down and told me that pursuing a PhD was a very long a painful process, it would take ten years, and at the end I would be poor, in debt, and probably teaching at some unknown college in the middle of nowhere (and almost certainly somewhere I didn't want to be). But if I really wanted to teach, I could go to law school instead, finish in three years, and be "less poor" and probably better off with less effort. So off to study for the LSATs I went! But a funny thing happened when I went to law school, I fell in love with the practice of law. So even though I went to law school NOT to practice law, here I am all these years later having loved a career of practicing law. You just never can tell.

Dang, THAT Is Irritating! (Or what frustrates me about people newly out of law school)

Kids these days! But seriously, the differences among my generation (Gen X) and younger generations have certainly created some interesting work challenges. What I've noticed over the last few years among many recent law graduates or lawyers early in their careers are two things: first, they think they know a lot more than they do. Unfortunately, law schools leave you ill-prepared for the actual practice of law. Most law schools do a really nice job of teaching you how to think like a lawyer. The Socratic method challenges your brain to continue exploring different avenues and permutations of possible outcomes, and IRAC is a fantastic method of breaking down and understanding a case. But law schools often don't give you a lot of the skills you need to practice law. How do you navigate the billable hour? How do you engage with your colleagues? When should you ask questions? (Pssst . . . the answer is ALWAYS.) What is EQ? How do you write a concise e-mail with the right amount of information and not too much explanation? WHAT DO CLIENTS REALLY WANT??? Unfortunately, these things are generally learned during the first years of practice by sucking on a fire hose and crossing your fingers while standing on one leg and hoping someone takes you under their wing. Second, these same folks expect rocket movement up the proverbial ladder regardless of competence or skillset, but merely as a matter of course and expectation. I've had many conversations with new lawyers who expect to work 9-to-t, no weekends, but still make General Counsel within a few years. This is not only unreasonable, it would most likely be malpractice. There is absolutely nothing wrong with demanding a work-life balance, and with having high expectations. But the expectation that a recent graduate will achieve partner or GC status (or CLO or top dog or whatever) as a matter of course is simply hubris.

Also, I forgot to mention that I am highly annoyed by poor grammar. Please learn the difference between which and that. Know when to use a semi-colon and a colon. And the use of a period is not "aggressive."

The Importance of Empathy, Listening, Asking, and Giving Advice

I think that when most people think of lawyers, these four words probably don't come to the top of their minds. But in actuality, these "soft skills" are really an integral part of being a truly effective lawyer. You shouldn't underestimate the power of empathy. Whether you're a litigator litigating a high-stakes trial or an M&A lawyer negotiating a definitive agreement, or an employment lawyer negotiating a termination agreement, having empathy, and stepping into the shoes of the other party can help you come to a solution more quickly and with less conflict. Empathy should not be viewed as weakness, but as understanding; it's one of the traits that truly brings out our humanity, and should be revered in legal practice.

Likewise, Listening is a vital part to the practice of law and is something I use every day, not only in the practice of law but in the management of my team. As an example, when I actively listen to my clients, it allows me to better map out my thoughts and figure out how to attack any issues. It demonstrates to my clients that I'm engaged in the discussion and that I care about their issues. And it allows me to determine what additional information I need to figure out a resolution.

This leads me to the next crucial core skill of Asking. Knowing when and how to ask questions is an important lawyering skill. It sounds cliché but the only dumb question is the one you don't ask. The only way to make sure you have the full picture is to make sure you get all of your questions asked, and answered. Of course, there's a nice and efficient way to do this, and there's a poorly planned and annoying way. Choose the former; make sure you choose a time that is convenient, and when the person from whom you need the answers can be engaged and won't be rushed. Try and ask your questions in a methodical order, so they build on each other (and not haphazard). Be specific if you need a specific answer, or be broad if you need more of a story or narrative. There's an art to this, which you can improve over time. But planning is important.

Last, knowing when and how to give advice is the core of the practice of law. Often, people don't want the advice you have to give. You've probably heard the phrase Don't Kill the Messenger? Understanding when and how to give advice is vital to being an effective lawyer. Giving advice that might be difficult to hear is definitely a skill. If you have some advice that you know will be challenging both to deliver and to hear, practice giving it first, more than once. Listen to how you sound, and then massage your tone and delivery. It might sound silly, but your tone and word choice will be important to ensuring that the message you want to deliver is both heard and understood.

Boy, That Was a Doozy

Not really. I don't have many regrets from law school. I'm probably one of the few people who admits to actually loving my law school experience. At the time, however, I could not have predicted my future as a business lawyer. In law school I thought I might work for the government or do public interest work. It never occurred to me that I might need a background in business. Looking back, the one thing I probably would have done differently is applied for the joint program with Berkeley's school of Business and attempted the condensed JD/MBA program. My husband (also a General Counsel, of a tactical gear company) has a JD/MBA and assures me I'm not missing anything, but I think that having the financial education would have better prepared me for my life as a General Counsel and given me a leg up when I am wearing my "business hat."

I think another mistake I made was choosing my first-year elective based on the subject matter. I chose employment discrimination because I thought it would be a fun sexy subject! Unfortunately, the professor was deadly boring. I learned that no matter how sexy the subject, it cannot survive a poor professor. When you have a choice in classes, make sure you do your diligence on the professors before you choose.

I really wish I had taken Federal Taxation. No, Really!

As I stated earlier, I could never have predicted that my life would take the road it took. If I knew then what I know now, I 100% would have taken Federal Taxation. Yes, tax. Having a basis in tax earlier in my career would have been very helpful.

Moot Court Prepared Me for Life. Legal Writing Prepared Me for Art

There are a lot of useful courses in law school, but a few stand out for me. I am sure that philosophically some people believe that the usefulness of classes depend on what area you plan to practice. But in reality, I think that most subject matter classes teach you how to think like a lawyer, and the subject matter is somewhat interchangeable. That being said, I think torts stands out to me as being particularly good at providing a great platform for legal analysis. Moot Court, however, stands out as the series of classes that really honed my "lawyer" skills. It gave me the opportunity to put legal research skills into practice, and the writing and re-writing of briefs gave me the opportunity to understand the process of creating and refining legal arguments and the art of storytelling. Last, "moot court" forced me to learn public speaking skills and to learn to think on my feet. If you survive Moot Court and can stomach the public speaking aspect, I can't recommend enough going through the competition process. At UC Hastings, it's truly a competitive sport where the preparation process requires you to look at every possible angle of an argument, to argue both sides of a case, and to argue the same case over and over until you feel almost over-prepared for oral argument. This allowed me to gain a confidence in public speaking that I believe I would not have been able to gain in another way.

Learning how to write like a lawyer is extremely important. It's crucial that law students and new lawyers understand how to write for different audiences. When is a memo the right deliverable? (Hint: for a General Counsel, pretty much never.) When will a concise e-mail do? (For me, almost always.) How do I get 1000 words worth of ideas fit into space for 250? Your Legal Writing class is your introduction in how to communicate like a lawyer, and it's a very important part of the process of becoming an actual practicing attorney. A really good piece of legal writing is definitely like a piece of art.

My Life Is a Series of Accidents, but I'm Fine

I went to law school to become a Professor, but instead I'm a General Counsel. And that was not in any way by design. My professional life, and to some extent my personal life, has been a series of falls uphill. It wasn't always pretty, but somehow it all worked out!

My second-year summer I clerked at a small boutique law firm in San Francisco that practiced some entertainment law, some political law, and some bankruptcy. A weird mix, but it was interesting work. They made me an offer, but I held off on accepting while I looked into clerkships. I had some reservations, but ultimately accepted the offer. And then two weeks before the Bar Exam the firm decided to split and "revoked" my offer (legally, this was not possible, since you can't revoke an already-accepted offer, but I digress. . .). In any event, after the Bar Exam, six weeks in Europe, convincing my entertainment law professor to get me a gig in LA with his friend on a film, and then doing some freelance law and motion work, I threw caution to the wind and applied for a job for which I was completely unqualified, at a firm in Seoul, Korea. It was an incredible elite firm in Asia, and I was lucky to call it my home for about 2½ years. The experience I earned there helped pave my career.

Fast forward almost two decades, during which I experienced a series of personal tragedies and professional nightmares, including being laid off from a tech firm shortly before 9/11, but in every single case where I landed next was almost always unexpected and most certainly better than where I was before. I've led a charmed life of always falling uphill.

So how good was I at predicting what I was going to do? It appears I failed miserably. But this failure feels pretty damn good.

I know I've made a lot of mistakes, but if I don't remember them, I assume they weren't important. . .

In terms of lawyering mistakes, I am sure I made more than a few in my first job, but I guess they weren't that important because I don't remember them now. They probably seemed earth-shattering at the time! Some mistakes I remember at later jobs that still haunt me. . . #1: using autofill on Outlook and sending an email to cousin Cameron instead of to client Cameron. TURN OFF AUTOFILL. This is a common mistake and can be devastating. What if the e-mail I sent to cousin Cameron instead of client Cameron had hypersensitive super confidential information in it? Grand-scale mistake.

#2: traveling to a new city for meetings, not understanding traffic patterns, underestimating how long it would take to get to the meeting and showing up late. ALWAYS LEAVE EXTRA EARLY. Go find a Peet's coffee, or hang out in your car. It doesn't matter. Don't be late.

Don't Leave the House Without Lipstick—The Best Advice

I always say trust your gut. Intuition is there for a reason. It's primal, it's intended to protect you FROM EARLY DEATH. So if you're feeling like something's not quite right, trust yourself.

Also, when I was in college, I was an intern at the LA City Attorney's office. One of the Law Student Externs told me that when considering what job to take, the people are more important than the practice. If you have amazing colleagues, then no matter what type of law you're practicing, you'll enjoy coming to work each day. But if you have horrible colleagues, not even the best work can save you. This has held true for me to this day.

Last, my mother always told me never to leave the house without putting on lipstick. I don't think this was really about the lipstick. Something to think about.

You Have to Wear a Skirt, and Other Bad Advice

I went to Law School in the 1990s, and the legal profession was still very, very sexist. Maybe it hasn't changed very much, but back then career advisors were adamant that women wear skirt suits to job interviews. And skirt suits also meant pantyhose. Do you know what skirts and pantyhose meant to 25-year-old Jolene? It meant 25-year-old Jolene was insanely uncomfortable, hot, fidgety and unhappy. One hundred percent this does not lead to a good baseline for an interview. Ultimately, you need to be at your best in an interview. You 100% need to look professional, and oftentimes that requires a suit. But to be at your best, it's my opinion that you need to be comfortable in your own skin. After a few hit-and-misses, I ditched the pantyhose, and sometimes even ditched the skirts in favor of a beautiful dark pantsuit. Still professional, but very me. When I went to work in Seoul, where skirts and pantyhose were the norm, but the six-day work-week and turning off the air conditioning at 6pm in the summertime was also the norm, I rebelled and ditched the panty-hose and sometimes even wore tank tops under my suits and took off my jacket when they turned off the air. But they got used to it.

If Someone Tells You They Are Happy All the Time, They Are Lying

I don't think anyone could honestly say they were happy in their profession 100% of the time. But I've had and continue to have a wonderful career, and I have much for which to be thankful. I've had different roles over my career, and there have been pros and cons with all of them. I think I'm most happy when I'm learning, and growing, when I'm working with bright and talented people, and when I feel like I'm helping others in one form or another.

In my current role, I've had more opportunity to work as part of the executive team and to work on cross-functional projects. I really enjoy delving into new areas and to see things from different perspectives. I also love tackling problems and finding creative solutions, and I enjoy the process of working through issues in a methodical way. The other part I've really loved about this current role is building a team from scratch. It's allowed me to be slow and methodical in the design of a "perfect legal department," finding the right personalities and the right expertise to fit the business. Then working with each member of the team on personal development, and on team development, has been personally very satisfying.

I would be remiss if I didn't mention that I strive always to try and balance the ever-moving scales. I love work, I love family time, and I also need time that's just for myself. It's a constantly moving target, but I am happy in my profession because I'm able to feed all three of these aspects of myself well enough at any given time. They don't all get the right "care and feeding" at the same time, but over a period of time, they seem to do ok. When things aren't going right, I force myself to take a step back and review whether all three pieces are getting the care and feeding they need; if one or another is not, then it's time to make a change.

If you could go back and tell yourself something about the transition from law school to the practice of law what would it be?

You will experience life to the fullest. You will have great love, great loss, tragedy, and triumph; you will fail, but you will pick yourself up off the ground and learn from that failure, and you will ultimately succeed. So during these early years as you're just starting out, make sure you are kind to yourself, and kind to others. Don't worry about what everyone else is doing, and instead follow the motto you will one day tell your kids when they are having a tough time: Do your best, and get a little better every day.

Guest Chapter 9

Name: Gregory Mann

Current Position: Associate Chief Counsel with the California Department of Fair Employment and Housing (12 years with DFEH)

Former Post-Law School Positions: Associate with Jones Day (2 years); O'Donnell & Shaeffer LLP, mid-sized elite litigation firm (4 years); O'Donnell & Associates, small, elite trial firm (2 years), and Lapidus & Lapidus, small litigation firm (1 year). Co-owner and general counsel of Our Music, Inc., defunct music and media start-up (1 year).

Legal Practice Areas: Litigation: civil rights (employment, housing, public accommodation discrimination); general business; intellectual property.

Law School and Year: University of Michigan, 1998

Time between undergrad and law school: None. Although I went straight from college to law school, I suggest taking at least a year or two after graduating college to travel, volunteer, and work—i.e., gain life experience—before going to law school. The maturity and experience gained by living as an adult in the "real world" outside the academic bubble enhances the law school experience by providing some real-world insight for your legal education. I also think time away from school rejuvenates our ability to learn and builds an appreciation for attending law school.

Short background on why I went to law school

I grew up 15 miles east of downtown Los Angeles in a diverse working-class neighborhood. My parents did not go to college, but they firmly believed in the American dream and instilled in me from a young age that I would attend college. A career in law or medicine would be my ticket to wealth. Arguing came natural to me, so I gravitated toward the law from a young age. When I got to high school and learned about Thurgood Marshall, *Brown v. Board of Education*, and how lawyers used the law to fight for justice and equality, my goal was to become a civil rights lawyer. I clerked for the ACLU of Southern California the summer after my first year of law school, which confirmed civil rights law was my future. It took 11 years of working at private firms, paying off my loans, and taking a break from litigation, but I finally found my way to the Department of Fair Employment and Housing and became a civil rights lawyer. I have never regretted trading higher pay for career satisfaction.

How have you used (or not) the core concepts of lawyering as this book proposes: Empathy, Listening First, Asking Questions, and Giving Advice?

I use these concepts daily in representing victims of discrimination. Every lawyer, and certainly every litigator, uses these core concepts regularly. You cannot adequately represent clients without listening to them, asking them questions, and giving them advice. Doing each of these things with empathy makes each more effective and provides insight otherwise missed. Empathy is also crucial to building trust with clients (and witnesses), which is essential to providing them your best representation. When approached with empathy, clients and witnesses open up when discussing the facts and their motivations, which helps avoid damaging surprises. Employing these core concepts also makes clients feel heard, which makes them more receptive to your advice. Practice these concepts in all the legal work you do and you will reap major benefits.

Most useful classes in law school, and what class(es) did I wish I had taken while in law school? In or outside the school? What about today?

As a litigator, the most helpful classes were the core first-year classes: Contracts, Civil Procedure, Torts, and Constitutional Law. Those classes provided a foundation upon which to build my legal education. Litigators use concepts from those classes throughout our careers, regardless of practice area. For example, settlement agreements are contracts. So even though I no longer litigate business disputes, I still frequently deal with contracts. Another helpful class with long-lasting benefits for all litigators is Evidence. Additionally, I gained practical skills and real experience in the Family Law clinic, in which I represented foster children. Representing clients with significant interests on the line, and engaging with real lawyers in court exposed me to the actual practice of law and the pressure and satisfaction of using my education and skills to advocate on others' behalf. If you want to litigate, take a clinic. It may well be your most rewarding class in law school.

As a civil rights lawyer, Constitutional Law, Civil Rights/ Section 1983 Litigation, the Fourteenth Amendment, and Employment and Labor Law were crucial to my development. Although I spent a decade in private practice litigating business disputes before I applied the information I learned in those classes, I was so grateful to have taken those classes because most of what I learned came rushing back to me once I started working at the DFEH. It is obvious, but if you want to work in a certain area of law, take classes in that area. While you will likely not be limited in your career options if you do not take classes in the area of law in which you want to practice—on the job learning/training is most important for lawyers—having the knowledge you learn from those classes will help you, even years later.

I knew I wanted to be a litigator so I did not take Negotiations. But I wish I would have! Most cases settle, and they settle through negotiations. Take a mediation class. You will learn about listening, empathy, and asking questions, all of which are crucial to representing clients in any situation. Take at least one undergraduate class or a class at another graduate school if that is an option. And take classes that interest you! Most of the knowledge you need to practice law you will learn on the job. So do not hesitate to take a few classes that interest and engage you.

How did you decide what to do post-law school? With hindsight, how good of a job did you do?

Although I always wanted to be a civil rights attorney, graduating with six figures in debt meant I had to postpone that dream. Loan repayment programs were in their infancy in the late 1990s, so I did not see a realistic option for pursuing my passion in a non-profit or government job while paying down my loans and building a strong financial foundation for my future. Being at Michigan, with several hundred employers from firms coming to campus to interview, I got swept up in on-campus job interviews and ended up at Jones Day as a first-year associate. But I never intended to even attempt to become a partner at a law firm. My plan was to make a big firm salary, pay off my loans, buy a condo, become financially stable, then leave firm life to become a civil rights attorney. Although my plans evolved and I took some unexpected detours along the way, after a decade I had reached my goal when, fortunately, a friend called to inform me about an opening at the Department of Fair Employment and Housing. I have been there ever since pursuing my passion for civil rights.

My plan was solid, and I was able to bring it to fruition by sticking to it, being financially responsible, and staying true to my values even while working at firms that did no civil rights work. In hindsight, my plan worked well, and I am very proud I stuck to my values and avoided getting caught up in making big firm money or the big firm lifestyle. It was not easy to leave firm life for a job making less 11 years out of law school than I made as a second-year associate. But despite seeing my big firm friends succeed financially in ways I likely never will, I never regret my decision to follow my passion for civil rights law.

Biggest mistake you made while at your first job

My biggest mistake at my first job was not building strong enough relationships with senior attorneys and not finding a mentor. Don't get me wrong, I had good relationships with several senior associates and a few partners. But I did not work hard enough to strengthen those relationships, and I did not maintain them once I left Jones Day. At my second job I found a strong, experienced mentor, whose support proved invaluable throughout my four years there. He taught me how to litigate and lead, and he supported me within the firm. His friendship and mentoring was essential to my development as a lawyer and a man. Find mentors, within or outside your organization, and build those relationships with regular communication. It will pay huge dividends over the course of your career.

Best advice you received or have given for those coming out of law school

I received lots of professional advice before starting my first legal job, most of which I promptly forgot. However, the best advice I received was from a senior associate while I worked as a summer associate the summer after my 2L year: pay attention to detail. After editing a memo I drafted, he provided those simple words of wisdom, which I took to heart and have practiced throughout my career.

Paying attention to detail has paid major dividends. I noticed immediately that something as simple as using proper citation form and formatting resulted in fewer revisions to my written work, which built trust in my work with senior associates and partners. At my second firm my co-workers immediately noticed my attention to detail, and I became a go-to editor of briefs, even for cases to which I was not assigned. This helped me gain the respect of my peers and build relationships with co-workers. A crucial aspect of being a successful junior lawyer is gaining the trust of senior lawyers. Paying attention to detail is a fundamental means by which to do so, and it is completely within your control.

Another great piece of advice I received was to build and maintain a network of colleagues. As an introvert, I have always found this difficult. But I try, and it has been integral to my career. Aside from my first two jobs, my other jobs came through referrals from colleagues. I have been recruited and nominated to boards, invited to speak at seminars, and asked to provide training to attorneys and laypeople by members in my network. In fact, I was invited to write this chapter by a dear friend from law school. Regardless of what you do in your career, your network will prove essential to your opportunities and success.

Lastly, be—or at least act—excited about your work, especially when working with others. Before doing civil rights work I rarely got excited about my work. I worked hard and did good work, but without any passion or excitement. Although I got along well with almost everyone I worked with, I never seemed to click when working with a rainmaker who loved practicing law and always seemed excited to be in the office. He would eagerly ask me about an assignment, and I would calmly provide an update without matching his level of excitement or interest. Our working relationship was fine, but I was missing out on the opportunity to work closely with, learn from, and hear the stories of one of the best litigators in the country. One day

I was in a particularly good mood when asked by this partner for an update, and I provided the update with much more enthusiasm than usual, meeting his level energy and interest. The gleam in the partner's eyes brightened, he engaged me in a lively discussion of the issues, and we clicked as we had never done before. From then on I met this partner's level of energy and enthusiasm—even though I was often simply faking it. Yet, simply pretending to be as interested in the matter as that partner had the real effect of increasing my actual enthusiasm. And it greatly improved my working relationship with that partner, which later led to a job when he opened a boutique trial firm. If it does not come natural to you, as it did not for me, fake it until you make it. You will be amazed at the benefits.

Worst advice you received or have given for those coming out of law school

"Do whatever it takes to satisfy your client." That is terrible advice! Your clients do not know the law, may be focused on ends other than obtaining justice, and do not have to live with the implications to your professional reputation caused by unethical, irresponsible, or inconsiderate behavior on your part. Rather, show empathy and support to your client; help them understand that you are invested in their success. Listen to them and ask questions to understand their underlying interests. Use your knowledge and experience (and that of your colleagues) to advise them of their options, the costs associated with pursuing each option, and your best estimate of each option's success. But you must always maintain control over legal strategy and decisions. And you must protect your integrity and professional credibility regardless of what a particular client requests.

How have you remained happy in your profession? Have there been times when you were not? If so, what did you do to improve your situation?

Maintaining professional happiness, or at least contentment, is crucial to a happy—or whatever your goal may be—life. Like litigation, my professional satisfaction has waxed and waned throughout the years. Although a big firm salary enabled my financial stability, the practice did not inspire or satisfy me. I found it incredibly difficult and unrewarding to bill 2000 hours a year representing large corporate clients and very wealthy individuals. But I did *pro bono* work for my firms, volunteered outside the office, and joined organizations in pursuit of my passion for civil rights. I moved from a big firm to a medium-sized firm, which improved my satisfaction. Then from the medium-sized firm to small firms: another improvement. It was not perfect, but it balanced my goals, and I always looked forward to the day my sacrifices would pay off. And they did! After a decade, including a few interesting and fun detours, I got my dream civil rights job.

But even dream jobs have their ups and downs. Whether it's a new administration or boss, a different assignment or responsibilities, or any of the inevitable changes that occur in your professional and personal life, satisfaction can fade to disillusionment. But fear not, there will be a new administration or boss, a different assignment or responsibility, or some other change in your professional or personal life that will be a catalyst to get you back on the road to satisfaction. When my motivation subsides or my frustration begins to dominate, the thing I always remind myself of is that I am helping people who need help and supporting the long arc toward justice. It's not a magic elixir of happiness, but it helps.

One or two books I recommend: *Getting to Yes* (Roger Fisher and William Ury). This is not a secret or a surprise. *Getting to Yes* is a must read whether you want to litigate, negotiate, or mediate. Learning to discover and then focusing on people's underlying interests is crucial to practicing in any area of law. So too is knowing that there is almost always a solution to every problem and a resolution to every dispute. Whatever you choose to do in law, this short book will provide useful insight. Read it every few years and take it to heart.

Guest Chapter 10

Name: Nicole Day

Current Position: Associate Director, Legal Counsel – Product at Twitter

Former Post-Law School Positions: Director, Legal Counsel at Epsilon Data Management, LLC; Associate at Holland & Hart LLP; Associate at Davis Graham & Stubbs LLP; Associate at InfoLawGroup LLP

Legal Practice Area: Technology. I started my legal career in privacy and security compliance, then transitioned to technology transactions, privacy, and advertising. I now focus on the product side of in-house work, advising product and engineering teams as they build.

Law School and Year: University of Colorado, 2010 (J.D.); University of Colorado, 2011 (LL.M. – Information Technology and Intellectual Property)

Time between undergrad and law school: 1 year (taught English in Brazil)

One or two books I recommend: *Burnout: The Secret to Unlocking the Stress Cycle* by Emily Nagoski and Amelia Nagoski – Great for women who feel stressed, overwhelmed, uninspired, tired, or any combination. With burnout so rampant in the legal profession, particularly among women, I recommend this book to all of my female colleagues.

Short background on why I went to law school

I went to law school because I had absolutely no idea what to do with my life. When I graduated from college, I knew almost nothing about available professions, or about the world generally, making it nearly impossible to stake out a path that made sense for me. My father is a lawyer, so when I started to panic about what to do after my teaching gig, I took my father's advice and applied to law school. "Just because you go to law school doesn't mean you have to practice law," he said. "A law degree will give you a leg up in any field." I'm willing to bet you've heard some variation of this platitude (no offense, dad).

My first year of law school was a disaster. I disliked most of my classes, and after I blacked out from fear during mock oral arguments, I realized I'm not suited for a courtroom. I was nearly ready to throw in the towel when I took an intellectual property survey course the second semester of my second year. That is when I discovered the overlap between law and technology, and met the professor who inspired me to pursue it.

What frustrated me most about coming out of law school and/or what frustrates me with regards to people I work with or hire who are newly out of law school

I think the first year of law school is mostly a waste. Forcing students to take classes they may have little or no interest in can severely demotivate. There are ways to provide law students with proper fundamentals and set them up for bar exam success without dictating an entire year's curriculum. I find it incredibly frustrating that after three years, many law school graduates lack basic core skills necessary to practice law. Sure, they can tell you about the rule against perpetuities, but they can't negotiate effectively or conjure persuasive arguments on the fly. I can tell you with 100% certainty that when I wrote the prior sentence, it was the first time I used the phrase "rule against perpetuities" since 2010.

As for recent graduates, I've found they tend to overstate what they know and overestimate their skills. There's always more to learn, and it's perfectly fine to admit you're unsure about something (or everything, as was the case when I was a first-year associate). When you're fresh out of law school, your superiors don't expect you to know everything. They expect you to ask questions about everything—substantive issues, client relationships, processes. . . everything. It's far better to own up to not having an answer and take the time to ask questions and conduct your own research than to provide an incorrect or incomplete analysis.

How have you used (or not) the core concepts of lawyering as this book proposes: Empathy, Listening First, Asking Questions, and Giving Advice?

I've already touched a little bit about how important it is to ask questions generally. This is particularly true in technology-based or adjacent roles. Products are multifaceted and constantly evolving. As product counsel, being curious is essential: asking questions until you understand all of the ins and outs of a product is essential in order to conduct a thorough analysis of how the law applies. This ties in well with listening first—make sure you give your clients ample time to explain what their problem is, what their product is, etc. You'll be surprised by the volume of information people divulge when you keep your mouth shut. As a general principle, people love talking about themselves. Give them the opportunity to talk, and when it's your turn to ask questions, they'll be happy to answer them because you've demonstrated your ability to listen.

Of the four core concepts, I believe empathy is the most important. Empathy is essential to being a good person, which has been instrumental in my professional success. I won't pretend all stereotypically successful lawyers are good people—that's just simply not true. To me, "success" is a lot more than becoming a partner at a big law firm or General Counsel at a large company. To me, it's about finding work you think is interesting and challenges you, and doing that work with people you enjoy being around. That can be hard to find, particularly in the legal world, and I wouldn't have found it without the real relationships I formed with clients and colleagues along the way. People are drawn to goodness, and being empathetic is a strong signal.

Biggest mistake(s) you made while in law school

Name a mistake to make in law school, I probably made it. A big one was not attending enough lunch hour events my first year, I think doing so would've helped me get a better sense of different legal practice areas. Another was failing to seek out a mentor early on. Find a teacher who seems interesting to you and go talk to them. Ask what they like and dislike about the law. Tell them what you're interested in outside of law school. They may have some great ideas about areas of law you can explore that integrate your interests.

What class(es) did I wish I had taken while in law school? In or outside the school? What about today?

Think about what you're interested in outside of the law. Do you like sports? Computers? Fashion? Cooking? Whatever you're interested in, it has a nexus to the law. I failed to realize this until pretty late in the game. Figure out how your interests and the law intersect, and take classes that boost your acumen in those areas to set you apart. For example, if you think technology law is for you, skip the law school mixers and take some computer science classes. Basic knowledge about things like programming languages, algorithms, and data structures will put you way ahead of the curve.

Most useful classes in law school

Introduction to Intellectual Property Law and Computer Crime. Introduction to Intellectual Property Law is what introduced me to the overlap between law and technology. Computer Crime is what cemented my interest in technology law, specifically privacy issues that arise in the context of technology-based investigations. These two classes were vastly different from the other classes I took during law school because I actually enjoyed the readings. I listened to those instincts.

How did you decide what to do post-law school? With hindsight, how good of a job did you do?

Because I discovered the intersection between technology and the law the second semester of my second year, I didn't feel like I had enough time to take all of the classes that interested me before graduation. My teacher-turned-mentor suggested I stay another year to get a specialized LL.M., enabling me to complete additional courses, write and publish a thesis, and land my first job with a small, niche privacy and security law firm.

Biggest mistake you made while at your first job

I rushed and made silly mistakes because I was overly concerned that clients would complain I billed too many hours per project. If you work at a law firm or other place that requires you to keep time, don't look at the clock. Your managing partner/manager will write off time if they need to; you don't need to focus on whether something is taking you too long. Take the time you need to do your job thoroughly and completely.

Best advice you received or have given for those coming out of law school

"Don't be afraid of the red pen." When I worked as a technology transactions associate, I did a lot of work for an incredible partner who would mark up my drafts with a red pen. The first time the partner reviewed one of my drafts, she handed my draft back to me and it looked like a crime scene. Sensing fear and panic in my eyes as I began to flip through it, the partner told me not to be alarmed by the amount of red. She then took over an hour out of her day to explain her edits and answer my questions. This happened over and over, with the amount of red decreasing each time. The red pen isn't to be feared if you take the time to learn from it. But if you don't invest in learning from your mistakes, you'll never escape them.

Worst advice you received or have given for those coming out of law school

"You have to work at a law firm first." While the training you can get at a law firm is difficult to replicate elsewhere, and law firm experience may give you a leg up in the applicant pool, working at a law firm isn't a necessary evil. Internships can be a great way to get your foot in the door. Taking a position that is legal-adjacent—such as a policy or compliance role—is a great way to get in-house experience right out of law school that can be parlayed into a legal career.

How have you remained happy in your profession? Have there been times when you were not? If so, what did you do to improve your situation?

Being a lawyer is terrible. Of course this isn't true for everyone, or even for me all of the time, but see what happens when you ask attorneys whether they agree with this sentiment. Whatever professional legal path you take, you'll inevitably experience one or more commonalities that bolster this sentiment: long hours, difficult clients, antiquated and/or vague laws, unfairness, demoralizing situations. . . the list goes on.

So if being a lawyer is terrible, how have I remained happy? I found an area of law that centers around something that interests me (technology), and I took often-necessary steps to land a position at a place where being a lawyer is the least terrible. Product counseling is the most technology-heavy, creative role I've had during the course of my career. It's extremely difficult to land a product counsel gig straight out of law school, however. Many tech companies look for applicants with prior law firm experience, with brownie points going to those who've worked both at a firm and in house. So that's what I did. The training I received at law firms, and the in-house work I did after I left law firms behind, is what landed me where I am today. That, and being myself in interviews.

If you've always wanted to be a lawyer, good for you. That was never me. I'm not even sure I want to be a lawyer now. What I do know is that my job is not my life, and the ability to spend time with my family and pursue my hobbies is paramount for me. If you're like me, find a place that prioritizes work/life balance, and do what it takes to get there.

If you could go back in time and tell your younger self something about making the transition from law school to the real world, what would it be?

Surround yourself with people you actually like. Enjoying the company of your colleagues will have an enormous impact on your emotional wellbeing, which in turn will increase and improve your relationships, which in turn will impact your professional success.

The first step toward surrounding yourself with people you like is being 100% yourself in interviews. If you act the way you think someone wants you to act rather than like yourself, or you're nervous, or you overstate or otherwise misrepresent your knowledge and experience, it's only a matter of time until your facade crumbles. Be true to yourself, and see if you genuinely connect with the people interviewing you. If a connection isn't there, move on. It'll be better for you in the long run.

Guest Chapter 11

Name: Lindsey Beran

Current Position: Assistant United States Attorney, Northern District of Texas

Former Positions: Federal judicial law clerk (x3); Trial Associate at Jones Day; Trial Associate at regional law firm Hughes & Luce, which was subsequently acquired by K&L Gates

Legal Practice Area: Currently, criminal law. Previously, affirmative civil enforcement (ACE), with a focus on healthcare fraud and grant fraud, and general commercial and business litigation

Law School and Year: Southern Methodist University, Dedman School of Law, 2006

Time between undergrad and law school: One year, during which I worked as an assistant at a law firm doing general odds and ends and making sure I wanted to be a lawyer. I also spent that year traveling, relaxing, and laughing with friends with close to zero responsibilities.

One or two books I recommend:

1. *Just Mercy* by Bryan Stevenson. This book helped reinforce my perspectives on empathy and the need to better understand others' situations. It is a reminder of the two great lotteries in life: where and to whom you are born. We have no control over either and they dictate so much of what happens in an individual's life.
2. Any funny book. I have lots that fall into this category—*Girls in White Dresses* by Jennifer Close, *Bossypants* by Tina Fey, both Mindy Kaling books, and probably more. A more instructive

or poignant book may be what is expected here and my husband, who is thoughtful but slightly overzealous when it comes to book gift giving, has given me way too many of those. But if a book makes me laugh out loud, I will read it again and again and give as a gift to just about anyone.

Why law school?

Simple: because I wanted to be a lawyer. I have met many lawyers who went to law school for one of the following reasons: (i) they did not know what else to do, (ii) they figured anyone could study for the LSAT regardless of their college degree, (iii) they thought it seemed like a profession where anyone could make decent money, or (iv) they thought it would allow them to put off the real world for another three years. But for me, I wanted to be a lawyer. My mom was a nurse and my dad was a doctor, but I was too squeamish for the medical profession. My mom eventually took a position as a legal nurse consultant, and I spent significant time at her office (after having spent a significant number of Saturday mornings at the ICU nurses' desk). I like to talk, confrontation does not bother me (note: that confrontation does not bother is different from saying I like it), and I am competitive. That said, I have an ability to turn each of those components off when I need to do so, so long as I have an outlet for them. Being a lawyer has given me that outlet. I did not fully appreciate it until later in my career, but being a trial attorney was the perfect fit.

New lawyer frustrations—for me and working with baby lawyers

Even though I knew I wanted to be a lawyer, it took time to realize what specific legal position would bring me professional enjoyment. I graduated top of my class, could carry a conversation, and wanted to stay in the Dallas area, so I was fortunate in that job offers were plentiful. I took a job with a regional law firm so I could get on-my-feet experience. But before I started, it was swallowed whole by a large international firm. I did not get the experience I wanted and did not work on many cases that interested me. I raised my hand at every opportunity, but never spoke up or went to the lawyers who were doing the work I wanted to do. I was too afraid of burning bridges and spent a long time thinking I was more important to a project or a partner than I actually was. But getting experience is the holy grail for young trial attorneys. And it was incredibly frustrating not to get it right away.

Working with new lawyers, they want experience before they are ready for it. HA! It was true for me too in that I wanted to question witnesses before I learned how to review documents, how to craft an outline, how to ask the question a second time (better), or how to recover from an answer I did not expect (note: you move on and decide later whether to circle back). New lawyers should watch, listen, learn. For that matter, all lawyers should try to do those things. I also find that new lawyers are not quick to own up to, appreciate, or learn from mistakes. The best advice I received as a baby lawyer is to immediately say when something is your fault. How can anyone quibble with you? You may take a few harsh words, but it will benefit you in the long run, and it can normally be fixed.

How have you used (or not) the core concepts of lawyering as this book proposes: Empathy, Listening First, Asking Questions, and Giving Advice?

I would like to think that I use these core concepts every day, though not as often I could. I work and interact with a unique subset of people: criminal defense lawyers, government lawyers, law enforcement, and individuals and companies who have been charged with, convicted of, or accused of some sort of wrongdoing. I try to listen to everything everyone says. Listening serves many purposes: you learn more if you listen more, you unsettle people if you are not talking, and people want to talk when they feel heard. People who listen can also form questions, take notes, remember spoken words, determine what information someone wants to provide and what they do not want to provide, and that carries forward in any area of law—depositions, witness interviews, internal investigations, corporate acquisition negotiations (I would assume). If you are not listening, you may anticipate the answer and miss what the responder is really saying.

Empathy plays a big role in my current position, but I think it carries over to all we do. Having the ability to step back and try to understand where someone is coming from, whether that is a boss, a partner, a spouse, an agency head, an agency director, a managing partner, a son or daughter, a ranking officer cannot be overstated. Everyone brings their baggage to the table and it can only serve you to try to look at the issues from their perspective, even if you do not ultimately agree with them. I tell opposing counsel regularly, even though we may not agree does not mean I do not like you or you are (or I am) a bad person; it just means I understand what you are saying and why, but we just see things differently. I think that having acknowledged our differing views, and the fact that I looked at things from their perspective, makes the working relationship better in the long run.

Biggest mistake(s) you made while in law school

I'm going to swap out the word "mistakes" for "regrets" in this question. And the answer to that question is none. I have no regrets about law school. I focused, worked really hard, graduated at the top of my class, made a handful of some of my very best friends, and had a good time along the way.

What class(es) did I wish I had taken while in law school? In or outside the school? What about today?

I wish I had taken a public speaking or debate class. I tell my children that my job is one-third writing, one-third public speaking, and one-third negotiating (really, heated discussions). I wrote extensively in high school and college and "negotiated" my entire life (starting with my parents), but I think a public speaking class or club would have given me more confidence for speaking and presenting my ideas in the courtroom or elsewhere.

I also wish I had taken some sort of psychology class. So much of what we do involves getting into the heads, the psyche, of others, what makes people tick, what connects with people, what will people on juries care about in terms of facts and nullification. More than anything, it interests me now on a level it did not when I was in law school.

Most useful classes in law school

I did a criminal clinic my third year of law school, and it was hands down the most useful class I took. By the time I graduated from law school, I tried two cases, negotiated several plea deals, and argued a suppression hearing. I lost both trials and the suppression hearing. But getting on my feet, picking a jury, questioning witnesses, there was no better learning experience for me. Any class that gives you the opportunity to put your learning into action and try what you want to do when you grow up is a class worth taking.

How did you decide what to do post-law school? With hindsight, how good of a job did you do?

I kept changing jobs until I loved getting out of bed every morning and going to work. I worked in big law, which I did not mind for a few years, because I worked with intelligent and gracious people, friends, and mentors. But I realized I wanted to have control over my cases, I wanted to be in the courtroom, and I wanted to experience the thrill of victory (or the agony of defeat). I also wanted to do something that felt worthwhile to me because that was important to the person, wife, and mother I wanted to be. It seemed like a natural fit to become a federal prosecutor, because I loved practicing in federal court. It took me longer than I would have liked, but I was patient, and I took my opportunities when they came. I listened to the advice of mentors and friends and by hard work, luck, and good timing, I landed right where I want to be. I doubt I will be a prosecutor for the duration of my career, but I can say without a doubt it will be the best job I will have ever had. Being a prosecutor allows me to interact with a wide swath of people, to help people who have found themselves making bad decisions, and to flex my competitive spirt when necessary. In hindsight, that combination is exactly what I wanted, and needed, to do as a lawyer.

Guest Chapter 12

Name: Robyn T. Williams

Current Position: Co-Chair of the Trademark Practice Group at intellectual property boutique Devlin Law Firm headquartered in Wilmington, DE

Legal Practice Area: Intellectual Property and Business Law. The practice is highly diversified due to my pre-law experience in risk management and business analytics.

Law School and Year: Thomas R. Kline School of Law at Drexel University, 2016

Time between undergrad and law school: Four years. I continued working in risk analytics after completing my undergrad degree.

One or two books I recommend: *The Tipping Point* by Malcolm Gladwell. I've read this book a few times and it's an interesting account of how being in the right place at the right time with adequate preparation can catapult you into your mission. It is a must-read for anyone interested in the thorough rationalization of seeming random success and events. The book sheds a wonderful light on the concept of "the flow" and how finding your "flow" and being adequately prepared can transform your seeming simple existence into something monumental. Bonus: Gladwell's *Revisionist History* podcast is equally interesting and enlightening.

    Long Walk to Freedom by Nelson Mandela. I found this book at Half Priced Books. Oddly enough, after my initial purchase I did not think I would get through the nearly 700 pages for at least a month or so. To my surprise, I ended up reading the book in one weekend. The book is an account of Mandela's life, which I found to be extremely rich with experience and eye-opening. He touched on many topics, including propaganda and media spin, political masquerading, the delicate nature of race relations, and perseverance from his heart and wise eyes. Once I finished the book, I passed it on to a missionary. The gift of knowledge is its ability to be spread.

Short background on why I went to law school

I went to law school as a second option to medical school; it was always a toss-up between the two. My educational trajectory was never traditional. My mother saw at an early age, a special gift inside of me, and so delicately nurtured it throughout my younger years into adolescence. As I grew older, I was able to hold onto my special gifts. I choose to work before going to law school. Choosing to work before law school gave me the unique opportunity to look at the world from a different vantage point. A point from which I could truly see, know, feel, and understand the inequities in the world. I saw inequality due to race, class, and education and from there my mission was set, to advocate for the people. The more I had real-world experiences, the more I decided law school was for me and the rest was history.

What frustrated me most about coming out of law school and/or what frustrates me with regards to people I work with or hire who are newly out of law school

The culture that surrounds law school. Law school does not teach students to work cohesively toward a common goal. Instead, it fosters highly competitive behavior that carries over past graduation and into the workforce.

Students leave law school with a hyper-competitive frame of mind and then are expected to work together on matters and research and be "collaborative" in the workforce. The workforce essentially becomes a breeding ground for brownnosing and competitive overachieving. In essence, it's law school over again—except this time the stakes are higher.

There is a substantial difference between the pressure of getting grades and (for example) saving a criminal's life or a company's assets. The practice of law can be a pressure cooker. When one adds competitive behavior with the overachieving pick-me-ism to the stress of being a lawyer, an unnecessarily contentious work environment with monumental stress is created—a breeding ground for disaster. I think we need to more educate educators on how to change this culture.

How have you used the core concepts of lawyering as this book proposes: Empathy, Listening First, Asking Questions, Giving Advice?

The core concepts of lawyering outlined in this book apply to many of life's other pursuits. The ability to have empathy is a good trait for any human being to exhibit and utilize throughout life. The act of listening first and talking second precipitates being a truly empathetic person. Any empathetic person who listens first and talks second is far more likely to ask thoughtful questions that usually lead to advice—unless it's unsolicited and unwanted.

Empathy

Empathy, and intuition led me to the practice of law. I have always been an advocate for whomever I felt had the lesser advantage in any situation, the David and Goliath-type situation. Be it the smallest kid in the lunchroom or the least intelligent person in a discussion, I have tended to always advocate for the person seeming to need a little push or a helping hand.

My innately empathetic nature translated well to my legal practice. A substantial portion of the people I work with are looking to protect or defend ideas and creations that are uniquely their own. There is a special significance that people and entities seeking to protect or defend have about their connections with this thing—if you will. Whether an idea springs up overnight, or it is someone's life's work, these ideas and creations are special.

It is my position that you cannot truly be of complete service if you are not empathetic to the plight that led them to you. The path to seeking legal representation typically starts with hard work, dedication to a craft or task, sacrifice, large time and monetary expenditures, and investments in what they hope materialized from the thing that is unique to them for which they are seeking protection and/or defense. All these things must be taken into consideration to facilitate a reciprocating dedication to the client. Simply stated, empathy is paramount.

Listen First, Talk Second/Ask Questions

Part of being an empathetic creature involves receiving the information coming from the person on the other side of the conversation. Actively listening is a good way to receive the information. If you're lucky you can pick up on nonverbal cues too.

While listening, it is best to be attuned to what is being said and communicated as well as what is not said. I have found that the things that are omitted usually turn out to be equally important. Keying in on the omitted parts of the conversation will allow you to ask pointed questions and give feedback that solicits further dialogue by way of a statement.

If you've listened effectively, the conversation should blossom into a productive dialogue where you, the attorney, have gathered information that facilitates questions and feedback that will help the client fully communicate the crux of the matter. The back and forth of listening, and then talking, should go on as long as is necessary to make sure you fully understand your client, their position, where they are truly coming from, and what led them to you.

Always/Usually Give Advice

This advice step can be tricky. I have identified a *full spectrum of people* in my practice. The range includes the person who has done their research and knows more than you and ultimately will not take your advice or has to be convinced; the person who knows their thinking or position is incorrect but still want you to fit a square peg into a round hole and is willing to take your advice under advisement; and the person who has done no research at all and dumps facts in your lap and just wants you to give advice on how to fix everything.

As a counselor of law, part of your job is to give advice. A therapy almost as you will. If you practice steps 1 through 3 outlined in the core concepts of this book, you will be able to advise all three of these types of individuals.

Bonus Concept: Be Objective—Must Seek Balance

Some of us geeks started our educational journeys in the fields of math and science. Unlike humanities and other subject matters that are highly subjective, math and science-related degree courses are fundamentally rooted objective concepts and established methods for problem-solving. I have found that remaining objective during the entire course of dealing with a client helps to properly navigate their matters and affairs.

Taking an objective position leads you to root your advice in facts and factors beyond just examination of the other side of the argument in litigation and helps to remove any subconscious bias you might have otherwise.

Biggest mistake(s) you made while in law school

A person entering law school without help or mentorship is truly in uncharted, shark-infested choppy waters. The biggest mistake I made in law school was not tapping into the many academic boosts and supplemental mechanisms that some of my counterparts were utilizing. I was already several steps behind from the get-go.

I was unaware of the scores of supplements and treatises available on the market. I tried the traditional approach of listening in class and studying the material. This works with math and science— show up for class, do the work, and study hard and you're good to go. This did not work so well for me in law school.

Imagine being in an ultra-competitive environment where the grades you earn have the potential to dictate your immediate future. (Sidebar: No one tells you that the grades you receive the first semester of law school typically dictate if and/or where you will be able to have a summer associate position.) Some of my classmates had been preparing for law school for a large portion of their academic careers. They'd been coached and prepared by their parents who were attorneys and judges or mentors who had shown them the ropes.

Not only were my peers aware of legal supplements, but they had also read, studied, and did all the fact patterns in anticipation of law school. I had not.

Then, there were the pre-law-school tutors. Perhaps, I should have known such a thing existed, but I was unaware. It had not occurred to me that I could have elicited a tutor before law school, which would have greatly increased the chances of avoiding the "deer in the headlights" feeling I experienced during my first week.

What classes do I wish I'd taken?

I was very deliberate about my law school career. I went to law school with a purpose and to achieve a goal. Because I was focused on what I intended to do after law school, I focused my coursework on what I intended to do—intellectual property and business law. I have zero regrets regarding my law school coursework.

It is my opinion that a person should be a lifelong student, and I continue to take classes and I seize every opportunity to learn. No regrets here.

Most useful classes in law school

The most useful classes in law school were the classes that deviated from the standard casebook and instructed from the perspective of the real world. Because my coursework was focused on intellectual property and business, I was fortunate not to spend too much time with casebooks.

I can recall there being two different criminal law classes taught in two different ways by two different instructors. One class was traditional and followed a casebook and explored the history of the model penal code and criminal law theory. I hated it at the time.

The other did not follow a typical course and instead taught from a practical perspective. The class was divided into two sides: the prosecution and the defense (they switched mid-semester). The students were required to prepare and argue a case from both sides. I always felt like this was far more useful than reading cases about criminal law.

I no longer feel that one was better than the other. I wish there was a blend. Having taken the traditional criminal law class has enabled me to be able to have policy discussions about changing criminal legislation. This is a useful skill when you are trying to effect change in the criminal justice system through policy reform. Although, I never had the opportunity to argue a case from the side of the prosecution or defense. I am confident this would have proven an equally useful skill set.

How did you decide what to do post-law school? With hindsight, how good of a job did you do?

I entered law school with a plan—I wanted a seat at the table. Because my undergraduate coursework focused on hard sciences, I knew I was going to focus on intellectual property. I did not know how the practice of intellectual property law would get me a seat at the table, but it did. It had not occurred to me that my experience in risk analytics coupled with knowledge of intellectual property and business law would make for a great due diligence skill set. It was around the deal table that I found my seat.

There is nothing that I would have done differently in hindsight. I made good career path decisions. However, had I been independently wealthy or of substantial financial means when I entered law school, I would have been a public defender. Not because I feel that all the accused are innocent, but due to the way the system is set up, laws being skewed in favor of lawmakers and prosecutors, and district attorneys having a plethora of resources at their disposal. Now, I focus a substantial portion of my *pro bono* practice on criminal justice reform and reducing the recidivism rate.

Biggest mistake you made at your first job

The biggest mistake I made at my first job was lacking the ability to read the egos in the room (real or electronic). It is my opinion that any legal associate must be able to read and cater to the egos of the people over them. Because I did not follow the typical path to law school, I was far past a twenty-something who was still wet behind the ears. In other words, I was a full-grown adult (redundancy intended). The problem with this is you cannot read the egos in the room because (to the point of my first legal-related job) it had not mattered.

I can recall making the mistake of hitting reply all on an email chain and criticizing the opinion of someone with more letters behind their name than my own. This person called me immediately and let me know that they were not to be criticized before the group and my reply was inappropriate. In my previous career, I was used to voicing my perspective without there being any hurt feelings. It didn't take too long for me to figure out that would not be the case anymore.

I am glad to have encountered that situation early. It taught me a lot about dealing with egos.

Best advice you have received or have given for those coming out of law school?

There is no advice that I have been given or received. All the advice that has come across my path has been situational. I consider no one piece of advice I received to be any better than the other. Rather than reflecting on a piece of advice, I'll reflect on what I've learned, which is to do what makes your heart happy.

I'm sure somewhere there is a quote by someone far more poetic than what I can communicate, but the short is, do what you love. Although no one has ever given me this advice, nor have I given it, until now, it is very important.

I had a colleague very early on who started down the intellectual property path with me. They too had a background in hard sciences. This person was very sharp and would have made an excellent intellectual property litigator. I saw them two years after we'd worked together and they'd switched practice areas from IP to civil rights law and they were beaming. When I asked about the reason for the switch, they told me that they felt more rewarded by this career path. I was so jaded at the time that I thought this was, for sure, crazy. Now, I know that it wasn't and in fact, I'm really happy that this person found their way to a practice that makes their heart happy.

Worst advice you have received or been given out of law school?

Referring back to my statement, I believe advice is a situation, so no one piece of advice is worse than the other. Rather than stating the worst piece of advice, I'll discuss the advice I wasn't given and that is to attend law school where you'd like to live.

While I was in law school, we engaged in many networking events, gatherings, and social things in service of getting to know people in the legal community. This is very helpful if you plan to practice in the community where you attend school; not so much if you don't. Unless you are moving back to a place where you're from and/or have connections to the legal community, it is good practice to go to law school where you intend to live and work.

How have you remained happy in your profession?

I have remained happy and satisfied with the fact that I am helping people and advocating for them when they need it. This carries me through the day and the rough patches.

The practice of law is difficult. It requires a lot of commitment and dedication for a substantial portion of your waking hours. There are also some things that you will not find favorable. For these reasons, it is necessary to find something that propels you and keeps you happy. Without it, you're doomed.

Younger self to old self about the transition?

Take a vacation between taking the bar exam and starting work. I wish I did this. It was a huge mistake. In hindsight, I should have taken 30 days off and tended to my mental well-being and fatigue.

Guest Chapter 13

Name: Alfred Levitt

Current Position: Chief Executive Officer for RPTC Inc. and President and General Counsel for Hugo Enterprises LLC. RPTC Inc. is the private trust company for the Ricketts Family and holds assets including the Chicago Cubs and an extensive portfolio of investments. Hugo Enterprises is the holding company for the operating businesses and investments of TD Ameritrade Founder, Joe Ricketts.

Former Post-Law School Positions: Clerk for the Honorable J. William Ditter, U.S. District Court, Eastern District of Pennsylvania (1994-1996); Litigation Associate at O'Melveny & Myers (1996–2000); Partner at Boies, Schiller & Flexner (2000–2007).

Legal Practice Area: General Counsel. Started as a commercial litigator.

Law School and Year: Temple University, 1994

Time between undergrad and law school: None

One or two books I recommend: I don't like reading books. For a long time, I thought this was a sign of being dumb. Then I discovered Audible and I found I love books, just not reading them. Favorites include Earnest Hemingway, *For Whom the Bell Tolls*, James B. Stewart, *Den of Thieves*, and Amor Towles, *Rules of Civility*.

Short background on why I went to law school

My friend Scott Gant once said to me, "Law school is the first resort of the generalist." In my case, it was more like the first resort of the clueless. As college graduation approached, I didn't have a master plan. In fact, I didn't have any plan. My brother and uncle were lawyers, so I figured, why not. I was rejected at every school to which I applied except Temple University (and Villanova, which waitlisted me). So off to Temple I went. The school and experience changed my life. They taught me how to think. And once I figured that out, the pieces started to fall into place.

What frustrated me most about coming out of law school and/or what frustrates me with regards to people I work with or hire who are newly out of law school

The fact that Judge Ditter offered me a job out of law school felt like a miracle, so I had zero frustrations. I was thrilled with the opportunity and experience. A federal clerkship is the greatest thing a litigator can do to sharpen his toolkit. I got to see and learn how decisions were made. My clerkship was like a postdoctoral degree in practical decision-making. Temple had been good at teaching me the law and how to think, but I needed the clerkship to learn how to apply those things. I remember one time during a case the judge came back to chambers and said, "That woman should get some money; figure it out." The judge relied on us in many instances to build scaffolding around his innate sense of right and wrong, and through that process, I began to learn about the real drivers underlying decisions.

As far as frustrations today, I work with a lot of younger lawyers. It's a different time than when I joined the profession. And while there are many extremely bright, talented, hard-working young lawyers, the pathological focus on client service feels diluted in many cases as compared to when I began my career.

I hear a lot about work-life balance. That wasn't a big thing when I began practicing law. As Don Flexner said to me when I interviewed with him, "This is a service business, and it's not for everyone." He was right, although I didn't fully get it until about 5 years after he said it.

It sounds a little harsh, but as a consumer of legal services in a time when rates for those services have skyrocketed, I don't care a lot about the work-life balance of outside counsel. My expectation is that questions will be answered quickly, clearly, and accurately. It's how I approach my client relationships and it's what I expect from lawyers who work with me. It's a service business, and it's not for everyone.

On another note, escalating compensation and billing rates have fundamentally changed law. More than transforming it from a profession into a business where young associates at big firms need to bill huge hours to support their salaries, those rates have also made it harder for young lawyers to build their own client relationships. It's difficult for an associate billing $500 per hour to originate new business or take on smaller matters. But as my friend and former client Rich Baer emphasized to me years ago, building those client relationships is incredibly important; just as important as being a great practitioner.

How have you used (or not) the core concepts of lawyering as this book proposes: Empathy, Listening First, Asking Questions, and Giving Advice?

I think that those four concepts perfectly encapsulate what being a lawyer is, or what it should be. It's hard to do all four well, but if you do, that's the game. Even three out of four make you a solid lawyer.

It starts with empathy. Whether your client is being sued, or is suing, or is involved in an important transaction, she is under stress. Often intense stress. Empathizing with your client's predicament and experience is hugely important. It not only builds trust with your client—a critical element of a successful attorney–client relationship—it informs your approach to the matter.

Empathy can, however, be taken too far. It took me some time as a younger lawyer to strike the right balance between empathizing with my client's situation and maintaining some objective distance. I had to work to find where I "ended and they began." If a client is going to trust you, you have to show genuine empathy but in a way that preserves your ability to provide clear and unemotional counsel.

Listening is also essential. A lawyer needs to give people the chance to talk through what they are experiencing. Through active listening, you better understand your client and the matter on which you're working. Listening builds human connection and sharpens your focus. (Fun fact: listening is pretty good for your marriage too.)

I think asking questions as a lawyer is a notoriously difficult thing to do. People are often concerned that asking questions will make them seem dumb and diminish their authority. I have learned to ask a lot of questions and not to care how it makes me look. I've found that asking the "dumb questions" often is the single best thing you can do to provide good counsel and representation. Keep asking questions and listening carefully to the answers until you understand the issues.

As far as giving advice, this is what lawyers get paid to do. When you do it, give practical advice. I still get too much talking at me from lawyers. On highly technical issues—issues where I don't have a good grounding in the underlying law—I want clear counsel on what the lawyer thinks I should do. Caveats are fine, but at the end of the day, you're being paid to offer informed, smart counsel. On issues that involve a business judgment, I want the tradeoffs framed in a way that permit me to make an informed decision. And when I'm the lawyer, that's what I try to do.

The wrapper around these four concepts are authenticity and integrity. By authenticity, I mean speaking and behaving in a way that is honest and never phony. That often takes courage as there's something of a fake it 'till you make philosophy in the law. My view is that people can spot a phony a mile away. (It's what juries do, by the way.) Speak honestly to your colleagues, your clients, and yourself. People will trust you more for it.

And then there's integrity. None of the four concepts matter if you don't conduct yourself with professional and personal integrity. That means doing the right thing and not cutting corners, even when doing the right thing isn't easy. It can be a "small thing" like how you complete your time sheet or treat colleagues. It can also be a "big thing" like how you handle a conflict of interest. And often doing the right thing is most difficult when the stakes are high, but that's when it matters most. In the end, high-integrity people generally succeed.

Biggest mistake(s) you made while in law school

I didn't have confidence during my first year. I was too focused on what everyone else was doing. When I started to run my own race, I did better. I didn't do study groups or share outlines, or anything. I just put my head down and did the work. It proved to be a successful recipe that has guided my career.

What class(es) did I wish I had taken while in law school? In or outside the school?

If you might want to go into commercial litigation, take accounting for lawyers or finance for lawyers. I wish I had taken more (um, any) economics or finance courses. When I practiced law at a firm, my work was focused almost entirely on matters that involved complex financial issues—e.g., antitrust, securities fraud, business disputes. I had been a creative writing major and felt adrift in the deep end of the pool. I had to learn on the fly while litigating cases. It would have helped to come to the practice of law with a stronger foundation (um, any foundation) in these concepts. By the time I worked on the Cubs acquisition, I had gotten better.

Most useful classes in law school

Federal Courts. For commercial litigation it is super helpful. If you don't take it, you'll miss the issues. And it's still useful to me today despite not having set foot in a courtroom in 15 years.

How did you decide what to do post-law school? With hindsight, how good of a job did you do?

For some people, it can feel like there's a well-worn path: do well in law school, make law review, join a big firm or clerk. I tried to follow that path, which I thought was the only one. It worked out great for me. But the truth is, there are many ways to apply the disciplined approach to thinking law school teaches you. Keep an open mind about your career, particularly in the early years, and don't put blinders on.

Biggest mistake you made at your first job

The biggest mistake I made in my first job was citing to the wrong case in a draft opinion. It almost embarrassed my judge. And while the mistake got caught, it was horrifying: in a clerkship, the clerk is supposed to protect the brand of the judge. It didn't happen again.

Best advice you received or have given for those coming out of law school

There's not a lot of people who will stay up at night worrying about your problems. Maybe your parents. Maybe your spouse. To be a great lawyer who connects deeply with his clients and colleagues, you need to care deeply about their issues. Get into work early. Stay late. Solve your client's problems.

Worst advice you received or have given for those coming out of law school

I didn't get bad advice. I was lucky. I also didn't get a lot of good advice. Truthfully, most lawyers are terrible managers, unskilled at giving structured feedback or sustainably mentoring in a way that works. Don't worry about it. Figure things out for yourself.

How have you remained happy in your profession? Have there been times when you were not? If so, what did you do to improve your situation?

I have a personal failing: I'm wired to be a Golden Retriever; I like a pat on the head when I do a good job. It isn't a good thing; you surrender a lot of power in your relationships when you crave positive feedback. I've had hard times when I've gotten smacked upside the head rather than patted. It often didn't seem "fair" at the time.

Careers inevitably have ups and downs. There were times when I wasn't sure if the law was for me. Over the course of the past almost 30 years, however, I always come back to loving my job. I'm not much of an everyday lawyer anymore but the diversity of my work keeps me happy and interested. I love solving complex problems.

Then again, I also like solving small problems, including fixing my client's WIFI in his New York apartment.

If you could go back in time and tell your younger self something about making the transition from law school to the real world, what would it be?

Be authentic with people. Authenticity builds trust and this business is all about trust and deep relationships with clients, bosses, and colleagues. Lawyers are insecure and pretend too much. It's corrosive to building lasting relationships. And most importantly, be resilient. Life directs a lot of negative feedback at you. Don't let it get you down. And when it does, listen to Toots and the Maytals.

Guest Chapter 14

Name: Nicholas (Nick) Troxel

Current Position: Partner and Co-founder of Troxel Fitch, LLC, a law firm built by entrepreneurs, for entrepreneurs

Legal Practice Area: Corporate, Securities, M&A, Real Estate

Law School and Year: University of Colorado, 2017

Time between undergrad and law school: Three months

Books I recommend:

1. *The Untethered Soul* by Michael A. Singer – True happiness is the most important, and often most fleeting, part of life. Without happiness, everything in your life will suffer, including your professional pursuits and your personal relationships. This book will help you better understand who you are and what makes you happy. It will help you free yourself from the constraints of self-doubt and negative emotion. I would recommend it to all, but especially young lawyers and law students, a population known for unhappiness and overthinking.

2. *Difficult Conversations* by Douglas Stone, Bruce Patton, and Sheila Heen – As humans, we are driven by emotion. Even those among us who claim to be driven purely by logic are, at their core, driven by primal emotions. These emotions, or fear of experiencing these emotions, often lead us to avoid certain situations and conversations. This book will teach you how to handle difficult conversations that are needed to address situations like issues with an underperforming business partner all the way to issues within a romantic relationship that is on

the rocks. These skills will be invaluable for your legal practice as well as your life.

Dedicated to my parents, Amy Struthers and Charlie Troxel. This would have all been a dream without your unwavering love and support.

When you ask the question "How Do I Become a Great Lawyer?" you will likely get a different answer from everyone you ask. The story of how I ended up where I am today starts in Seward, Nebraska, a small town 30 miles west of Lincoln, Nebraska. I had just ruptured the L4/L5 disc in my lower back while maxing out on squats during football spring conditioning my freshman year of college. After breaking my right ankle my junior spring of high school, my left ankle my senior fall of high school, and then breaking my hand my freshman fall of college, I experienced the moment that all athletes someday face. I looked at myself in the mirror and I knew it was time to hang up my cleats. But where would I now place my focus, my drive? What would be my new mission?

That was the day I decided that I wanted to attend law school. I looked up the best law school in the country and told myself that day that I would go to Yale law school. At the time, I knew there was a low likelihood that I would actually get into Yale, because it is not common for someone to get into Yale that simply decides it would be cool to do so on a whim. However, in life I have always believed that you should aim as high as possible and never stop believing in yourself, so that even if you come up short, you'll find yourself a lot further along than you may have initially imagined. To this day, I've never seen a brick wall that I didn't feel like I could run through.

My plan was to get an undergraduate degree in accounting, get a law degree, work for a few years as a lawyer to get startup capital, and then start a business with the foundation of accounting and legal knowledge. I moved back to Lincoln, moved back in with my parents, enrolled at the University of Nebraska, and decided that I would apply every ounce of focus and drive I had to academics. My first semester I had a 4.0 GPA for the first time in my life, and at that point my dreams started to seem a little bit more real.

As undergrad progressed, and I continued to get straight As, I decided that instead of trying to go to Yale, I wanted to move to Los Angeles, attend USC or UCLA, and become a Hollywood attorney.

I applied to only schools in LA or San Diego until my mom urged me to apply at University of Nebraska and one other law school that was within a day's drive. One of my oldest friends had just moved to Denver so I chose CU Boulder, the highest-ranked law school in Colorado. However, two months before I was set to graduate from the University of Nebraska with my undergraduate degree, I started to have cold feet about going to law school. I wanted to "find myself" and applied to the Peace Corps. My dad convinced me that I needed to do my due diligence and at least visit some of the schools I got into. I begrudgingly agreed, and ended up visiting CU because they offered me an almost full-ride scholarship, something that made the thought of diving into law school feel less scary.

I remember the first time I crested the hill leading into Boulder on US-36 for Admitted Students' Day like it was yesterday. I can still see the sun shining on the flatirons on that perfect April day. I was seated next to a kid from Florida named Josh Fitch that day at a table with Brad Bernthal (a professor at CU law school who teaches Venture Capital as well as the Entrepreneurial Law Clinic) who told us all about Boulder's entrepreneurial culture and how the law school embraced it. Little did I know that this interaction would change the trajectory of my life forever. I remember getting home the next day and telling my dad, "I found myself, I'm going to CU."

Attending law school is an interesting and transformative experience. I remember showing up late to the first day of class in a t-shirt and sweatpants with a huge beard, and people looked at me like I was crazy. I have always marched to the beat of my own drum, and law school is a place where you have drilled into you that you need to think a certain way, act a certain way, and look a certain way. I was determined to never buy into this mindset. However, I, like so many others, "drank the Kool-Aid" and bought into the idea that the only path to success was to get into the top 10% and work for a big law firm. This was the biggest mistake I made in law school, other than listening to Jason Mendelson (one of the authors of this book) when he told me to shave my beard and buy into the corporate attorney look (haha).

While I didn't always love law school, I was determined to "win" at law school, and to me that meant getting a job with the highest-paying corporate law firm I could. I knew I would need to study hard and make as many connections as possible. I applied the same academic work ethic I had used in undergrad and ended up doing very well. Other than my second semester 1L year, the first snowboard-ing season I had ever experienced, my grades were in the top 10%. Even with that hiccup I ended up ranked in the top 15%. My favorite classes were without a doubt Venture Capital, Legal Negotiations, and Legal Ethics. Venture Capital because it was what introduced me to the startup world in earnest, as well as introducing me to Jason Mendelson and deepening my relationship with Brad Bernthal, who would both end up being great mentors. Legal Negotiations was a life changer because it taught me about so much more than just negotiating. It taught me how to communicate and navigate com-plex situations and relationships in all facets of life. Legal Ethics with Peter Huang was another life changer. Professor Huang focuses his course on mindfulness, happiness, and fulfilment within the legal profession, because he feels that instilling more of these traits in lawyers will naturally result in fewer lawyers being involved in shady and unethical situations. I loved this course because it was the first time I had ever learned about this kind of thinking. I had always been a generally happy and fulfilled person, but I was surrounded by law students and lawyers, and most seemed pretty miserable. It was refreshing and just what I needed to start seeing the practice of law in a different light.

I was planning on taking a couple of classes in the business school to better understand the numbers side of business law, such as cap table management, how different types of securities were priced, and the tax ramifications of using different types of securities. I ended up not taking these courses when I learned that the grades for these courses would not count toward my law school GPA. Remember, at the time I was focused solely on having as high of a GPA as possible because that meant "winning." What knowledge did I miss out on by having such a narrowed view of success drilled into me?

In law school and in life, learning goes much deeper than your coursework. While in law school I made a concerted effort to build relationships with attorneys who practiced in the areas of law that I wanted to pursue. Further, I tried to get as much time as possible with anyone who I admired or resonated with on a personal level, by any means necessary. I remember noticing that Jason Mendelson would leave my Venture Capital class and take a specific route through the courtyard at CU. I started eating breakfast in the courtyard at a bench directly in his path just to have as many chance interactions as I could. I showed up to events that I had no interest in attending just because I knew someone that I wanted to interact with would be there and I might be able to catch a quick conversation on their way out. I used to take the bus to Denver and back two to three times a week to meet people for coffee just to pick their brain. Every time I met someone I resonated with, I asked them to introduce me to others who may continue my pursuit. Sure, part of the reason I did this was with the hopes of getting a job, but the biggest reason I craved these interactions was to observe and absorb everything I could from these people. I wanted to see how they thought, how they spoke, and how they moved through life and the law. I believe that having this mentality, that you can always learn something from everyone you meet, that you should always be in pursuit of perfection, is what led me to the success I enjoy today. Many of the individuals I met during this time ended up being great mentors. Some even hired Josh and I to perform contract work when we were first starting our firm.

After graduating I thought it would be easy to get a good job and the path forward in life would become clear to me. The day after graduation, I interviewed with my first-choice big law firm and figured I was a shoe-in. I had the grades, I made the connections, and I felt like I rocked the interview. I never heard back. No yes, no, or we're still thinking. I have never received a response to this day. Admittedly this left me feeling unfulfilled and lost. I didn't understand how I could have achieved my dream and still feel like a failure. I received other big law job offers, but nothing made me feel the burning passion I was chasing.

Looking back, this was a blessing in disguise. It allowed me to reflect on what I really wanted out of my life and who I wanted to be. I come from a big family, and my parents always told me that life was about more than money and status. Life is about happiness, fulfillment, and spending time with people you love. I remember speaking with my mom while in this state of feeling lost and she reminded me of my original plan of becoming an entrepreneur. She made me realize I had lost my way. I had forgotten who I was and let the bubble of law school convince me I needed to go a certain route. I realized I would never have the life I wanted working for a big law firm, or anyone else for that matter. I realized that I wouldn't find what I was looking for unless I was the captain of my own ship.

Josh had decided months prior that he was going to start his own firm whether I wanted to do it with him or not. I remember Josh used to randomly say, "Troxel Fitch, I'll give you your name first!"

Over the course of six months, my self-reflection and Josh wearing me down led me to have the confidence to take the leap into starting Troxel Fitch, LLC. Josh's willingness to believe in me and what we could do together is what has led me to realize my greatest potential. I am grateful beyond measure and will forever be in his debt.

Now I don't want you to think it has all been sunshine and rainbows. Being your own boss is awesome, but sometimes it is scary as hell. When Josh and I first started the firm, we were broke. We drove Lyft and ate canned beans to keep the lights on. But we had a lot of fun along the way as well. I remember the first time I paid myself $1,000. The feeling of signing my name on a piece of paper and that paper then becoming valuable nearly brought me to tears. Success and failure is all relative. One thing is for sure, if you want to start a law firm right out of law school, you have to change the way you view mistakes and the way you view failure. I have made more mistakes in starting and running this firm than I could count on 10 pairs of hands. However, there is no failure unless you quit. If you refuse to lose, if you refuse to give up, you can never fail. Spend the extra hour researching, ask the extra question even if you feel dumb, go to every networking event you can and lean on mentors. Josh and I started the firm in November 2017, and we committed to each attend 150 networking events in 2018. We were anywhere and everywhere small business owners might go to network, shaking hands and kissing babies. Not only did this help us grow our business, it sharpened our ability to walk into a room and confidently talk to hundreds of people. Don't be afraid to curl your toes over the cliff's edge and dive in. It's just life, we're all going to die someday anyways. Do you think you'll remember the failures you had along the way or regret not pursuing your greatest potential?

The concepts that Jason Mendelson brings up in this book are spot on and I use them every day in my practice. Clients, and people in general, know when you actually care about their problems and when you are faking it or simply don't care. When you are speaking to another human being in real life, and you treat the interaction like you are analyzing a fact pattern from your legal writing professor, you are going to have a tough time. This is often why so many lawyers have a hard time bringing in business, and, if you didn't know this already, it doesn't matter how good of a lawyer you are if you can't convince clients that you are the lawyer they should pay to help solve their problems.

Many lawyers only think about legal issues from a theoretical perspective, as if they were trying to write an A+ memo, instead of trying to put themselves in the client's shoes and solve a real-world problem for them. Here's a fact I hope more law students and lawyers will take to heart: 99% of clients have no clue what the difference between an A+ lawyer and a D- lawyer looks like. The law is a foreign language to non-lawyers. Clients want a lawyer who listens, understands their problem, and explains a solution to that problem in a digestible manner. Ultimately, clients hire you for the peace of mind you bring them, and feeling confident that you care about their problem is the first step to giving them that peace of mind.

In sum, looking back I wouldn't change a thing. I run a successful law firm where I make more money than most of my law school classmates and I never work on powder days. I am the master of my own destiny and the sky is the limit.

I would implore you to remember that no one has lived this life before. We're all making it up as we go. Stay true to who you are and who you've always been. If you treat people right, work hard, and never stop believing in yourself, I promise you that you will find happiness, fulfillment, and success.

Remember, you can do whatever you set your mind to in this life. Never forget that.

Name: Josh Fitch

Current Position: Partner and Co-founder of Troxel Fitch, LLC, a law firm built by entrepreneurs, for entrepreneurs

Legal Practice Area: Corporate, Securities, M&A, Real Estate

Law School and Year: University of Colorado, 2017

Time between undergrad and law school: Eight months

One or two books I recommend: *Untethered Soul* by Michael Singer: The existence of the body and mind are obvious. Gyms and fitness programs are everywhere to tend to the body, and we are put in school almost immediately after birth to tend to the mind. I think most people would acknowledge the existence of the soul, but other than what happens to it when we die, there isn't much out there about what to do with it, how to understand it, or how to manage it. I consider this book a user manual to the soul, and a guide on how to understand to the pit in your stomach, or the flutter of your heart.

Essential reading for those who want their place in the world to sync with their place in the cosmos.

How to Win Friends and Influence People by Dale Carnegie: In contrast to my first recommendation, which is more ethereal, this book is worldly and practical. This is a user-guide to human interaction. Like the unbreakable laws of physics, this book describes the laws of people. If you want to know how to navigate the world with social skill, finesse, and delicacy, look no further than this book.

> *Dedicated to Timothy James Fitch*
> *Nothing Ventured. . . Nothing Gained.*

In starting a firm directly out of law school, and finding success, it sometimes feels awkward. Nick Troxel and I have found success beyond our wildest dreams, and we are often asked about the foresight it must have required to become such "innovators" or "disruptors" in a traditional legal field that is averse to change.

In truth, Troxel Fitch was born as a reaction to a legal world that seemed unwilling to accept us unless we "fell in line" and as a passion project to a life we knew must exist, even if at the time it was elusive. More than evolution, it was rebellion.

My law school experience was characterized by the feeling of being misplaced, and stifled. I came to law school seeking the skills to become an entrepreneur. I grew up playing sports, and learned that to become a master of your game, you must also master the rules; only with an awareness of the boundaries can one operate fully within them. I figured that a legal skill set would complement my other talents to make me an effective businessman. Yet in law school I felt that my other talents were viewed as a distraction, and that succeeding in this grade-based environment would require me to abandon the things that made me who I am, and focus solely on the class rank, the pursuit of the big-law job, and the glorification of "the grind." I felt I understood the law (and the world) well, but didn't see the point in stressing myself to near insanity just to be ready for a cold call about some unrealistic nuance to a legal minutia posed in a theoretical world that would never exist in reality. In short, I was frustrated because I felt like I got it, I understood it, but was being asked to worship it, to sacrifice myself on the alter to it, and was ultimately cast aside for my recognition of the absurdity of it.

I greatly enjoyed some of the same classes that Nick has mentioned, and would add that the Entrepreneurial Law Clinic with Brad Bernthal was an incredible experience, but otherwise I basically kept to myself and focused on getting the job done. I finished law school somewhere around the top half of the class, with my will to live and self-esteem still intact, and I considered that a win.

Deciding what to do post-grad was informed by the truths I had found, and a new truth I was desperate to find. During my time in law school I met with many practicing attorneys to decipher what type of life lay ahead for me as a lawyer. With a precious few exceptions, I found that I could be well-compensated, or happy, but likely not both. From my perspective, most of the "high-powered attorneys" were miserable, and those who were happy had essentially stepped off the ladder and abandoned the climb to the top. When I met with recently graduated colleagues who took the big firm route, I found shells of their former selves. They were overworked, struggling in personal relationships, unmotivated by the monotony, and criticized to the point of losing confidence. What a shame! These are extremely talented individuals, with ridiculous focus and drive, a lucrative skill set, and more potential than can be quantified. Why were they so broken? What kind of system is this that takes such wonderful people and extracts everything to the point of leaving nothing but the will to survive?

I wasn't quite ready to abandon my grand ambitions, but I also wasn't willing to sacrifice the joy in my life for the money in my wallet. I was torn between the means and the ends, trying to decide between two unappetizing choices.

Then my life would change forever. Two weeks before my final exams of 3L year, my older brother, to whom this chapter is dedicated, passed away. Tim, as both an example and at times a counter-example, had been my role model, my teacher, my fearless protector, and my champion. Despite Tim living a life of struggle, faced with harsh consequences for every misstep, he took special care to ensure he imparted the lessons derived from those consequences on to me. From a young age I was imbued with wisdom far beyond my years, which I did nothing to earn, paid for by my brother's suffering. Although I was jaded from law school and beginning to succumb to the idea of sacrificing a few years in the name of professional progress, Tim encouraged me to be brave with my talents, and be fearless in pursuit of the life I wanted, even if others were unwilling or unable to do the same. Even if doing so might subject me to rejection and ridicule.

Carrying the weight of immeasurable grief and fighting tears that were never more than a blink away, I hid in the corners of the law school library so I could study without being noticed, free from interactions that would require me to summon a strength I no longer possessed. I began to ponder the brevity and fragility of life, and the value of each and every moment. As the weeks passed, the notion of surrendering even a day to the lines on my resume became repulsive. After exams I resigned myself to the solitude of bar prep, and in that solitude discovered the question that would reveal to me my life's second truth. What type of man am I? Am I the type of man who will waste the wisdom of my brother's legacy and retreat to the safety of convention, or do I have the courage to pursue the life I want, despite how uncertain and terrifying it might be, and honor his legacy?

With that monumental motivation, I determined that I would start my own firm, in hopes that I could build a life of joy and fulfillment, and also ambition and achievement. I was going to harness my talent to build a beautiful life in honor of my loved ones who were deprived of that opportunity, or fail gloriously, knowing I had the courage to go down fighting. That very well might have been the result had Nick not agreed to join me. I consider Nick's willingness to join me in this foolhardy endeavor one of my life's great blessings, and we could never have accomplished what we have without his drive, resilience, and, most importantly, loyalty as a friend.

Now, resolved to start our own firm straight out of law school, and clueless as to how to actually accomplish that, we devised our method.

More important than any other specific skill one gains in law school is the ability to learn. Law school teaches you to identify the question, identify the authority, find the answer to the question, and identify the next question. This applies just as much to digital marketing and bookkeeping as it does to income taxation and civil procedure. Combine that ability to learn with the humility to drive Lyft and eat ramen as a licensed attorney, and you've got a powerful combination, not to mention a lucrative skill set. If you can use that skill set to your own benefit, you can learn anything entrepreneurship demands of you, and the price-tag of legal services is high enough to keep you afloat as you figure it out.

As we struggled to get our firm off the ground, we devised a three-pronged attack.

For the first prong, we worked with legal insurance providers doing simple debtor defense work. There are a variety of firms with whom you can simply sign up, and they will send you cases. Basically, when someone didn't pay their credit card bill, they got sued, we filed an answer in defense, and then assisted the settlement negotiation in exchange for a modest fixed fee. This required nothing in the way of business development, and was quick and easy from a legal expertise perspective. The primary objective of this prong was to keep the lights on while we nurtured our fledgling firm.

For the second prong, we worked with a variety of mentors as subcontractors, handling excess work at a very reduced rate in exchange for mentorship and guidance. As licensed attorneys, our work was valuable, and we charged a paralegal rate, so there was benefit to both sides. Our mentors got cheap labor, and we got valuable knowledge. While we performed elementary transactions on our own, we got to assist with sophisticated transactions under the tutelage of our mentors, and use the skills learned for our own benefit. We were extremely lucky to have brilliant and generous mentors who worked with us not only for the professional support, but from the good of their hearts, to help us succeed as people. One such mentor to whom we owe a tremendous debt of gratitude is Stan Doida, who showed us not only how to practice law, but how to operate a law firm, and how to be an upstanding professional. The primary objective of this prong is replicate the mentorship you might find in a big firm in an outsourced, networked fashion. The revenue is secondary to the education. If you find yourself a mentor like Stan, consider yourself extremely lucky.

Finally, the third prong is developing your own client base and providing services at your full rate. This takes time, as initially you have no reputation, and no experience to which you can speak. However, if done correctly, the first two prongs will support you as you slowly climb this hill. Your first clients will choose to work with you because they trust you. They trust you will listen to them, work diligently to understand their business and their problems, and that your zealous effort and attention will overcome your lack of experience. Take extra care to ensure this is true, and dedicate your whole soul to serving and protecting those who have bet on you. This is where you plant the seed of your reputation, and that seed will either turn into a tree that bears fruit, or be the placeholder for your firm's grave. In time, when you have given your everything to prove yourself and do right by your clients, your client base will grow, as will your income, and you can begin to phase out the first two prongs on your way to a self-sustaining firm. This is the final prong and eventually overcomes and eliminates the other two, until you now have a successful law firm. The primary objective of this prong, and of owning a firm generally, is to do great work, treat people right, and benefit your community. At all times beware of what you don't know, and what you don't know *that you don't know*. Be ferocious and humble as you investigate the gaps in your skill set, and seek always to improve. You won't have a firm above you to review your work and monitor your mistakes, and your clients don't know how to catch them. Honor this trust and autonomy with vigorous and honest self-evaluation. You can't always be perfect, but you can always be improving.

If done right, you will find yourself in the position Nick and I now find ourselves; living a life of full-autonomy, proud and fulfilling achievement, and joyful balance. It fills me with gratitude to look back on the path taken and the lessons learned on the journey to now. I can confidently say I wouldn't change a thing. I have never sacrificed a day to the misery of the heartless grind, I am happier than I ever imagined, as well compensated as I could want, and with limitless potential. I am the sole master of my destiny.

I never thought this life possible, and I wouldn't dare ask for more.

In writing this chapter I hope that my story may inspire others to be brave in resisting the deleterious pressure the legal profession places upon us, and be confident that your skill and drive is sufficient to build your own beautiful life, however that may look. The view is clear atop the shoulders of giants, and the road they walk is well-worn and paved by years of tradition. However, if you seek the freedom and excitement that comes from blazing your own trail, you mustn't be afraid to put your feet in the dirt, and venture into the unknown. Let your legal education be your compass, and I hope this chapter might serve as a torch to light your way when the path seems dark.

If you've gotten this far in the law you already have the skills required for this adventure, so happy trails, and Godspeed.

Guest Chapter 15

Name: Emily Galvin Almanza

Current Position: Founder and Executive Director, Partners for Justice; former public defender

Former Post-Law School Positions: Senior Legal Analyst, The Appeal Media; Criminal Defense Attorney, the Bronx Defenders; Clerk to the Honorable Thelton Henderson, U.S. District Court, Northern District of California

Legal Practice Area: Criminal defense, criminal legal policy, civil rights and human rights

Law School and Year: Stanford Law, 2010

Time between undergrad and law school: 3 years (writing and wandering around)

One or two books I recommend: *Just Mercy* by Bryan Stevenson, *Evicted* by Matthew Desmond, *Ordinary Injustice* by Amy Bach, *Misdemeanorland* by Issa Kohler-Hausmann, *Privilege and Punishment* by Matthew Clair, and the collected closing arguments of Clarence Darrow.

Short background on why I went to law school

I almost didn't go to law school. It wasn't something I planned, or had aspired toward. I went—as many people do—because the thing I was doing wasn't working out, and a lot of people I admired told me you can do anything with a law degree. (In hindsight, I think that's pretty terrible advice, since for most people, a law degree saddles you with the kind of debt that forces you to be a lawyer no matter what.) But with my job going nowhere and having been accepted to a great school, I got in my car and drove from Los Angeles to Palo Alto to see what law school was like.

More interesting than why I went, though, is why I didn't turn my car right back around and drive back to LA. At the event welcoming 1L students. Professor Lawrence Marshall stood up and told us that when we became lawyers, we would have to be licensed, because our minds and our mouths would be weapons. I decided I wanted to turn my mind and mouth into weapons as expeditiously as possible, and use the force that gave me to push for liberation and mercy. Our criminal legal system, up close, is as far from justice and equity as a system could be: targeting Black, Indigenous, and other people of color, low-income people, and allowing police and prosecutors to exert enormously outsize power to spur forward a machinery of punishment built more for efficiency than righteousness. I wanted to put my body between that system and the people it sought to harm. And luckily, I was in a school that enabled me to do so: where I could get a 1L job in a public defender office, where I could spend most of my time back on campus representing people sentenced to life under California's draconian Three Strikes law, and teaching criminal law to incarcerated kids. I won some cases. People came home. Families were reunited, new futures unveiled. To help people come home was all I wanted to do, and if law school let me do it, well, I was happy to be there.

What frustrated me most about coming out of law school andor what frustrates me with regards to people I work with or hire who are newly out of law school

The space in which I most frequently encountered new lawyers was the criminal courthouse: young prosecutors learning the ropes by arraigning cases, handling simple pretrial hearings, and occasionally covering their colleagues' calendar calls. The most frustrating thing was the degree to which they had emotionally removed themselves from what they were actually doing.

The practice of law is a confrontation with human narratives. Things find their way to court because something went wrong between people, and now will require other people to engage in a highly ceremonial process to find an outcome that we imbue with social legitimacy. In criminal law, the law brings us stories of absolute tragedy, and also stories of incredibly petty transgressions and police-manufactured crime. At least three-quarters of the things that find their way into criminal court probably don't really need to be there (arguably, with robust community-led practices, almost none of this stuff needs to be there, but that's a topic for another treatise). For experienced lawyers, the "weight" of a case, or its relative worth, is obvious: when you've seen real harm, you no longer find misdemeanor fistfights particularly compelling, let alone petty theft or drug possession. But new lawyers often act as though their job is to treat every case as earth-shattering, which means I would often walk into court and find myself facing a 25-year-old first-year prosecutor who wanted to lock my client in a cage for selling bottled water without a license in front of the soccer stadium.

Among our own side, mentoring and helping young lawyers learn to appropriately value the matters in their hands is easy—we can have frank conversations and offer advice and guidance. But when the relationship is adversarial, it is difficult to offer advice and have it be taken. When the power given to a lawyer vastly outstrips their experience—when, for example, with a few months on the job, one has the power to separate a new mother from her baby over stolen diapers—that lawyer's personal maturity level and ability to retain their human common sense in spite of adversarial urges or a perceived professional duty is essential. Watching young lawyers forget the degree to which their every choice can alter the course of someone's life and cause irreparable harm was my greatest frustration.

How have you used (or not) the core concepts of lawyering as this book proposes: Empathy, Listening First, Asking Questions, and Giving Advice?

Yes, all of them, together, in every single client interaction—and now, teaching them as I train non-attorneys on how to build a fruitful relationship and get results.

When you enter a relationship with a client, no matter what identities or lived experiences you may share with that client, there will always be a power imbalance: you are the lawyer, and they are the person who needs a lawyer. This fundamental fact is one of the single biggest barriers to deeply effective lawyering, as it must be overcome to build the kind of trust and partnership that you will need to get your client to be honest with you about their struggles and concerns, their hopes and priorities, and, in some cases, their larger goals or plans.

The best lawyering, after all, happens in *partnership* with the client rather than on their behalf. They are the expert of their own life, and almost certainly the expert in the situation you'll be litigating, so they hold crucial information regarding the case before you. But case-related information isn't the ballgame: they also may have priorities that surprise you, fears they need allayed, a vision of what success looks like that may differ from yours. The concepts outlined here are an excellent toolkit to get yourself out of the way, listen to, and learn from your clients, and then, once you're truly informed, be able to give the kind of *personalized* advice that defines a good lawyer. No one wants one-size-fits-all counsel.

As a public defender, one is often meeting people on the worst day of their lives. On top of that, one is entering the conversation as a stranger in a suit who may hold very different identities from the other person. I need to very deliberately do things to make my clients feel safe being honest with me, a stranger who they met (usually) on a really bad day. I have found the best way to do that is to listen. Listen deeply. No presuppositions. And then ask the right questions to help my client feel able to tell me not just what is going on in their case, but what's going on in their *life*, so we can make better decisions together. A person with both a family court case and a criminal court case might get a better outcome in criminal court playing the long game and pushing the case to trial, but if a swift resolution means getting their kids back home, that is almost always the most important thing to a parent. So my legal judgment about what's best in the case (trial) has to take a backseat to what's most important to my client (the kids). Priorities aren't always immediate, either—knowing, for example, that a young client has a dream of going to college (and needing loans to do so) or becoming a security guard (for which he'll need a specialized license) or joining the military (much more difficult with a record) will materially impact the strategic decisions we make in the case. I need to know all of it to be a good lawyer, and give good advice.

Biggest mistake(s) you made while in law school

I was so focused on representing clients and fighting cases, I don't think I spent as much time as I could have getting to know my professors. And they were *incredible* professors, many of whom I now count as dear friends, so my lack of attention to the hours they offered me, the conversations they were open to. . . it feels like such a needless missed opportunity. There are very few times in life when one is in the company of so many great minds, and has access to them. I wish I had given myself the time to learn from them outside of class—maybe even outside the law—instead of impatiently shoving myself toward the bar exam.

What class(es) did I wish I had taken while in law school? In or outside the school? What about today?

Again, going back to the professors—there are no classes I regret missing for the subject matter, but there are professors with whom I wish I had studied. Pam Karlan, for example, is one of the defining legal thinkers of her generation. As a 2L, I didn't feel adequate. I didn't take her class, and I really wish I had. Just to have gotten to watch her think out loud for a few hours a week.

Also, if you have a chance to learn Spanish, learn Spanish.

Most useful classes in law school

Beyond classes that put you in rooms with professors who excite you, I would say the best learning opportunities come from clinical practice. Ideally clinics where you get to take on real clients—volunteering to fill out domestic violence restraining orders or benefits applications in a come-and-go community clinic is virtuous and, yes, informative about how to interview a client and navigate bureaucracy, but there is something tremendously different about representing one person over a longer period of time.

Additionally, clinical work teaches you the things you will otherwise be most insecure about when you leave school. School generally does a great job of teaching you how to do research and write things, but where do you stand when you go into a courtroom? What are the "magic words" you use to introduce yourself on the record? When do you stand up and when do you sit down? Because courtroom moments involve a great deal of pressure and adrenaline, getting proactive about practicing them while you still have the safety net of a nearby professor is useful.

How did you decide what to do post-law school? With hindsight, how good of a job did you do?

Because I spent so much time in law school trying to work as a lawyer rather than being a student (for better or worse), my path after graduation was clear to me. I wanted to be a public defender so badly that I actually lobbied my school to create the first Stanford Criminal Defense Fellowship, so that I could find work in an industry that does not often have positions for post-bar, pre-license graduates. In hindsight, I was able to make an informed choice not just because of my prior work in the field, but because I spent one summer of law school at a big, multinational law firm: Kirkland & Ellis. I spent my 1L summer at the LA County Public Defender fighting for kids and, ultimately, second-seating a murder trial, which ended in a wrongful conviction I would spend the next decade of my life fighting to rectify (and ultimately we did bring my client home). But after the incredibly emotional experience of ride-or-die public defense, I needed a breather for my heart. So I went to a big firm, where I knew my brain would be busy and my heart would be uninvolved.

I learned some surprising things that summer: that misogyny in big law is real, that I weirdly love antitrust, that a trip to the LA Gun Club is *not* a great work outing, and that in spite of the financial promise of a firm, doing work without my heart's involvement is not for me. But had I not tried it out, I wouldn't have had such certainty at graduation.

It's worth noting that I only had the freedom to make that choice because I went to a school with a glorious debt-forgiveness system. I knew that I could take a job as a public defender and my school would have my back, paying back my loans for me every year as long as I worked in the public interest and made a lower salary. The freedom that affords its graduates, in my opinion, is the biggest benefit to the school: its graduates can afford to follow their dreams and be happy lawyers instead of taking a job just for the paycheck.

Biggest mistake you made while at your first job

When I think of decisions I made in that first year that I would make differently now, it's hard to call them mistakes—after all, almost every single one of them led me to where I am today, and taught me things I needed to know. Most of the big screw-ups I came closest to were driven by passion: wanting to go too far investigating a case, or making choices that were expeditious but risky. Luckily, I had a great colleague at the time who would remind me that no case was worth my license, so no, I shouldn't go over and chat with the complaining witness one-on-one just because she was open to it, I should leave that to the investigator. No, I shouldn't sneak into the crime scene and snap a few crucial photos even though the DA wouldn't give us access to it, I should litigate the issue properly.

(That colleague is now my husband and I am still licensed.)

Best advice you received or have given for those coming out of law school

Be the lawyer you would want to have.

Even if you are privileged or lucky enough to have never been in that position, we have all been in crisis. No one is exempted from pain and disaster. We have all had the sinking feeling in our stomach of something going really, horribly wrong. We all know what we want in that moment: safety, trust, someone who will *really* listen, choices, information, a modicum of control over what happens next. Digging into the universality of our own human experience, and thinking deeply about what it is you have reached out for when you were lowest or most afraid—that's the best guide on what you should do as *counsel*.

Worst advice you received or have given for those coming out of law school

Lawyering is such a rigorously ceremonial profession that most of the advice we receive pushes us toward blind professionalism at the expense of humanity. Lawyers so often strive to be perfect instead of striving to be effective—thinking, for example, about the law underlying a judge's ruling and failing to consider the judge's mood, the context in which the conversation is happening, the rhetoric guiding the tenor of the conversation. We as a society have, for better or worse, created a system of justice that is made out of humans. Human decision-makers, fact finders, arguments, fears and flaws and dreams and mistakes at every layer. Law school rarely reminds you of this.

Much of the advice you get will push you toward behaving as though it is the *ideas* that matter most, the arguments and statutes and citations. Don't fall for it. Humans are flawed, so is the practice of law, and the more you lean into that—and are strategic about it—the more effective you will be.

How have you remained happy in your profession? Have there been times when you were not? If so, what did you do to improve your situation?

As a trial lawyer, I was happy because I cared deeply about my clients, and wanted to be the lawyer they were hoping to have. Regardless of the outcome, when I could make someone feel safe, informed, and in control of their choices, I felt I was able to offer a form of empowerment to the people this system seeks to crush. The goal was to win, yes, but also to rob an oppressive system of the tools it uses to churn out punishment: to let my client's story, goals, struggles, achievements, and dreams be so unavoidably present and amplified to decision-makers that they could not comfortably dehumanize the people whose lives they impacted. I was happy because I was forcing the powerful to listen to the people they sought to disempower, which felt inherently good. And I won almost all my trials, which helped.

Stepping back from trial practice was an incredibly tough decision, and one that I worried would rob me of some of that joy I kept in my daily practice. But the decision was driven by the larger mission-orientedness that fueled my happiness: as a lawyer, I always believed that it was my job to defend *a person*, not a *case*. That meant that whatever the person was struggling with—complex, intersecting problems, multiple demands on their attention, conflicting needs, the horrible emotionality of it all—was also my burden and my responsibility. I never felt comfortable saying, "Sorry, that's not my area, best of luck," when asked about access to food stamps or housing trouble. I wanted to say yes to my clients, yes to their requests, and let *their* priorities and goals guide the process as much as possible— even if their priority was not the case on which I was assigned.

I went to work at Bronx Defenders so that I could practice this way, on a collaborative team of multidisciplinary professionals, lawyers and non-lawyers, all working together to ensure that our clients were represented in this fuller, more empowering—and more effective—way. But thinking back on my trial practice in California and my time as a student, when I had done defense work in 12 California counties and New Orleans, I couldn't help but feel frustrated that lawyers everywhere weren't able to practice this way. Overburdened and mandated to focus exclusively on criminal matters, defenders were unable to be truly client-centered. So I decided to leave practice, and try to build something better.

Now, I run a program called Partners for Justice, which I cofounded, and which helps any public defender become holistic—rapidly and with enormous support. We recruit and train brilliant early-stage professionals, people who might one day be the next brilliant generation of lawyers, organizers, and leaders, and embed them with public defenders across the country. There, they operate as a plug-n-play wraparound service team: connecting people with housing and jobs, getting people into treatment, hooking up benefits, chasing down civil rights claims, fighting for licensure and against school suspension and more. When they collaborate with lawyers, they get better results inside *and* outside the courtroom, which, of course, means clients are more likely to walk away with their lives—and futures—intact. I'm going to keep doing this until every person in America can access a wraparound public defender.

If you could go back in time and tell your younger self something about making the transition from law school to the real world, what would it be?

Savor it. And embrace the adrenaline.

Guest Chapter 16

Name: Jennifer R. Zimmerman

Current Position: Managing Partner, Dolan + Zimmerman LLP; co-chair of Colorado-Criminal Defense Bar, Boulder; owner, Boulder Wine Merchant; founder Boulder Burgundy Festival NFP

Former Post-Law School Positions: Of-Counsel at Jurdem, LLC; associate attorney at Berg Hill Greenleaf & Ruscitti LLP; adjunct professor at Front Range Community College

Legal Practice Area: Criminal Defense Attorney

Law School and Year: University of Colorado, 2007

Time between undergrad and law school: 2 years (paralegal)

One or two books I recommend:

1. *Just Mercy* by Bryan Stevenson – If you want to defend the accused, it is important to remind yourself of why you are doing it and how a zealous attorney can make a difference to an individual and effect genuine change in a community. In addition to being a wonderful read, this book highlights both the human story of criminal defense and the complicated and nuanced procedural issues that make up the heart of the criminal justice system.
2. *Cross Examination: Science and Techniques* by Larry Pozner and Roger Dodd – The definitive book on effective cross examination techniques.

Short background on why I went to law school

After working as a paralegal at first a small firm and then a large firm, I knew I was as smart and driven as the attorneys and decided to apply to law school. I assumed I would become a civil litigator specializing in construction law, like one of my long-time mentors. I clerked at the same firm where I was a paralegal and was extended a job offer as a lawyer after my first year in law school. I had every intention of spending my career at that firm and was committed to jump onto the partner track even before I graduated from law school. After accepting that position I began working with the criminal defense partner at the firm so that I could get courtroom experience (something that is surprisingly difficult to come by in civil litigation). As I learned more about criminal defense, I realized that I felt more inspired working with individuals and handling cases that mattered to individual people's lives. I also fell in love with the intricacy of the constitutional arguments and the importance of holding the government to its burden when it accuses an individual person of a crime.

What frustrated me most about coming out of law school and/or what frustrates me with regards to people I work with or hire who are newly out of law school

By the time I graduated from law school, I had spent five years with my firm—first as a paralegal, and then clerking for all three years of law school. I was quite familiar with the firm, the people, the internal policies, and the cases. Even so, nothing prepared me for my first year as an attorney. I realized that I had no idea how to be a lawyer or how to advise clients. I remember talking with a friend who had just begun her medical residency and wishing that there was a formal apprentice program for lawyers. Instead, my first year out of law school was a bit of trial by fire. I was given cases as soon as I passed the bar, and I was expected to handle cases on my own, and to know when I needed to ask for help. Although I made mistakes, I learned quickly. The realization that individual clients were relying on me to tell them what to do with serious and complex cases was terrifying and exhilarating. It inspired me to learn as much as I could as quickly as I could so that I could more confidently and accurately advise my clients. Although I originally thought the most daunting part of my job would be court appearances, I quickly learned that court was the easy part. The preparation, research, writing, and connecting with clients so that they trust you is the real work, and the work that makes the job worth it.

I have been most frustrated with new lawyers at our firm doing three specific things: (1) Not taking ownership of clients. Young lawyers often treat work as specific projects with a limited scope, and don't spend the time to consider how their work would be integrated into representation of and advocacy for the client. When a new lawyer assumes that his or her work is complete when a project is done, that lawyer fails to take the client into account. They need to consider how to convey that information to the client, the impact it may have on them and the case, and the follow up work necessary to zealously advocate for a client accused of a crime. (2) Attempts to save face. In our firm we often discuss the fact that mistakes are unavoidable, and that what matters is confronting them and working as a team to ensure that those mistakes never impact our clients or their cases. It is frustrating when young lawyers are afraid of the personal consequence of their mistakes and, as a result, fail to proactively address missteps. As an attorney, you must be confident enough that you can identify a mistake when it happens, and address it in a way that maintains focus on your client. (3) Not doing complete research. I am always available to help young lawyers. I do, however, expect that they try to find their own answers before coming to me because that is how you learn to be a lawyer. When a new lawyer asks me about a rule or statute, I expect them to have already read the statute and its annotations, and be able to have an intelligent conversation about what they have found, what they think the answer may be, and the answers they are still trying to find.

How have you used (or not) the core concepts of lawyering as this book proposes: Empathy, Listening First, Asking Questions, and Giving Advice?

I have used these concepts throughout my career. As a criminal defense attorney, I am focused on representing individuals in matters that can have a serious and negative impact in their lives.

My clients are stigmatized in the community because of their charges, and often have underlying mental health and addiction issues.

Empathy and listening rather than jumping in with advice based on the charges has been a core value of our firm. Taking that approach has allowed us to ask relevant questions and ensure both that our clients feel heard and that we are in possession of the best information to advocate on their behalf.

Starting with empathy, listening, and asking questions creates a strong attorney–client relationship so that when it is time to give advice (which it always is at some point), the client feels confident in our services and expertise and can take steps to make an important and consequential decision in their lives.

I believe that part of my success as a lawyer has been based on these concepts. This is both because listening and asking questions creates an appearance that I am confident and knowledgeable so that the client can accept my advice, but also because having a framework for interacting with clients where they get to tell their story and feel heard helps them feel secure.

I have seen this same phenomenon play out with young lawyers as well. Having the innate ability to empathize with and listen to clients facilitates a strong attorney–client bond. Once that bond exists, even a young lawyer appears confident and knowledgeable to her client and can provide solid legal advice.

Biggest mistake(s) you made while in law school

The biggest mistake I made in law school was spending more time working than at school. I clerked throughout law school at the firm I ultimately worked for and focused almost entirely on the future.

In hindsight, I should have spent more time getting to know my classmates. What I learned later in my career is that those relationships are valuable. Now that I regularly interact with opposing counsel and judges who were classmates, I realize how beneficial that connection is for getting complex matters resolved. While neither a judge or prosecutor would ever do something unfair or unethical for a law school classmate, that history can ensure that you get the benefit of the doubt when you genuinely need it.

What class(es) did I wish I had taken while in law school? In or outside the school? What about today?

In law school, I should have taken more varied courses, and not limited myself to the areas I believed would be my focus. More breadth of knowledge about different areas of law allows a lawyer to spot collateral issues that may otherwise not seem relevant.

At this point, I wish I had more experience in business management and economics. The business side of law is something that most lawyers will encounter at some point in their career. I had to learn about these areas through trial and error after my partner and I opened our own firm. I know we both wished we had some background in general business concepts, like business and revenue models, and in general management.

Most useful classes in law school

The absolute most useful class I took in law school was the criminal defense clinic. I spent a year representing indigent defendants in minor criminal matters and had the opportunity to appear in court doing everything from bond arguments to motions hearings and trials. Appearing in court is something that can only be learned through experience. Graduating with some knowledge about the logistics of court and the way the rules of evidence worked in practice allowed me to start my career with more confidence.

How did you decide what to do post-law school? With hindsight, how good of a job did you do?

I had committed to a large law firm prior to graduating and, at the time, believed I was going to pursue a career in complex civil litigation. I had planned to use criminal defense as a way to gain courtroom experience and set myself apart from other civil litigators. After law school, I quickly realized that I preferred criminal defense work.

In hindsight, I stand by my choices. I was able to gain valuable experience in both civil and criminal litigation at that firm, and also learned a fair amount about the workings of a law firm. Those three things, in combination, contributed to me having the drive to start my own law firm.

Biggest mistake you made while at your first job

I made big mistakes at my first job. The first was making personal sacrifices that didn't matter to the firm. For example, I chose not to take a honeymoon after my wedding because I didn't want to miss work. I realized later that the partners would never have noticed if I took time off for that, and certainly didn't notice that I chose not to take time off. In hindsight, I realize that as long as I was producing high-quality work and hitting my hours, there was far more flexibility than I understood at the time.

The second big mistake I made was not asking enough questions. I incorrectly believed that I should have known everything already, and was worried that the partners would lose confidence in me if I asked too many questions. As a partner at my own firm, I know that part of a partner's job is teaching, and that they are happy to do it. As long as you research your question to the best of your ability first, a partner is always happy to help you get the rest of the way there. Law is a collaborative job that works better when lawyers ask questions.

I also found myself scared to ask a question that I thought, "I should know." I would fake my way through some things hoping that I'd either learn along the way, or wouldn't get caught. I was lucky on the latter, but in hindsight, I didn't deliver the client service that I should have.

Best advice you received or have given for those coming out of law school

The best advice I ever received is to make myself indispensable. That can mean different things in different contexts, but in law it means taking complete ownership of your own work. If you are confident enough in yourself and willing enough to ask questions that a partner can give you a task and know that you will either come back to them with a question or a finished product, you will become indispensable. The most valuable employees I have ever had are those to whom I can delegate work and then completely forget that works exists because I am confident that they have it under control.

The second-best piece of advice I received is to always bring a notebook, a pen, and a calendar. If you have those things, you will be prepared to take notes and calendar deadlines. It also ensures that you appear prepared for anything from a client meeting to an internal firm meeting. When I meet with an employee and they come into my office without a notebook it makes me wonder if they understand the nature of this particular job.

Worst advice you received or have given for those coming out of law school

The worst advice I ever received is that meeting your hours goal is the only thing that matters. Quality of product and reliability both matter more than the sheer number of hours billed. While a new lawyer needs to be cognizant of any firm requirement, including hours, the specifics of the case and the client, and not your personal minimum billable requirement, should be driving your work. As long as you can make yourself indispensable through the quality of your work and taking ownership of your projects, most partners maintain some flexibility in hours requirements.

How have remained happy in your profession? Have there been times when you were not? If so, what did you do to improve your situation?

This is a hard career, and the work of continuing to find it rewarding takes effort. There are times where it feels like you are expending an amount of effort that is unsustainable, and there are times when it feels like it is busy and flowing and fun. I think finding some modicum of balance is especially hard for young lawyers who feel like they need to prove themselves.

I have, on balance, been happy in this career. I have found it consistently rewarding, intellectually interesting, often fun, and sometimes funny.

What I have learned over the course of my career in a larger firm, a small firm, and my own firm is to prioritize things that make me feel good and be honest with myself about what those things are. For me, I realize that taking time off of work to ski with my children is a priority. I leave work early every Friday in the winter to go to the mountains with my family. I also learned that taking time off to exercise is not a valuable use of my time. That is something that I can accomplish early in the morning when it does not impact my family or my job.

I have also learned that everything ebbs and flows, and to try to be okay with both of those things. There are times when I feel like I am working 24 hours per day and cannot catch my breath, and then the next week I take extra time off to see my family or take some time to myself. Law is a demanding job, but also has more flexibility than many other careers. Adapting to the changes in weekly, monthly, and yearly cycles allows me to find balance between family and work obligations.

Perhaps most importantly, I have learned that who you work with matters. Surrounding yourself with colleagues with whom you can be honest and vulnerable creates a stronger foundation for a career. We have set up a firm where we are able to provide outstanding work for clients and enjoy our time at work. We spend a significant portion of each day talking creatively about cases and laughing. When it comes down to it, we also have shared values regarding the importance of prioritizing clients and providing exceptional representation. I am confident that part of the reason we have been able to get great outcomes for so many clients is our shared values and work ethic, and the fact that we know we can rely upon each other.

If you could go back in time and tell your younger self something about making the transition from law school to the real world, what would it be?

I would have told myself to invest in myself instead of in a firm. I would have focused more on enhancing my legal skill and knowledge in order to make myself a better lawyer, and less time worrying whether I was living up to the expectations of the firm.

I also would have better preserved my time with my family and friends. Those are the people who are there for you when work is hard and whose grace you need when you have to cancel plans in order to work.

Guest Chapter 17

Name: Margot S. Edwards

Current Position: Wealth Advisor at JP Morgan Private Bank

Former Post-Law School Positions: Partner at Holland & Hart LLP; Member of Firm Management Committee; Adjunct Professor at University of Colorado School of Law; Judicial Law Clerk, Justice Gregory J. Hobbs, Colorado Supreme Court

Practice Area: Member of the Private Client Group, which focuses on estate and gift tax planning for individuals and families with substantial wealth

Law School: University of Colorado School of Law, 2006

My Practice Area and Why I Love It

My practice area is intensely personal. It addresses money, death, and private family matters. Clients share information with me that they do not share with anyone else—their hopes and fears about their children, their marriage, their business. I listen first, and the listening is perhaps the most important part of my role. Clients need to share in a confidential, nonjudgmental setting in order to work through whatever is on their mind.

I often then make recommendations, and ultimately give the client peace of mind that they have done or are doing everything they can to address their goals. Whether the clients' goals are the goals I would choose is not relevant. I do guide clients based on my experience and observation, but ultimately clients are human and they each have their own perspective.

The other significant feature of my practice area is that it requires deep tax expertise in an area of the tax code that most people never think about. This creates a balance between intellectual challenge and human relationships that I believe is unique. The blend of personal relationships with intellectual complexity is what I love about my practice.

Your First Client—the Partners

One thing that I wish all new associates understood is that partners are your first clients. Partners are people and are under significant pressures. An associate who makes the partner look good is like gold. Associates should empathize with partners and apply that empathy when doing their work. Put yourself in the partner's shoes and think about what would be helpful—and then do it.

An excellent associate anticipates the next thing a partner will need, beyond what they requested. If you can anticipate the next logical step, you will thrill the partner, and, frankly, get ahead of the next task you are likely to be asked to complete. The best associate also considers not just the task assigned, but the goal the partner is trying to achieve for the client. This sometimes means that you should make suggestions or find information that the partner didn't request.

When turning a project in, provide the partner with everything they need to review it. If there are other documents, statutes, or cases that would be helpful to have handy, include them with the work product you have prepared. Often these items are available on an electronic filing system or otherwise, but don't make the partner search for them—that just means they must spend more time on reviewing your work. In addition, consider that partners often need to do work in locations that are not at their desk and may not have ready access to files. If you have given them a complete package, they won't need it.

Communication—a Key Feature of Every Good Lawyer

One of the most important features of a good lawyer at any level is communication. Clients are anxious about their deal, their case, their planning. They want to know that someone is thinking about them and that there is progress being made. Keeping in touch so that they know where their project stands is key. If a client emails to ask a question that cannot be answered quickly, respond anyway. It is perfectly acceptable to respond with a note that says something like "What a great question, let me think that through and get back to you in a day or two." That way the client is not left wondering if you received their email and if you are focused on their question or issue. They can feel reassured that you are, while you take the time to provide a thoughtful response.

Further, if you are not going to be able to complete something for a client in the timeline agreed upon, or otherwise in a timely fashion, tell them. Clients ask lawyers to handle their most worrisome matters and wondering where something is creates anxiety. Our job is to provide peace of mind, and so the best approach is to simply communicate about the delay and assure the client that their matter is important, even if it is taking longer than anticipated.

The same is true for associates working with partners (again, their first clients). Partners worry about their ability to review associates' work and provide it to the client in a timely fashion. Keeping them posted on your timeline goes a long way to helping partners plan and prioritize their work. It also gives them the opportunity to manage client expectations before a project is late.

Partners also sometimes forget when they asked for a project to be delivered to them. Believe it or not, they can forget which associate they assigned a project to, or even if they assigned it at all. An associate who communicates frequently about their work and the related timelines can really reduce anxiety and help a partner manage their client matters.

Focus on Your Development

Remember that every project is an opportunity to develop as an attorney. You should always exhibit intellectual curiosity about why you are taking a particular approach for this specific client. Why this document, or why are we including this provision in the document? If you don't ask these questions, you won't develop the skills to craft plans for clients on your own. Partners want to take the time to answer your questions—it means that you will be a better lawyer and even more helpful to them. However, they can sometimes forget what it is like to be an associate and so it is up to you to find a time and ask the questions.

One thing that I wish I had done differently is starting with the basics. My practice is focused on sophisticated tax planning, and that is where my training began. However, understanding the fundamental concepts related to estate planning is just as important. In my case, that meant expending some effort on learning applicable state law in addition to learning about tax. I took several approaches to filling in this gap, including CLE courses. For me, working on several estate administration projects permitted me to see how the estate plan worked out in a practical setting. Teaching Wills and Trusts also forced me to learn the fundamental concepts in a much deeper fashion—once you can teach something, you know that you actually understand it. Take the time to understand the core concepts, in addition to the most sophisticated ones.

Develop Good Habits

Something I did well as a young attorney is to develop good administrative habits. These continue to serve me well now, but it would be easy to stray from them if they weren't fully ingrained in the way I practice. For example, tracking my time daily is important. It avoids hours of going back through emails and calendars to determine what I did in a day. It also means that I capture more of my time.

Another example is doing a good job filing documents and emails so that they can easily be found later. Again, this is a quick task if done on an ongoing basis but saves time in the long run.

Third, I endeavor to return all calls and emails that require a response within one business day. This ensures that I am communicating with my clients in a timely fashion and not creating anxiety for them. It also means that the correspondence doesn't build up to a point of being overwhelming. Finally, it means that other members of a client team can keep moving forward, rather than waiting for a response from me.

You Need a Team

Finally, it is never too early to start developing your team. This is a hard job, and no one should do it alone. Having an assistant, paralegal, and other lawyers around you to help ensure top quality client service is critical. It is also important for your ability to create boundaries and to enjoy your work. In order to create such a team, it is important to integrate others into your client matters and to inspire their loyalty. Develop strong relationships with the people around you so that they want to help you—it pays off many times over.

Take Charge of Your Career

Being a lawyer is not easy. It is high pressure and demanding. Think continuously about what you want from your career and take action to ensure it goes the way that you want. Make sure you get opportunities to do work you enjoy with colleagues and clients who you like. Reach out to senior lawyers you admire and develop relationships with mentors. Your career is far too important to leave to chance.

Guest Chapter 18

Name: Jason M. Lynch

Current Position: General Counsel and Chief Operating Officer, Foundry Group, a venture capital firm

Former Post-Law School Positions: Partner, Davis Graham & Stubbs (Denver); Associate, Wachtell Lipton Rosen & Katz (New York); law clerk to the Hon. David M. Ebel, U.S. Court of Appeals for the Tenth Circuit

Practice Area: Today, general counsel. In private practice, I was a trial lawyer and litigator.

Law School/Year: Columbia, 2002

Time between undergrad and law school: Four years

No matter your practice area, it's a safe bet that there are many lawyers in your market who do the same legal work as you. Litigation, corporate, securities, M&A, employment, trust & estates, criminal defense, personal injury, intellectual property, real estate—it doesn't matter. Clients can choose among any number of lawyers to obtain the service you provide. Why would they pick you?

As you have read in this book, we believe that empathy is a core capability of a successful lawyer. This is true because more than anything else, the key to landing and keeping clients is *how you make them feel*. And empathy is a key to understanding what your clients are feeling. For clients, legal matters are often complicated, esoteric, overwhelming and can be episodes in their life or business where much is at stake but they have little control. The feeling you want clients to have is: "I feel confidence that this lawyer will take care of me and this problem or project I have. I don't have to worry about it." How can you make someone feel this way?

Let me tell you a story.

It is the summer of 1995, and I graduated from college a year ago. My girlfriend, Sarah (now my wife), and I are living in a little apartment in New York City on Amsterdam Avenue and 108th Street, combining the wages from our entry-level jobs to make ends meet. I'm working as a junior associate at a public relations firm. The city is full of energy, but we are not living a glamorous life. The summer, as it always is in New York, is hot and humid. We're not spending the weekends in the Hamptons. I'm starting to worry about the loans I took out to pay for college.

One day I arrive at work to the announcement that associates are being paid a mid-year bonus. The firm hands me a check that afternoon for $1,500. Fifteen hundred dollars! It was more money than I had ever had at one time. I show the check to Sarah when I get home that night and we stare at it gobsmacked. When we come to our senses, we know we should celebrate, and we decide to have dinner at a fabulous New York restaurant we ordinarily could never afford. A friend working as an editorial assistant at a leading New York restaurant guide tells us we should go to Union Square Café, the flagship for up-and-coming restauranteur Danny Meyer, which has been named best restaurant in New York several years running. We make a reservation.

We arrive that summer night in 1995 wide-eyed and intimidated. We haven't done much fine dining in the city during our college years there; we are not making enough money to eat out often. When we enter Union Square Café, the bar, which runs from the front door back into the heart of the restaurant, is filled two-deep with well-heeled Manhattanites: lawyers, socialites, bankers, corporate executives, and media types. A convivial buzz emanates from the dining rooms where, as we are led to our table, it appears we are the youngest people in the place by at least 15 years.

What is most striking is what happens next. A waiter welcomes us as we sit down and takes our drink order. Moments after opening our menus, water is poured and bread arrives at our table. We have a warm, friendly conversation about the menu with the waiter and place our order. The courses are perfectly spaced, and the staff checks in to see how we are doing at precisely the right intervals: not so often that we feel pestered, and just often enough to feel cared for. In other words, the staff treats us like everyone else in the place, with precisely the same thoughtful, pleasant, and attentive service and respect they dispense all evening long at every table.

Our insecurity dissolves. We relax and have a delightful meal, fully enjoying the celebratory evening we hoped for.

I don't remember what we ate or drank that night. But what I do remember more than 25 years later is how we *felt*: eager to celebrate a small victory but outside of our comfort zone, we were welcomed, we were cared for, we belonged. Because of how the staff at Union Square Café made us feel that night, we became devoted fans of Danny Meyer's restaurants, ate at them every chance we got, and told everyone we knew about our experience. It created a lasting devotion.

Years later I learned that our experience at Union Square Café was not happenstance. It occurred by design. Danny Meyer is an evangelist for the art of hospitality. He built his restaurants around it and a business consulting firm to teach it. I strongly recommend you read his book *Setting the Table: The Transforming Power of Hospitality in Business.*

Treat existing and prospective clients with true hospitality—with true professional *service*—and you will make them feel cared for. Taken care of. And that feeling is why they will pick you when they can choose from a hundred other lawyers in your market who perform the same legal work that you do. That is the power of hospitality and exceptional customer service, which is really a form of empathy in practice.

So, I challenge you to think about how you can bring this approach to service into your legal practice. You could:

- *Do things to show your client she is more than a billing input in a law firm's factory delivery of legal services.* Law firm practices often create this feeling by clients. Find ways to overcome that. A mentor of mine, the General Counsel of a prominent company, once said, "It amazes me that law firms where I spend hundreds of thousands of dollars per year in legal fees don't have a picture of me at the front desk when I come to the firm so the receptionist can greet me with 'Hello, Mr. _____. Welcome back,' each time I arrive for a meeting instead of asking me who I am and who I'm there to see."
- *Learn the idiosyncrasies of your client's work environment to discover ways to make their lives easier.* For example, at Foundry Group, the most common legal activity we engage in is completing early-stage investments in technology companies. There are a standard suite of documents that memorialize every deal.

But once a deal closes, our internal finance and audit teams need to be able to extract specific information from the legal documents. Lawyers who took the time to inquire about and understand how their work fits into our overall business process would know that organizing the set of closing documents a certain way would make our process meaningfully more efficient for us. An adjustment like that in service delivery can generate substantial goodwill from your clients because, even with small things, it shows you are paying attention to their experience of working with you and trying to make their jobs easier.

- *Refuse to settle for delivering mediocre service in the everyday things.* Meet client deadlines every time. Better yet, deliver work product early. Don't send documents saying, "Here is a draft which is still under review." Complete the review beforehand and deliver only what you feel is a final product, even if the client is expecting a draft. Be impeccable in how you deliver your work, even the things that are standard and expected.

As a new lawyer, you may not be in a position yet to direct how service is delivered to a client. But you can certainly employ these practices as an associate inside a law firm to establish a devoted following among partners. Just replace "partner" for "client" in this discussion above to prompt ideas for how to deliver exceptional service inside your firm. Knowing the idiosyncrasies of the partners you work for is as important and valuable as knowing the idiosyncrasies of your clients. And refusing to settle for mediocre in your regular dealings with partners will go a long way to cementing your reputation as an exceptional lawyer in your firm.

It should go without saying that empathy is not enough to win and retain clients or ensure advancement within a law firm. You must, of course, be knowledgeable and skilled in your practice area. You must be, and cultivate a reputation as being, an expert at what you do. Yet those attributes are the obvious things expected of a lawyer and are not enough on their own to cement your success. If you also embrace the importance of empathy, and use that as a foundation from which to deliver outstanding and hospitable service to your partners and clients, then you will truly distinguish yourself from the mass of lawyers competing with you. Trust me, very few lawyers approach their practice this way. If you do, you will win the devotion of partners and clients and a thriving and sustainable practice.

Guest Chapter 19

Name: Randy Klein

Current Position/Background: Principal at Goldberg Kohn, Ltd., a 90+-lawyer finance boutique based in Chicago. https://www .goldbergkohn.com/professionals-Randall-Klein.html.

I joined Goldberg Kohn in 1993 as a fourth-year associate, after a one-year bankruptcy law clerkship. Ten years after my clerkship, I recruited that judge to join Goldberg Kohn. I have been the Chair of the Bankruptcy and Creditors' Rights Group for the past 15 years. In 2021, I named a co-chair who I have trained since recruiting him from law school 20 years ago. We have 10 lawyers in our Group, with 5 women and 2 diverse, including one former judge who is of counsel. All of the current principals (except me) started their careers at Goldberg Kohn.

Law School/Year. Northwestern University School of Law, 1990

Legal Practice Area: Bankruptcy. While in law school, I thought I might want to become a real estate developer, so I took a summer position at a smaller real estate boutique and focused on real estate classes. By the time I graduated, however, inactive construction cranes filled the Chicago skyline. Real estate transactions came to a screeching halt, as did my real estate legal career. Instead, I was left to work on busted real estate transactions (office buildings, apartment buildings, hotels, retail, mixed use), workout, chapter 11 cases, and liquidations. Simply because I took a couple bankruptcy classes, I became the resident bankruptcy attorney at my first firm (with no mentor). My second exposure to restructuring occurred within the firm itself. With no real estate work, my first firm struggled to keep the rainmakers (construction litigators) happy. They left, partners and associates were dismissed, and I was asked to stay on board as part of a "ground-floor opportunity." No thanks. I interviewed for a bankruptcy clerkship and landed several offers in Chicago before accepting my one-year gig with Judge Barliant. I used that year to hone my writing skills and build my bankruptcy knowledge. Some of the opinions I drafted formed the basis for later legal strategies and other published articles. I had found my calling.

Recommended Reading. Anything unrelated to the law that allows you to relax and escape would make a good reading list. For me, I like the *Gray Man* series by Mark Greaney and the *Mitch Rapp* books by Vince Flynn. Espionage, special agents, formidable foes, where the good guys always seem to win. I also enjoy reading "inside baseball"-type books about restructuring, debt trading, and bankruptcy. The most recent one of those is *The Caesars Palace Coup: How a Billionaire Brawl Over the Famous Casino Exposed the Power and Greed of Wall Street* by Max Frumes and Sujeet Indap. I know a lot of the lawyers and judges described in that book; and reading about the strategies of billionaire hedge funds pitted against one another is a useful guide to anyone interested in what I do for a living. Importantly, get a good book on legal writing. Brian Garner is a big name in that area, and teaches the craft for any young lawyer (litigator or transactional). If you find his stuff to be too preachy or textbook, pick up *Nino and Me: An Intimate Portrait of Scalia's Last Years* (Garner's memoir of his friendship and co-writing experiences with Justice Scalia).

Why I Went to Law School

With an undergraduate degree in liberal arts, a minor in finance, and no appetite whatsoever for accounting, I thought about either getting an MBA, becoming a real estate developer, or going to law school. I didn't come from a family of lawyers (no immediate relatives in the law), had no real idea of what it meant as a profession, but did surprisingly well on the LSAT. So I made the choice to go straight from undergrad to law school.

Frustrations After Law School—For Me and New Hires

For me, I wanted to practice real estate law and focus on real estate development. The real estate recession of 1989–1990 meant I needed to do something else. I found myself thrust into the bankruptcy world without mentors. That was frustrating, especially because I really didn't know how to practice law, let alone a tricky discipline like bankruptcy. I had to figure out a lot of things for myself, by myself. Not exactly sink or swim. No one knew if I was doing anything right or wrong.

I never forgot what it was like to know very little; and, once I started hiring law school graduates, I took an interest in their development. I trained a number of the bankruptcy associates and the ones who took a real interest in being trained were the most successful. No one wants to have to spoon-feed new lawyers; and, equally inefficient are young lawyers who try to do everything themselves without knowing what not to do. Find a mentor. Not every senior associate or partner is good at mentoring. Those who are will have a reputation for it. Find him or her and be willing to be taught. A related frustration are the new associates who don't dig in. Practicing law is hard. You need to ask questions, ask more questions, and then when you think you have it figured out, understand enough to know that you should ask more questions. Take the hard road. Challenge yourself, even on what may appear to be easy assignments. A young lawyer who used to work for me told me that my problem was that I didn't coddle him. I told him that his problem was that he needed to be coddled.

How Have I Used Core Concepts of Lawyering?

There are different ways to define success as a young lawyer in a law firm, but for me I wanted to develop client relationships and bring in business. I found out early on that many clients want to know their lawyers personally, for them to be genuine and forthright, and to work hard, be dedicated, and produce great work product. Clients only interested in giving instructions and wanting work done quickly, no questions asked, were of no use to me. So over the years I found clients with whom I meshed on a personal level. The single most important attribute of my most successful attorney–client relationships was sharing my thought process with the client. We became a team. I'll never forget the day I spent half an hour on the phone with the new client explaining my thinking and my strategy. My client said, "Wait. Excuse me? You are actually *explaining* what you are doing and you are seriously asking me for input on your *legal strategy*?

You are officially my favorite lawyer and now I know why I don't like all of the other ones." For 20 years she and I have worked hand-in-hand on cases, allowing me to weigh-in on business points, and allowing her to help develop legal strategies. It makes us both better and makes the practice of law so much more satisfying. Of course, it doesn't hurt when she spreads the word within her organization that if you want something explained to you, call Randy.

Similarly, when a young partner asked me how I was able to develop so many clients at such an early stage in my career, I told him to find a target and dedicate himself to that client. Literally tell them that they are your most important opportunity and that you want to do whatever they need, whenever they need it, without charging them for every single phone call and email. Build the personal trust by understanding their business and letting them know that they can rely upon you. I suppose you can break down what I did, for myself and how I encouraged my colleagues, into the Core Concepts. They're all in there. It is truly a function of being a real person first and a lawyer second.

Biggest mistake(s) you made while in law school/classes you should have taken

My biggest is not fit for print. But I wish I took more practical classes that would translate into being a transactional lawyer. Most law schools, unfortunately in my opinion, are not vocational schools. You're told that you'll learn how to *think* like a lawyer. Maybe. Teaching me how to draft a contract would have helped a lot, too. I had no idea if I wanted to be a litigator or a deal guy. At one point, I wanted to be an antitrust lawyer. I did not figure out until later that bankruptcy (part litigation/part transactional) would be my specialty; therefore, I did not take advantage of more finance and restructuring courses.

Most useful classes in law school

I learned a lot from the Negotiations class, taught by a practicing lawyer (so it had immediate application to the real world). Also, I learned a variety of negotiation techniques. Most important, it taught me the power of leverage. During one role play module about the building of a mental health facility in a wealthy suburban neighborhood, I was given the role of the federal government. The materials stated that I should allow the parties to try to reach their own resolution but if they couldn't, and only to break an impasse, I could announce all federal funding for various resources for the neighborhood would be withdrawn. Instead, I walked into the session and immediately announced my position and then walked out. When I met the professor in the hallway, he was incredulous. He asked me why I didn't follow the instructions and I told him: I had the big club, so I decided to cut through all the b.s. and swing it. I aced the class. This class taught me how to understand all the parameters in a complex situation (asking questions) and to navigate my own course (giving advice), and to trust my judgment.

How I decided what to do after law school? Did I make a good choice?

As explained above, the options for a real estate lawyer and potential real estate developer were nil upon graduation in 1990. I realized I had a knack for complex, multi-party negotiations, research, persuasive writing, and creativity. All of these factors came together in the creditors' rights field. During my clerkship, I had opportunities to research and write about the enforceability of liens on intangible income streams. Once back in private practice, I wrote articles on the subject, gave presentations, and had numerous opportunities to litigate related issues. Eventually, I built a reputation for creative solutions and a willingness to make arguments that pushed the envelope. Clients loved being educated about the process and the risks of various outcomes. I helped them understand the uncertainty of bankruptcy in general and the value of reaching a compromise. They helped me understand their needs (such as not spending a lot of money on litigation, or booking a loss in a particular quarter). Thirty years later, having spent most of that time in the same field, I am confident that I made the right choice. I'm still learning every day, understanding the needs of new clients, and coming up with new, thoughtful answers. It's a fun and challenging practice area.

Biggest mistake you made at your first job

As a brand-new lawyer, I was tasked with working on a purchase of an apartment building (near Northwestern Law School). I learned about the archaic law of party walls and the weird world of title insurance, including how to read a survey. The buyer (our client) agreed to pay some of the purchase price over time. We were supposed to close on the first day of the month, with monthly payment dates in equal installments (part interest, part principal). But the closing was delayed. Instead of closing on the 1st, we closed on the 20th. I did not adjust the promissory note to make it "interest only" for 10 days, and start the amortization schedule with the first payment after the first full month post-closing. As a first-year lawyer, should I have known that? Probably not. I was supposed to have been supervised. And, incredibly, the lawyer for the seller refused to correct for the mistake, which he absolutely knew I had made before we closed. Ultimately, the business folks worked it out, but it did not stop the senior partner at my firm from making an example out of me at a full associate meeting. He thought it was a teaching moment. I was mortified. I learned the hard way to make sure I understood what I was doing and why; and, if I didn't, I should have been asking questions. I suppose in hindsight this incident had an impact on my decision to leave the firm to pursue my clerkship. It wasn't because I made the mistake. It was the way I was treated. After that, I aspired to be a better teacher and to encourage inexperienced lawyers to not stress out about what they don't know. Everyone begins with very little actual knowledge. You have to accumulate it; and senior lawyers need to be willing to teach, guide, and encourage. As I said, find your mentor. (And it goes both ways when you become a partner. Be a mentor. You'll be rewarded throughout your career.)

Best advice received or have given for new lawyers

Take seminars and read books about how to draft clearly and concisely. Edit, edit again, and edit a third time. But perhaps the best advice I've given over the years is this: Speed Kills. Do not make the mistake of stressing out and rushing your work product. Ask how long an assignment should take; ask for samples and precedent and then do the work thoughtfully and carefully. Of course, clients don't like to pay for excessive hours, so you have to learn to be efficient. Do not hurry. The worst thing is for a client to spot a mistake that was easily avoided. They want the work done efficiently and done right. Sometimes, rarely, a client will ask for a rough draft so they can provide input during the drafting process. That's OK. Embrace their participation and expect that there will be errors. The final product is yours. Always strive to do it right.

Worst advice received or given for new lawyers

Eager to receive reviews as a junior lawyer, I was told "no news is good news." That's unacceptable laziness by the senior lawyers. Do not accept that sort of feedback. Ask for more. What else could you have done, or done differently, or should you be doing? If you have free time, think about organizations to join, articles to write, and clients to contact. The practice of law requires you to be thinking all the time about what else you should be doing. You should be sharpening your skills with feedback from your mentors and from senior associates. Eventually, you will develop enough to be able to ask clients the same sort of questions: How are you doing/what else could or should you be doing to help them? You may need to develop thick skin to absorb criticism. Constructive criticism, especially from clients, will strengthen your client relationships.

How to remain satisfied practicing law; what to do when you're not

Find out what kind of practice area best suits your skill set. For some of my colleagues who are happy practicing finance, they love checklists. They are extremely organized and task-oriented. They can multi-task, and are most efficient when moving through an assembly line of documentation. That didn't work for me. I started out as a front-end transactional attorney. I was often bored and dissatisfied, wondering whether I was going to be stuck doing work I didn't enjoy. Luckily, my career started with disruption. I was forced to learn how to practice restructuring law, followed by my bankruptcy clerkship, and leading to my job at Goldberg Kohn. Bankruptcy and creditors' rights rarely present the same matter. Every case is different. Different structures, clients, adversaries, businesses, third-party issues. It's more like playing chess. Infinite moves and outcomes. The most successful bankruptcy lawyers are those who are best at thinking on their feet (in court or in the boardroom), being persuasive advocates, and solving complex puzzles. But it is also an extremely stressful practice area. Understand that it is important to work hard, and to also decompress. Unplug. Turn off your phone (or at least don't look at it for a while). Try to find time for your hobbies. For me, that means golf. Unlike some folks who are better suited to be musicians, golf has been my best tool to develop long-lasting work relationships. You get their attention for six or more hours, have fun away from the office, and learn about them and their families. You may prefer going to concerts, or giving one.

What would I go back and tell myself as a third year?

What no one ever told me as a new lawyer, and I wish they had, was that it is OK not to know what you're doing. It's also OK to feel that there is always more than you should be learning. Remember that you are the sum of your experiences; and for the practice of law, you know what you have done. No one is any different than you. Find the subject matter that is most interesting to you. Try to master it. Get your hands on practical guidelines, checklists, and examples. And build your own annotated set of documents. Whether litigation or transactional, there are basic outlines that are now available. The practice of law has changed. Today, you have third-party resources like Practical Law, or Bloomberg, to provide you with the templates. Do your homework and your research. And keep building your own experiences. Eventually, you will be an expert in one or more areas. You will be able to attract clients because they trust you with their projects. Build your knowledge, build your clients, and then as soon as you are comfortable that you have achieved your initial goals, train someone junior to you. Then, start the process all over again.

Guest Chapter 20

Name: Stacy Carter

Current Position: Chief Legal Officer and SVP of Business Affairs at Techstars

Former Post-Law School Positions: General Counsel and Head of People at Sphero; Associate General Counsel of Rally Software; Associate at Cooley LLP

Legal Practice Area: General Counsel. Started as a business attorney doing mergers and acquisitions (M&A) and startup work.

Law School and Year: University of Colorado, 2007

Time between undergrad and law school: 3 years (accountant)

Two books I recommend:
Five Dysfunctions of a Team by Patrick Lencioni – Simply the best book on leadership team dynamics. I read it annually.
Wild by Cheryl Strayed – A book about a woman's journey on the Pacific Crest Trail, and a good reminder that sometimes we all need to take a break and get away.

Short background on why I went to law school

I was a tax accountant at KPMG in Virginia before I went to law school. I had thought about going to law school for many years, but after becoming serious with a guy who was getting his PhD at University of Colorado (CU), I decided it was time to apply for law school in Colorado. The relationship didn't last, but law school and a new career path did. I assumed I would be a tax attorney, given my tax and accounting background, and after the first summer of law school, I actually went back to KPMG for a summer doing M&A Tax work. The summer after my second year, however, I decided to try a law firm experience. I went to work for Cooley LLP and quickly became seduced by the joys of working with start-ups. Cooley offered me a full-time position after graduation, which exposed me to the wide world of entrepreneurs.

What frustrates me most about people I hire newly out of law school

I currently lead the Legal team at Techstars. Techstars is a global accelerator and investor that makes 600+ investments a year in start-up companies that are incorporated in more than 20 countries around the world. We support the business with a fairly large legal team, or as I like to think of it, a small in-house law firm. My legal team of 16 is constantly growing so I get to work with new lawyers all the time. New lawyers are exciting to work with and tend to be very enthusiastic about working at Techstars, especially since they get to spend much of their day talking to our entrepreneurs around the world, helping them secure investment, and learning about the latest technology and products in our portfolio. Of course, there are frustrations working with new lawyers as well.

One of the biggest issues I see is misunderstanding or misalignment on the end goal. The end goal for a lawyer is a specific outcome that your client (either at a law firm or in-house) wants. The idea is probably not to offer the most detailed legal advice covering every risk and scenario or to make sure your email/memo/contract is grammar-perfect. If your goal is to get an investment or transaction or contract done, think about what you are doing and how it relates to the goal. Too often, I see junior attorneys spend too much time researching and running down issues that really are not related to the goal that the business or client is trying to accomplish. I always encourage young lawyers to ask their manager or business partner if they do not know the end goal.

A second issue I see is written products that are sloppy and not ready for senior review because the attorney has rushed to meet a deadline. A part of every professional job is your organization and time management skills. If you have a deadline, you should understand approximately how long it will take you to complete the project, including gathering information from others and managing your own proofreading. It frustrates me when an attorney misses a deadline because they could not get the information they needed for completing the project and waited too long to ask. I recommend one to two proofreads of an email or written project, but not more; perfection is the enemy of getting things done!

How have you used (or not) the core concepts of lawyering as this book proposes: Empathy, Listening First, Asking Questions, and Giving Advice?

Being a lawyer means that we are fundamentally in a client service profession. This is true whether you have law firm clients that pay you money, or if you are an in-house lawyer. As an in-house lawyer, I know my legal team is generally a "cost center" to the business, meaning that we are an expense to the business without a balancing revenue (at Techstars we are also part of the product delivery team given the number of investments we facilitate, but most in-house legal teams are fundamentally cost centers). The business must be our client in order to justify the expense of having an in-house Legal team. I believe a key part of providing good client service is empathy and asking questions. What is the business or the client's end goal? Why is that goal important to them? What is the Legal team's role in helping to achieve that goal? This does not mean the client is always right, but it does mean that you must deeply understand the client's point of view if you are to explain yours successfully (if you read the *Getting to Yes* negotiations book that Jason recommends, you will see this concept explained detail really nicely).

For the Techstars Legal team, one of our most important jobs is to work with our managing directors to help make accelerator investments in the 10 to 12 companies that the managing directors have selected to enter into their Techstars accelerator program. The managing director's goal in choosing these 10 to 12 companies is to select companies with the greatest opportunity for growth, future venture capital (VC) investment, and eventual liquidation through acquisition or IPO. Sometimes, in the legal due diligence process, a Techstars attorney will see an issue that would go against our rules for investment. While it is tempting to just let the managing director know that we cannot invest because of XYZ specific rule, the better way is to explain the decision is that this company is likely to be uninvestable by future VCs because of the particular issue (which is the genesis of why we have most of our rules). By showing empathy to the end goal of the managing director (investing in a company that will be able to grow and take lots of future investment), we can make sure we are aligned with them when explaining why the Legal team is taking a particular action. Shout out to my colleague Sierra Moller, who treats managing directors at Techstars as her valued clients, often by showing them incredible empathy.

Most useful class in law school

CU Law School has an amazing clinical law program for its students. Most lawyers I know who went to CU Law and work in the start-up field participated in the Entrepreneurial Law Clinic, which is a phenomenal program giving students the opportunity to work alongside entrepreneurs for school credit (helping them incorporate, issue initial founder stock, file their patents, etc.). In fact, many lawyers who I have hired over the years have gone through the Entrepreneurial Law Clinic and have loved it. Given I took mostly business law classes at CU, I decided to do something a little different my third year and worked in the Juvenile and Family Law Clinic, representing children who have been abused or neglected. While I have not needed to use any of the technical legal knowledge I learned while at the clinic, I cannot overstate the value in what I learned about client service and being partially responsible for a client's health and safety outcomes. The clinic taught me client advocacy, how to work with individuals who have truly been failed by others in their life, and of course, empathy. Even if you know the type of law you want to practice, I would highly recommend taking a couple classes in law school completely out of your comfort zone, particularly with types of clients that are completely different from ones you have experienced.

Biggest mistake I made at my first job

I am going to share two big mistakes that I made at Rally, my first in-house job. For my first year or so at Rally, I was responsible for negotiating most of our SaaS sales contracts with big (often Fortune 500) customers. After signing a contract that included a negotiated source code escrow provision, I was told by our engineering team that we could not meet the terms of the provision. I did not know ahead of time that we could not meet the terms because I had not done a thorough job of asking the right questions. There was really no excuse—we all worked in one big office together and I often played ping pong with these engineers during an afternoon break. While I had egg on my face in this particular instance, I learned a career-long lesson about making sure the business can actually perform what is agreed to in a contract.

Also during my time at Rally, I went on maternity leave after having my third kid. While out on leave, Rally was in the process of an initial public offering (IPO), and my boss convinced me to come back to work before the end of my leave part-time in order to work on a special project related to the IPO. I wanted to get public company experience, and I think I felt guilty for taking the time off, so I worked part-time the last ~six weeks of my leave. I have always regretted not having that extra time at home with my daughter, and I certainly have had more than enough opportunities to work and get public company experience since then.

How I remain happy in my profession

Early on in your career, you will hopefully have the opportunity to experience all sorts of different projects and types of work. At Cooley (first legal job) and Rally (first in-house job), I raised my hand as much as possible to volunteer for various projects. This led to public company work, tons of M&A, SaaS and licensing contract negotiations, employment law, among other things. I realized that I liked M&A, was good at negotiating commercial contracts, and had a passion for employment law. And, I learned that I really do not like real estate (reviewing leases) and litigation. While I cannot always avoid reviewing leases and litigation, as I get more senior and have an experienced team to support me, I am better able to choose what I want to focus my time working on. I encourage all lawyers to spend time early in your career figuring out what you like and what you are good at.

My second piece of advice for happiness in your career really comes from my husband. Whenever I complain multiple times (he listens supportively the first time) about the same coworker or work issue, he asks, "Well, what are you going to do about it?" While you will hopefully have plenty of mentors, friends, and family members supporting you in your career, you are ultimately the one responsible for your happiness at work. If you do not like something, you can choose to try to change it or to accept the issue and have a good attitude. Trying to change a problem can mean fixing a process, setting up working agreements with a coworker, or even finding a new job. Accepting the issue with a good attitude can be equally valid in certain instances, and remembering those words of wisdom have helped me remain happy at work time and time again.

Guest Chapter 21

Name: Nikki Stitt Sokol

Current Position: Director & Associate General Counsel, Litigation at Meta (Facebook)

Previous Positions: Mayer Brown (Chicago); Hogan Lovells (Boston, via merger with Collora LLP); Wilson Sonsini Goodrich & Rosati (Palo Alto)

Legal Practice Area: Litigation

Law School and Year: University of Michigan, 1998

Time between undergrad and law school: None

One or two books I recommend: *Becoming* by Michelle Obama; *To Kill a Mockingbird* by Harper Lee.

Why I went to law school

I decided in 5th grade that I wanted to be a lawyer, which is really rare these days. A classmate's parent came into the classroom to talk about the Fourth Amendment and search and seizure principles. I loved the idea of standing up to power and knowing my rights so that the police could not take advantage of me.

As a kid, I also felt a sense of deep injustice over the lack of rights kids have and the ability of schools and other adults to control them. This seemed to fly in the face of what I understood my rights to be as an American. Of course, as an adult (and parent) now, I feel a little differently about these issues, but at the time that was part of my initial motivation.

What frustrated me most about coming out of law school and/or what frustrates me with regards to people I work with or hire who are newly out of law school

Junior lawyers tend not to be concise. They've been trained to write long, detailed, analytical memos. What they miss is that in-house attorneys need tight executive summaries. It's hard to distill something down to its essence and explain it in simple terms. We want to know that the deeper analysis is there so that we can test the conclusions, but it's critical to convey the answer to the question in a concise way. And right at the top. Don't bury the lede.

How have you used (or not) the core concepts of lawyering as this book proposes: Empathy, Listening First, Asking Questions, and Giving Advice?

Empathy is one of the most important but often overlooked qualities in a lawyer. You have to gain trust with your clients. If they don't feel like you understand their concerns and that you're on their team trying to get them to a good place, you will not serve your client effectively.

This is particularly true for litigators. Litigation can sometimes be a crisis for a company. Individuals can feel like the future of the company is riding on their shoulders. At the very least, it's an inconvenient, uncomfortable, and uncertain process. If you don't understand the human experience aspect, then you'll fail to adequately prepare your client. Or at best, your client will walk away with a less positive feeling about you.

Always check in to see how your witness is feeling about the process and what you can do to make them more comfortable. You'll be surprised how much it will matter.

Biggest mistake(s) you made while in law school

My dad never went to law school (he's an engineer), but he always told me when I was in undergrad to pick my classes based on the professor, not the subject matter. As with most things, he was right, and his wisdom applied equally to law school.

The biggest mistake I made in law school was to ignore this advice and focus too much on the subject of the class rather than figuring out who the best professors were and take their classes no matter the topic. A magical teacher can open your eyes and engage you thoroughly in a subject you never would have expected to enjoy.

Bonus: The same rule applies at law firms. Pick your work (to the extent you can) based on the partner with whom you will be working.

What class(es) did I wish I had taken while in law school? In or outside the school? What about today?

I should have taken a negotiation class in law school. Whether you're a transactional lawyer, a litigator, or never formally practice, negotiation skills are useful no matter what. You can be the best brief writer and advocate, but at the end of the day most cases settle, and you'd be amazed how many litigators aren't good negotiators.

Most useful classes in law school

The most useful classes I took in law school were civil procedure and torts. Civil procedure admittedly is quite dry, but it is really the bread and butter of your daily practice as a litigator. You'd be surprised how many times I've been faced with a situation that would make a perfect civil procedure final exam hypothetical.

Torts was not enjoyable for me, because as someone who tends to the analytical, the concepts felt amorphous and uncertain—even unfair. But in retrospect, that class more than any other taught me how to think like a lawyer and how the law frames issues relating to fundamental issues of human interaction, like how responsible people should behave toward others.

How did you decide what to do post-law school? With hindsight, how good of a job did you do?

I wanted to be a trial attorney. I'd had visions of myself in a courtroom since I was in elementary school. When looking through firm profiles during on campus interviewing, I kept my eye out for inklings that a firm could provide me real trial experience.

The hardest question was the city in which I would do this. I was part of a dual career couple. My now-husband was in medical school while I was in law school. I went into fall interviewing my 2L year with no idea what city I would end up in because residency match results would not come out until the following spring. So I had to pick a handful of cities that we were both interested in, interview with firms there, and then pick one offer in each city, as allowed under a NALP exception for people in my position. (Actually, it was even more complicated than that because my husband is an identical twin, and so we had to factor in where his medical student brother might land, too.)

In the end, I got really lucky. I had an offer at a great firm in Chicago and my husband matched with a residency program there—and so did his twin!

In retrospect, I'm glad I started out at a large, brand name law firm. I not only got to learn how to be a lawyer from some of the classiest, smartest lawyers in the business—and even got to go to trial for three months in my second year—it gave me a platform from which I could have done anything, from the U.S. Attorney's Office to smaller firms to in-house practice to other government roles and beyond. And paying off those student loans early helped, too.

Biggest mistake you made at your first job

The biggest mistake I made early in my career was submitting a draft to a partner that was a half-baked brief that really was more like an outline with a few case quotes. I foolishly thought that when people said to send them a draft, that they meant a rough version of where I was trying to go with the document so that they could give me feedback. I quickly learned that "draft" meant the best, final product I could generate. Anything less was an "outline."

Best advice you received or have given for those coming out of law school

Try to take a job in the city or region in which you ultimately want to live. Don't go to New York or another large legal market just to get the big city law experience or briefly live in an exciting place with the idea that you will eventually move where you really want to settle down. Relationships are critical in law, and the sooner you can start to build relationships with people in the community you ultimately want to serve, the better for your career.

Because I married a doctor who had to move around as part of his medical training, I did the opposite of this. I have practiced in three different states (and taken three different state bar exams) and felt like I had to start over each time. I don't recommend it—and not just because taking so many different bar exams is no fun!

How have you remained happy in your profession? Have there been times when you were not? If so, what did you do to improve your situation?

I have remained happy as a lawyer by doing three things. First, I bring my authentic self to work. I don't try to be someone I'm not. And I don't pretend not to be a parent. Second, I make friends with the people I work with—meaning I truly connect with them on a personal level. I don't do this in the strategic, transactional sense to advance my standing. I find people I like and then invest in the relationship. It's so much more fun to go to work when you get to hang out with your friends! Third, I get to work on challenging, cutting-edge issues with really smart people for a client with a mission that's meaningful to me. I am constantly learning.

The times I have been most unhappy as a lawyer have been the times when I was doing work that I didn't truly enjoy but felt that I was "supposed" to do well. I am an extroverted person who loves to engage with others and figure out the real story behind the allegations. But when I was in a role in which I spent all my time alone in my office reading cases and writing briefs—doing what was considered really "prestigious" work—I was miserable and lonely. The lesson here is that you should figure out what you enjoy, and then do that. Because if you like it, you're probably good at it, too. Don't force yourself to do work you don't enjoy. In the end, it doesn't help anyone.

If you could go back in time and tell your younger self something about making the transition from law school to the real world, what would it be?

As my dear friend Allison Kluger at the Stanford Graduate School of Business always says, "Offer the solution, not the suggestion." A slightly different flavor of this is to identify solutions, not just problems. You'll be surprised at what you can achieve and what others will let you lead if you approach your work in this way.

Guest Chapter 22

Name: Ryan Day

Current Position: Senior Deputy District Attorney – 20th JD (Boulder)

Former Post-Law School Positions: Law Clerk, United States District Court for the District of Wyoming; Associate Attorney, Wheeler Trigg O'Donnell LLP

Legal Practice Area: Criminal. I am the office's primary "appellate" attorney, so I handle all level of criminal work—misdemeanor to homicide—at both the pre- and post-judgment phases.

Law School and Year: University of Colorado, 2010

Time between undergrad and law school: None

One or two books I recommend: *Dune* by Frank Herbert. Because you've likely received enough recommendations for lawyering and self-care books, you can still read for enjoyment, and it's a tremendous book. Also, if you're reading my chapter you might be a trial attorney and all trial attorneys should learn how to tell a good story. Reading is a good way to learn storytelling.

Why law school

I never seriously considered doing anything else. My dad was an attorney and he raved about it: Lawyers solve the world's problems! Lawyers uphold the rule of law! Lawyers keep chaos at bay! (Really.) I should have known better, but I wanted to be like him. Plus, I was always told I could do anything I wanted with a law degree. I suppose that is technically true, even if I've never met anyone who spent three

264

years and several hundred thousand dollars learning to "think like a lawyer" in order to become a marine biologist or basketball coach.

In any event, I enjoyed the work that went into becoming a lawyer—speech and debate, mock trial, the LSAT, law school, moot court, etc. I was pretty good at these, it turned out, and I liked them enough to stick with it.

What frustrated me most about coming out of law school and/or what frustrates me with regards to people I work with or hire who are newly out of law school

Law school did not prepare me for the day-to-day <u>work</u> of being a lawyer. Knowing the difference between horizontal and vertical privity was great for the bar exam but not for effectively communicating with the five partners I worked for as a new associate. I had no idea how to triage and prioritize when I became overwhelmed. Law school should include less theory and more practice. Medical and trade schools require students to complete a residency or apprenticeship, right? Why don't law schools?

As for new lawyers, I would like them to ask more questions. They should ask all of the questions. Ask to borrow my work product. Ask me to review with yours. And they should not be afraid to make mistakes and then ask me how to fix them. For whatever reason, new lawyers believe we expect them to know everything or we expect them to figure out things themselves. We don't expect those things! The hardest thing to do as a new lawyer is to use your time effectively, and the best way to use your time effectively is to ask questions.

How have you used (or not) the core concepts of lawyering as this book proposes: Empathy, Listening First, Asking Questions, and Giving Advice?

Empathy is the most important of the core concepts because it begets the others—we're far more likely to listen first, ask questions, and give genuine advice if we empathize with the person we're speaking to. Also, empathy builds trust and respect.

When I was a civil litigator, I did not use any of these concepts enough. (Civil litigation is, as a field, short on empathy and listening and constructive advice-giving.) Regardless, in retrospect, I would have been happier and found more success had I listened better and asked more questions. I was worried I wasn't a good enough lawyer to make it in that field and I was afraid that asking questions and making mistakes would expose me. For reasons I touched on earlier, I was wrong.

You cannot be a good prosecutor without empathy. Obviously, empathy is what allows a prosecutor to communicate effectively with a victim about the impact of a crime and to understand the victim's desired outcome. Less obviously, but just as importantly, prosecutors must show empathy toward defendants, who often commit crimes in reaction to their circumstances. People rarely commit crimes on their best day. Prosecutors have discretion to account for this and they should exercise their discretion empathetically.

Biggest mistake(s) you made while in law school

My biggest day-to-day mistake was treating law school like school, at which I had always treated with varying degrees of effort. Treat law school like a job—develop a routine and work the same hours every day.

I also wish I had been more introspective and thought critically about what would make me happy in my career. I pursued a clerkship and law firm gig because I thought I was supposed to, ignoring doubts about whether they were the right fit for me. I reasoned that these would give me greater opportunity down the road—and I was right—but the price I paid was several years of unhappiness. Know yourself and find something you like. There's no point in being unhappy because other people expect you to.

Most useful classes in law school?

Right now? Evidence. I'm a trial lawyer. But across my career, I'd say legal writing and appellate advocacy. You know by now that I'm not a great writer, but I was a disaster before law school. No matter your field you will research, you will write, and you will advocate. For me, these classes were maybe the only ones that taught me principles I've used every day in my ten years of practice.

How did you decide what to do post-law school, and in hindsight how good of a job did you do?

I applied to clerkships because I thought I was supposed to, and that they could open doors down the road. I still think that's generally correct, especially for aspiring litigators. I would recommend it for anyone who wants to be a trial lawyer.

It was the next job that I got wrong. I went to work at WTO because it was a premier litigation firm that would get me into court early in my career. The problem is, as I mentioned above, I should have known that a law firm practice was not a good fit for me on a personal level. I learned a lot and am grateful for that, but in hindsight I did a poor job of selecting a path that would make me happy. Being happy is everything.

Biggest mistake at my first job?

I mentioned this earlier, but I should have asked more questions. I was afraid that revealing what I did not know would undermine me in the eyes of my colleagues. The opposite probably was true—when I put my head down and tried to figure it out myself, I was more likely to waste time and make mistakes. I also probably should have been more empathetic toward the partners I worked for.

Best advice I got coming out of law school

This might be silly, but I vividly remember a senior associate advising me to remove the section of a motion that summarized the legal standard and replace it with argument—I didn't need to analyze the problem objectively, I needed to persuade. This was both an obvious and relatively small tip, but it highlighted for me how I had to shift my thinking now that I wasn't in law school or working for a judge. I give the same advice to new lawyers every year. The mental framework you applied to problems in law school likely won't work in the real world.

Worst advice I received coming out of law school

That I had to work in a big or "prestigious" law firm after law school. Don't pursue a job about which you might have reservations because it confers a certain "status" in the legal community. Think hard about what you'd like to do and go do it. Don't worry about what other people will think. (And anyone who tells you that you can't start somewhere small is just wrong. My wife joined a five-person startup after graduation and is now a senior attorney at Twitter. You can make it work.)

How have you remained happy in your profession? Have there been times when you were not? If so, what did you do to improve your situation?

Of course I've been unhappy. I'm a lawyer. I hated working in a law firm. I spent almost four years trying to convince myself that might change, like I'd wake up one morning excited to go to work. And I know people who were equally unhappy but stuck it out long enough that they couldn't leave for some reason—family, the money, clients, whatever. Luckily for me, other life events intervened and gave me a chance to look hard at myself and think about what I wanted in life. That led me to the DA's office, where on balance I'm very happy.

My advice is to be introspective. Lawyers spend all their time solving other people's problems. Make sure you spend time solving your own. Learn who you are and learn what you like. Then go find it.

Guest Chapter 23

Name: Tyrone Glover

Current Position: Founding Attorney, Tyrone Glover, Esq.

Former Post-Law School Positions: Attorney, Killmer Lane and Newman, LLP; Partner, Haddon Morgan & Foreman, P.C.; Partner Stimson Glover Stancil Leedy, LLC; Senior Deputy Public Defender, Denver Office of the State Public Defender; Attorney, Shepherd Ross, P.C.

Legal Practice Area: Civil Rights, Criminal Defense, Personal Injury

Law School and Year: University of Colorado, 2009

Time between undergrad and law school: 5 years (professional MMA fighter)

One or two books I recommend: *Autobiography of Malcolm X* by Alex Haley: A real-life story of redemption, inspiration, enlightenment, and embracing the personal authenticity of where you stand in the world at any given moment. This book reminds me that there is value in the path, and even as you grow and learn, you can do phenomenal things along the way. It also empowers me to self-reflect and not be afraid to break molds to progress in my own personal evolution.

Devil in the Grove: Thurgood Marshall, the Groveland Boys, and the Dawn of a New America by Gilbert King: When we think about our legal heroes, we mostly remember them in their most prominent career capstone roles. This book follows Thurgood Marshall when he was a scrappy civil rights lawyer as he defended four wrongfully accused Black boys in the Jim Crow south. His tenacity to prevail even in the face of credible death threats is inspiring to any lawyer endeavoring to take on unjust systems.

Short background on why I went to law school

As a Black man, I was made personally aware of inequality and prejudice at a very early age. My parents and grandparents tirelessly fought to break barriers and improve conditions for our family and in our society. It has always been very important to me to find some way to address these same issues. After college, when I was competing as a professional fighter, I saw up close the way systematic power dynamics could be used to exploit people. Many of my fight-teammates came from marginalized communities and were prime targets for being taken advantage of by more sophisticated promoters, agents, and even coaches. I recognized, on both a macro and micro level, the good that I could do by going to law school and using my degree, and the knowledge that came with it, to empower people against those who sought to subjugate them. So, I retired undefeated in my prime to go to law school.

What frustrated me most about coming out of law school and/or what frustrates me with regards to people I work with or hire who are newly out of law school

Law school felt very much like a bubble to me. I did not realize while in law school how the work we do as lawyers affects our communities and the people in them. The #1 core concept of this book is empathy. It requires you to understand where your clients are *coming from*. I think this feat is difficult for some when they first graduate from law school, unless during law school you explore the intersectionality of what we do in our profession and the role it plays in society. I find that newly out of law school lawyers don't understand the great influence our actions have on the day-to-day realities of our neighbors. Some lawyers never reckon with this and retreat to their own organization or practice ecospheres, as we have been conditioned to do by the law school experience, which is often removed from reality.

How have you used (or not) the core concepts of lawyering as this book proposes: Empathy, Listening First, Asking Questions, and Giving Advice?

Lawyering must be client centered. Which is why these core concepts are essentially the foundations of my law practice. As a litigator, and former professional fighter, my natural inclination is to jump-in and tussle. But what I have learned over the years is that I can best serve people by identifying and embodying in my practice just exactly what I am fighting for. I have a duty to seek justice for people. The concept of justice is personal and can be different for each individual. Trying to step into a person's shoes, to really hear them, and to identify what justice looks like for their unique situation helps me meet their needs.

Biggest mistake(s) you made while in law school

My biggest mistake was getting wrapped up in competing for what everyone else wanted in law school, as opposed to following my own gut and passions. Law school attracts high-performing competitive people. You very quickly figure out the highly coveted accolades—whether they be certain summer internships, spots on reviews or journals, big law interviews, clerkships, jobs at high regarded law firms, etc. I spent a lot of time competing for things that I had no interest in before law school. Then, after law school I grappled with exactly what I wanted to do with my law degree. I probably could have done some of that soul-searching work in law school and better directed my interests. There were classmates who were competitive about the things they cared about. My biggest mistake was that I did not unplug from the competitive grind to better understand what really drove me.

What class(es) did I wish I had taken while in law school? In or outside the school? What about today?

I wish I had done more clinics and taken more classes with adjunct professors. My law school had an amazing clinical program and great practicing lawyers and judges teaching every semester. Some the best interns and young lawyers I have worked with transfer their real-world clinical experience to being effective advocates in practice. I, wrongly, had the attitude that after graduation I would get my fill of practical lawyering and exposure to practitioners. I chose to take classes that were mostly academic focused. It wasn't until my 3L year that I took more adjunct classes, which helped refine and deepen my perspective for the cases I was studying in my more academic classes.

Most useful classes in law school

Constitutional Law, the foundations from which everything flows, knowing and understanding the history of our most seminal cases has certainly helped and been useful. **Trial Advocacy**, learning and understanding the foundational concepts of how to advocate and *stand up* in front of judges and juries not only helps me in the moment when I am doing it, but also in case preparation. **Venture Capital**, helping a person attain justice is not unlike leading an entrepreneurial dream to a place of success. VC taught me to focus on achieving a successful outcome for my clients through, defined goals, skilled negotiation, and staged strategic thinking.

How did you decide what to do post-law school? With hindsight, how good of a job did you do?

My decision post-law school was simple—I liked the firm I was working for, I liked the lawyers, and they offered me a job. I was happy to land somewhere I enjoyed working. Based on those criteria, I did a good job. But what I learned from that first job is that I needed to also have a connection to the work I was doing. I needed to feel like I was part of a greater purpose. So, I adjusted my criteria and left my law firm, where I was doing mostly business law, to go to the public defender's office. At the public defenders I found a welcoming community of lawyers dedicated to fighting for our indigent clients. In hindsight, my first law job, like all past experiences, has made me who I am today and was part of my process to realizing professional fulfillment.

Biggest mistake you made while at your first job

I perceived that asking for help was a sign of incompetence. I perceived that I needed to be practice ready and able to do the job on day one. I went to law school, passed the bar, and now I needed to be ready. I toiled on projects to get them right and would often deliver close to perfection where it was not needed or misunderstand the scope of the assignment because I was afraid to burden more senior attorneys with my inquiries. I quickly learned that by following up, asking questions, and consistently communicating, I could complete my assignments in a timelier manner and at the quality level they required.

Best advice you received or have given for those coming out of law school

There are three pieces of advice that I regularly revisit:

1. **Continuously evaluate what drives you.** Professional growth requires self-reflection. Often our reflections as lawyers look more like self-critiques. This piece advice reminds me to evaluate where I feel energized and driven in my practice. It is a kinder, more invigorating reflection and often helps me zero-in on the next steps in my trajectory.
2. **When stagnant, get to moving.** When I feel stuck, whether is it with a case or just generally with my profession, this piece of advice reminds me to not wait for inspiration, but to get moving and find my inspiration. Set up a coffee with a trusted advisor, get out and do something in nature, attend an interesting CLE or event, etc. Anything that isn't sitting at my computer feeling stuck.
3. **Read the rules.** Interestingly, lawyers spend a lot of time strategizing and trying to find solutions to certain issues when the answers are often written down in rules, practice standards, or holdings. Spending time on the front-end by simply "reading the rules" has saved me the heartburn of spending hours on a matter before finding some material clarity that I should have discovered much earlier on.

Worst advice you received or have given for those coming out of law school

"Only network *up*."

When building relationships in our profession, so much of the emphasis is on connecting with "the boss," only people with much more time into the profession than you. Building those relationships is important, but the relationships and work you do with your peers is just as important. After law school you will watch your peers and colleagues do great things. Having an authentic relationship you went to school, worked, and/or essentially came up together with someone is extremely underemphasized.

How have you remained happy in your profession? Have there been times when you were not? If so, what did you do to improve your situation?

I have not always remained happy in my profession, but I don't think that is a bad thing. I have come to learn that being happy professionally is as much about knowing what works for you as it is identifying what does not work. There were so many law practice choices that I had given little thought to before law school. Public or private? Large, medium, or small? Neutral or advocate? Litigation, transactional or other? Workplace culture? I did not have a strong reaction to or opinion of most of these until I had some experience. Where I am today is as much about what I like as it is about what I did not like. The key for me is, if you are unhappy, figure out how you can change your situation.

If you could go back in time and tell your younger self something about making the transition from law school to the real world, what would it be?

You don't have to be perfect. Just be the best version of your authentic self. And trust your gut, it's gotten you this far.

Guest Chapter 24

Name: William E. Foster

Current Position: Associate Professor, University of Arkansas School of Law

Legal Practice Area: Tax; Mergers & Acquisitions

Law School and Year: J.D., University of Arkansas, 2005, LL.M., New York University, 2006

Time between undergrad and law school: None

One or two books I recommend:

1. *The Checklist Manifesto* by Atul Gawande. This is an obvious read for transactional lawyers whose practice requires consistency, organization, systems, and redundancies to eliminate mistakes (e.g., leftover language from a prior deal, a missed document at closing) and to navigate complex deals. But all attorneys can benefit from the simplest tool—a basic checklist—to help sequence and prioritize tasks and to build in safeguards so they don't miss something (whether it's the fifth time performing this task or the five hundredth). Consistency is essential in any practice. Particularly early in your career, it's helpful to have the mindset of Steve Jobs when he was trying to set Apple products apart from its competitors: "We just can't ship junk."

2. *Educated* by Tara Westover. This stunning autobiography is essential reading for anyone pursuing higher education. The author overcomes unimaginable obstacles to even be in a position to apply to college. Many students find themselves in graduate school (including law school) more or less by inertia,

merely the next step in the path to. . . something professional. This book reminds readers of the privilege of pursuing higher learning and can help someone struggling with motivation to clarify their goals, priorities, and purpose.

It's often difficult to persuade lawyers to read anything outside of work other than the news because, well, they read all day for a living. But reading very good fiction or literary nonfiction is incredibly helpful for finding your voice as a writer and communicator. Lawyers trade in words, whether emails or motions or contracts, and they need to develop their own voice to be confident and effective word merchants. The more time a person spends reading quality writing, the sooner they'll find a voice, tone, and cadence that works for them.

Short background on why I went to law school

I planned to be a lawyer early in life, probably persuaded by my parents and decent verbal scores on standardized tests. But in high school, I met a few attorneys who actively discouraged every young person they encountered from joining the profession. They were unhappy and overworked and unfulfilled professionally. Around the same time, I started gravitating toward music, and for a few years wanted to be a professional saxophonist of some ilk (music educator? studio musician? successor to Lenny Pickett on SNL??). After studying music seriously for a while, it was clear that the road to a viable music career was uncertain (to be generous). Then, in my freshman year of college, my father lost his job. So I began to truly value financial stability, independence, and the perceived dignity of a profession. I shifted through a few other majors and eventually found government, history, and politics too enticing to ignore. During my junior year, my father took his own life, and that drive to become independent and self-supporting became an urgent need, both financially and psychologically. From that point on, I brought an earnest intensity and seriousness to my coursework, knowing that it was a lifeline.

While weighing graduate school in political science and law school, I received a letter of admission and generous scholarship offer to attend the University of Arkansas, signed by Associate Dean

Jim Miller. A that moment, I believed the stars had aligned for me in law.

What frustrated me most about coming out of law school and/or what frustrates me with regards to people I work with or hire who are newly out of law school

Coming out of law school, I felt sickeningly unprepared to draft documents. When I stepped into private practice, I felt like I understood the law, but had very little idea of how to do the basic tasks of a lawyer beyond writing memos to senior attorneys. Although between J.D. and LL.M. programs, I had taken at least five courses on estates and trusts, I had never actually seen a complete will or a trust, and had certainly never drafted any provision of one. So I felt clueless approaching documents, form work, and basic drafting tasks. One of my goals in shifting to a career in legal education was to ensure that my students had exposure to documents and realistic drafting tasks in the relatively low stakes environment of the classroom.

With new lawyers, you sometimes see an unfortunate degree of casualness about work quality and even getting the right answer on the law. Particularly at larger law firms, I think new lawyers tend to rely on the safety net of the senior attorneys and send unfinished work product upstream before it's ready. Almost everything I saw in practice would have benefited substantially from another read and round of edits.

How have you used (or not) the core concepts of lawyering as this book proposes: Empathy, Listening First, Asking Questions, and Giving Advice?

I wholeheartedly agree that empathy is the most important trait for being an effective attorney. In any practice setting, a lawyer needs to be able to efficiently convey ideas and rapidly process input, and understanding your audience is essential in both tasks. Whether trying to persuade an opposing party to move on their offer or convincing a client that their goals will best be served by shifting course, it is essential to understand how they perceive the stakes. To have a reasonable chance of success, the lawyer must be able to see the situation from the other person's point of view. It's common for lawyers to fall into the trap of trying to game out the scenarios guessing what the other party might do solely from a strategic standpoint. But human beings are complex, and their motivations are often nuanced. What one can discern about someone else from their position at an organization, from their web profile, or from their reputation in the community only goes so far. And while it's helpful to gather as much information as possible prior to engaging with someone, it's a mistake to assume that they will share the priorities of someone with (what appears to be) an almost identical background and status.

When I was in my twenties, I felt like I could read people very well, and I began most interactions loaded with assumptions about the other person. Because it often took several exchanges to reset my understanding, I squandered countless opportunities to make connections with people who could have been friends, advocates, and professional resources. Most emerging professionals now understand the baggage they bring to their interactions and are better equipped to navigate that environment. But starting with a (relatively) blank slate is only the first step. Empathy takes a sincere investment in understanding someone else, and the more one is motivated by finding leverage or weakness, the more difficult it will be to pick up on the nuances in their perspective that complete the picture. I promise it is always worth the time and energy to set aside ego and take a genuine interest in other people—clients, law partners, support staff, opposing counsel, everyone—to better understand your role and how to achieve your objectives.

Biggest mistake(s) you made while in law school

I honestly believe I got about as much as possible out of my J.D. experience. But in the LL.M. program at NYU, I did not take full advantage of the opportunities in that vibrant community. I approached that program like a trade school and tried to get what I needed out of it for practice and didn't engage much beyond the classroom. Looking back, I would have spent more time researching the professors and then trying to build relationships with them. Now in an academic career, I often read and admire the work of professors who were just down the hall from me for nine months, but of whom I was shamefully unaware at the time.

What class(es) did I wish I had taken while in law school? In or outside the school? What about today?

I wish I had taken Administrative Law in the J.D. program. That course was not on my radar, and as a tax lawyer, it's more relevant to me than Civil Procedure. I also would have narrowed my coursework, particularly in the graduate tax program. I took a very generalist approach, and got a sampler platter of tax classes, but relatively little depth. I would have benefited from taking additional classes in pass-through entity taxation and international taxation. Even though I'm generally in favor of students taking a wide swath of classes, I would have felt more comfortable having much deeper exposure to some areas.

Most useful classes in law school

Contracts and Debtor-Creditor Relations (Secured Transactions) were incredibly valuable for me. These classes were most useful because the professor taught us to approach a problem in a systematic way. There was a method, driven by the statute, to determine who had what interest and where they fell on the priority ladder. No matter how complex the fact pattern became, and no matter how many parties or transactions you added to the mix, if you were methodical in your approach and analysis, you would get a clear answer every time.

How did you decide what to do post-law school? With hindsight, how good of a job did you do?

Throughout my first two years of law school, I was open to just about any non-criminal practice. I was particularly drawn to medical malpractice defense and employment litigation. But in my summer experiences, I found that I didn't enjoy drafting motions and briefs as much as I loved working with contracts and any kind of transactional issues. When interviewing for associate positions, almost every firm asked me if I had any interest in tax (perhaps because I wore glasses?). At first, I said no, preferring to focus on business and transactions more generally. But there was clearly a need in the region, and after the fourth or fifth time I was asked about tax, I decided to look into graduate tax programs.

From the graduate tax program, I faced a difficult decision of whether to go back to Arkansas and practice in a more general transactional and tax practice or to stay in New York and focus exclusively on tax in M&A transactions. I chose to return to Arkansas, and although there were many very positive aspects to my practice experience there, I regret not working in a major market for at least a few years. In smaller markets, it's often nearly impossible to focus exclusively on tax issues, or even to narrow the scope of tax work you do (e.g., corporate tax vs. estate planning). Many others, including most of my students, would prefer the variety in the smaller market. For me though, I would have benefited from the ability to focus my attention more narrowly.

Biggest mistake you made while at your first job

I was not good at communicating with the senior associates and partners at the firm. I tried to be extremely responsive, produce excellent drafts, and to make it easy to work with me. But I should have been more proactive at times by asking to get involved in the projects and deals that particularly interested me, and I should have kept at least one senior lawyer consistently updated on my workload. That lack of information flow contributed to a lot of inconsistency from month to month on my billing and project load.

Best advice you received or have given for those coming out of law school

My favorite law professor, Robert Laurence, often told us we had to develop a patience with partial understanding. In other words, there are a lot of concepts you are not going to understand perfectly the first time you encounter them. And it almost always takes a lot of reading and research to put any particular legal issue into context. It takes patience and a recognition that you will often have to invest significant time and deep thought to develop an understanding sufficient to give decent advice.

Worst advice you received or have given for those coming out of law school

It was common advice in the mid-2000s to buy as much house as you could possibly afford as soon as possible. Hopefully after 2008, people have backed off those suggestions.

How have remained happy in your profession? Have there been times when you were not? If so, what did you do to improve your situation?

I definitely had tense moments in practice and times when I felt incredibly insecure. My saving grace was having a friend at another law firm, out of state, with whom I spoke regularly. That friend understood the players and personalities at my firm but did not have to operate in the same market, so she could provide candid advice. She would also let me know when I needed to deescalate and take a step back from a situation before making it worse. Everyone should have a friend outside of the law firm they can turn to for advice, venting, and honest guidance.

If you could go back in time and tell your younger self something about making the transition from law school to the real world, what would it be?

A friend's father once advised a group of recent law graduates to save half of their money from every paycheck, starting with the first one. Although that may not be feasible for grads carrying a ton of student loan debt or those with high costs of living big cities, there's a lot of truth to the sentiment. Law graduates often have a great deal of delayed financial gratification, but they can start building long-term security by refraining from taking on large financial commitments for several years and by stockpiling cash as soon as possible. With financial security comes options.[10]

---

[10] As one of my undergraduate professors so eloquently put it, "Life is like a shit sandwich. The more bread you have, the less shit you have to eat."

CHAPTER

17

What Clients Want

W hen we decided to write this book, we listed the attributes we
disliked about "how to" books. One of the leading frustrations was
reading from authors who thought they knew everything. We don't
know everything and that is why we invited so many guests to join us
in the previous chapter.

Although we've been copious users of legal services our entire
professional lives, we didn't want to be the sole client view in this
book. We went out and interviewed folks who hire lawyers and asked
them about their experiences.

We chose from a wide range of people. There are CEOs, general
counsels, a public relations executive, an academy-award winning
movie producer, venture capitalists, an author, a convicted felon who
spent over two decades in prison, and even an inductee of the Rock
& Roll Hall of Fame. If nothing else, this shows the type of network
you can acquire one day as a lawyer.

We asked them specifically: What types of lawyers do you like the
most and which do you like the least? We also promised to keep their
names anonymous, so that they'd be completely honest and transparent. We even left in the profanity. We talked about whether we
should do this, but it felt disingenuous changing the quotes. Plus, if
the issue rose to the level of profanity, maybe we should all pay attention to it. Besides, as a lawyer, you are going to hear these words.

In short, you are about to get a masterclass in what clients like
and dislike about lawyers, except there is no way they'd tell their
lawyers this in person. To note, these are *not* transcribed from

interviews. These are written quotes that we were given, over email, without any edits.

As *Law & Order* would say: "These are their stories."

What Clients Liked

"It's really important that lawyers understand business goals and risk levels, and that those change over time. I think lawyers should be somewhat more conservative than the CEO and organization, but not wildly out of step."

"For me, this is simple. The best lawyers flag the challenges for you and then get creative on figuring out how to solve for them. The worst lawyers just flag the issue, tell you whatever you're trying to do can't be done, and stop there. Lots of people (lawyers and non-lawyers) just tell you what the problems are but don't give you options or solutions. I always find that lazy thinking. It's easy to lob in grenades from the peanut gallery. The harder work is then figuring out the best path forward."

"I appreciate lawyers that dig in, drive the client and keep the process moving forward. The best lawyers are highly organized and extremely communicative. They take the time to assess your knowledge about a given situation and then raise your level of understanding."

"I like it when I'm given a range of possible options, and the pros and cons to each one. Then together we can focus on the right approach."

"What clients love and inevitably feel are the best lawyers are the Clear Communicators. They constantly keep their clients updated on everything that is going on and what has been filed. The gold standard ironically is to keep it short and simple. Bullet point key issues and at the end briefly outline potential outcomes, good, bad, and otherwise."

"I love it when lawyers understand the business problem I'm trying to solve and become a thought partner in how to solve it rather than just blindly applying their legal opinion, absence of context. For complex, multi-step projects (like a venture financing): I like when lawyers clearly lay out steps, timelines, and communicate regularly about status."

"I like the ability of a good lawyer to help me make risk-adjusted decisions. The worst is when you get in a mode "the lawyers will or won't let me do it." It's never black and white and a good attorney encourages you to assess risk and make the right decision for you."

"Assuming they're helping me negotiate something out, I want someone who's done deals like this before. Ideally, they also know the other party or the other party's lawyers. They should be able to provide some insights as to what is important to the other party, where we can negotiate, and where dealbreakers might be. They are a negotiation partner, not someone I've hired to do a task."

"I've had lawyers who were dealmakers by nature and the opposite. The dealmaker was sometimes too eager to make compromises, but because I understood all the aspects of the deal he was fine taking my "no" as an answer. The other lawyer was a Doberman—enjoyed the fight more than making the deal. This was important with a lot of our Hollywood deals because the other side was that way too. My lawyer had a reputation as a fighter, so they paid attention to us. Again, because I understood all the parts of what we were negotiating on I was able to weigh out the risks and decide where to stand firm vs. give a little. To do so, I had to disagree with my lawyer a few times and tell him to back down on certain points. He would explain the risks and make sure I understood, and then move ahead. We worked well together, but if I just followed his lead we never would have closed a deal."

"Responsiveness is key. An attorney that gets back to me in a timely manner always earns my respect. Even if it's "hey, I'm a bit tied up for now but will get back to you shortly," I appreciate it. When I reach out and don't hear back from my attorney, I can't trust that they give a shit about our relationship, and I have fired counsel because of this in the past."

"Being a technical person, I like the specificity of language that lawyers use. It's very similar in structure you will get from a software engineer. The two professions are remarkably close in some ways."

"Having a great lawyer is one of the most important elements in my business of music and for any business you might be in. A great lawyer will help you navigate the difficult language of law in your best interest and a bad one could advise you to sign something that could come back and cause problems later. Choose wisely."

"Understanding my business they are representing is important but very rare. What are the drivers of growth, and what will potentially derail, etc. This allows them to actually make recommendations instead of just dumping a bunch of options on me."

"Being insanely meticulous with details so I can trust that I don't always have to be. I'm the CEO. Especially when starting a company, I have every function reporting to me, and details can fall through the cracks. Reminding me of important things and following up is super important."

"The lawyers I've liked working with are ones who explain the options and help educate me about what we're doing. I want and need to understand whatever the nuances are of what we're talking about. I even want to understand all the boilerplate stuff because it's there for a reason and I want to know why. Hopefully I only need to learn all that once and we can build on it from there. For example, the entertainment industry had very different boilerplate than the advertising industry and different expectations of IP ownership. The differences were significant but buried in decades of standard practices."

"Best traits are advocacy, integrity, and accessibility. I want to work with lawyers that have solid knowledge of their practice, are able to resolve things quickly, and provide sound advice and offers up scenarios that could occur."

"Two things stand out for me. 1) Empathy – the understanding that lawyers are expensive for companies and to maximize staying focused, minimizing extra work and being a thoughtful partner to the company. 2) Speed and responsiveness – making the client feel like the lawyer is on top of and ahead on things so the client doesn't need to keep track and check in."

"I need to be able to trust that my attorney knows when I needed to be reined in vs. when I have room to make my own decisions. This means they need perspective on what kind of advice is needed. Knowing when to provide "this is what you have to do" vs. "here are the legal parameters, but there's a comfort zone here for your interpretation" is super helpful."

What Clients Didn't Like

"I get too many ridiculous questions from younger lawyers. More seasoned lawyers can moderate the ridiculous questions arising from said lawyers and can guess 90% of the correct answers."

"It frustrates me when my in-house lawyers don't realize that they are in the client service business, meaning that we need to be responsive and clear in our advice and work. The best compliment my team can receive is someone actively seeking our advice because they know that we will be additive and won't block what they are trying to achieve."

"I become frustrated with verbosity and trying to look smart knowledge vs briefness and business guidance."

"I like it when I'm explained something in plain language. It's amazing to me how often I get thrown legal jargon, which makes the topic confusing, especially when citing rules and regulations. Fine to cite a regulation, but explain it to me in plain English."

"Lack of detail and sloppy mistakes."

"My biggest irritant has been lawyers who aren't timely. Particular example was a trust attorney who was taking way too long turning around changes for us. We pushed back and got excuses about "work from home" (during COVID) making it more difficult to access docs. That may be the case, but then they need to set our expectations properly rather than not delivering when they said they would. Oh, then there was that time a law firm decided not to work with me anymore because

I wasn't going to be a big enough client moving forward. Fuck those fucking fucks. (You may not want to quote that part.)"

"The most common and by far the worse is the Non Communicator. They tell you next to nothing but your charges and your court date. They could be really good lawyers and extremely busy fighting for their client. But from that person's perspective, who is waiting for events to unfold that will certainly change their lives forever, that absence of communication is a clear sign that the lawyer is doing little to nothing. Then there is the Volume Communicator. This kind of lawyer confuses the act of sending clients everything they file with actual communication. Such a thing is good for their clients' files but let's face it, they might have to hire another lawyer to explain what half those filings are and what they mean."

"I can't stand it when my attorney nitpicks details, or at least if/ when I don't understand the point behind the nit."

"I hate legal mumbo jumbo. It's the lawyer's job to explain it to me in a way that I can understand."

"It's frustrating when lawyers do extra work that isn't adding value or don't clarify what is needed to make sure the deliverable is on scope and keeps costs low. It's also frustrating when clients have to keep checking in on the progress of work a lawyer is doing because the lawyer is not proactive in communication or moving at the past of the business."

"It frustrates me when senior lawyers join client calls for perception's sake, but they do not actively contribute to the conversation. If a junior lawyer is running the show, don't charge the client for perception."

"Conflict-avoidant lawyers. How can you be a lawyer and avoid conflict?"

"I hate how there is very little feedback on billing and time spent until the surprise invoice arrives. If I'd known you were going to spend 4 hours reviewing that contract and emailing me, I never would have sent it over; the deal is immaterial to our business!"

"I want my lawyer to feel like a loyal guard dog protecting me during a conflict. More important, when a company is bigger and starts to have things like lawsuits, employee issues, etc., come into play. I've had too many conflict-avoidant lawyers."

"Me finding mistakes they've made in legal documents."

"I absolutely cannot stand it when legal bills are a surprise. Give me a quote for something, then let me know when we're getting close to going over that amount, then let me know when we're 10% over, 20% over, etc. We had an acquisition once, where we were told "it would be about $250–$300K." Bill came back at $750K. WTF? Yes it ended up being a complicated M&A, but they should have been communicating with us all along, rather than receive a shock like that."

By no means do we consider this an exhaustive list, but there are some common themes that present themselves. In no particular order of importance:

1. Be a teacher. Clients are smart. Leaders are curious by nature. They don't just want you to do the work, but learn in the process.
2. Communication is key. Don't speak in legalese. Keep in contact about the issue at hand. It is all about quality of communications over volume.
3. Understand their business. Even folks talking about hiring litigators want you to understand their business. Law firms talk about this all the time, but few lawyers actually listen to this advice.
4. Focus on the problem, not the small stuff.
5. Be responsive. Make your clients feel valued and that you care about them. We've talked about empathy a lot, but here it is again being asked for by the clients.
6. Be creative. Find solutions to the problem, not just identify the problem. This is perhaps one of the biggest differences between average and great lawyers.
7. See around corners. By learning the business, being empathetic, and getting to know your client, you can predict future issues and strategize accordingly.
8. Be a partner. People want partners not hired guns.
9. Be careful with billing. Communicate so no surprises happen.
10. Deal with conflict. Be willing to step up on behalf of your client.
11. Play the long game. The lawyer who dropped the client (and the client's reaction with many F-bombs) creates a long memory. This client would later go on to be a leader in a large venture capital firm and never used the firm again. Ouch.
12. Don't make mistakes. Clients finding mistakes is always a bad thing.

We think the biggest piece of advice is, as much as possible, put yourself in the shoes of your client all the time, every time. What would you want in your lawyer if you were on the other side? It's not rocket science, but you do need to be thoughtful.

CHAPTER

18

Law School as a "Second Career"

I t's an age-old question: should one take time between undergraduate school and law school to work elsewhere, or plow straight through? Are there any real outcome differences between these two populations?

If you are reading this while in school or after, your decision has been made. But that doesn't mean this chapter is irrelevant to you, it's just that you have fewer decisions to make.

We would like to explore the two situations taking time off most effects the outcomes: entrance into law school and the first job post-graduation.

Entrance into Law School

According to the admissions folks we spoke with (who will remain anonymous), if you have the grades, application, and LSAT that rank near the top quarter or so of the prospective class, baring anything abnormal, you'll get accepted. In other words, if you are top 25% going into the application process for that school, you should feel very good about your chances of getting in.

If you slot in the other 75% (and note that can include being significantly better than average), then all the other factors start to come into play. Other factors can include undergraduate university, geography, race, gender, age, military background, prior work experience, and other factors.

We know you cannot influence your race, gender, age, and undergraduate university (assuming you've graduated already). You probably have little ability regarding geography and veterans represent a small percentage of law school applicants and is always seen as a positive.

What one can control is whether to take time between the undergrad and law school experience. The feedback we got from admissions folks was very consistent.

1. It can't hurt. Literally nothing you can do will hurt your admission chances. Clearly jobs that point to your interest in law (paralegal, legal intern, etc.) all corroborate a story of why you want to go to school, but we were told that folks who took a year to travel, ski, work as a brewer, learned to cook, etc., all allowed the candidates to paint a picture of "I'm ready to do this" assuming the application told what they thought was a sincere story.

2. It probably will help. Some of the schools we spoke to said prior work experience helped the admission process because they believed this candidate pool would be more mature and have a greater chance of employment post-law school. Remember, law schools are partially ranked by employment numbers, so they aren't just accepting you as a legal student, but also looking at your future career opportunities and how that might affect their rankings and their fundraising prospects years down the line.

Anecdotal information seems to suggest that those who did something after undergrad but before law school experienced less stress their first year at law school. This might be attributed to either having experience in the real world to cope with new and stressful situations or having gotten into a healthy headspace by taking time off before the three-year slog of law school.

We were fortunate enough that two law schools gave us the data they track regarding this subject. One school that wants to remain nameless saw a marginal increase in grade performance from those who took time off, but it was not a massive amount. Northwestern Law, Alex's alma mater, has found that work experience greatly improves student outcomes, such that it has almost become a de facto requirement for admittance. More than 90% of incoming NU Law students have at least one year of work experience. Alex was one of the few in his class who did not have work experience, and at times during the critical first year felt that lack acutely.

Getting a Job

Unlike law schools that gave a neutral to positive review of prior work experience, we found no employers who didn't rate prior work experience as important.

Given some of the topics that we've discussed around lack of empathy and experience, having any work experience looks good on a resume. If you survived or thrived other professional ecosystems, it's one less risk factor for an employer to consider. Particularly, service industry jobs are valued, as being a lawyer is a service industry job as we've mentioned before.

Besides the experience, we learned that some employers prefer older employees as they believe they are less likely to turnover having more life experience and perhaps obligations like supporting families, etc. Those life "handcuffs" can keep you tied to the desk.

When asked if deciding between identical candidates on paper with one having work experience and one not, the universal answer was to take the person with more experience.

If you are reading this while in law school and have no prior work experience, please don't freak out. Our advice to you is the following:

1. Get great grades in law school.
2. Get out of the law school and do something like volunteer work to show good character.
3. Sign up for clinics and seminars to gain real-life legal experience.

CHAPTER

19

How to Be a Happy Lawyer

Being a lawyer is a tough job. It's mentally and physically demanding. The stakes are high a lot of the time. You have pressure to perform, and failing isn't really an option, although it happens. Nobody is perfect. Many lawyers we know are not happy in their professions. Is it a majority? It's unclear, but it could be. Fortunately, our guest authors don't fit into that group.

Jason was sitting on his porch one day meeting with his trust and estate lawyer, Margot Edwards (who is also one of the guest authors). While Margot doesn't normally make house calls, a certain global pandemic was in full force, and she did what any good attorney does: improvise. When Jason told her about this book, she immediately asked if there was a chapter on happiness. Jason responded there would be now! Thanks Margot.

We began to reflect on our careers and spoke to others. We asked the question of what has kept us happy (or not) all these years. When we were junior folks no one, not even ourselves, cared about this. It certainly was a different time, but happiness wasn't something we talked about openly. It was too close to the subject of mental health, which was extremely taboo at the time.

But times change and today we are fortunately moving in a direction where these subjects can be discussed. Being happy isn't just about you being happy, mind you. While that's massively important, being happy will also make you a better lawyer. Being happy will give your brain creative space to figure out problems. It will allow you to be more empathetic. It will allow you to be more humorous and perhaps make a client feel just a bit better in a difficult time.

Happiness is not just a selfish state of being, rather it will allow you to perform your best. And we won't even begin to discuss the impact it will have on your friends and family, which in turn will feed back into your happiness flywheel.

Not everyone is wired the same way and so telling anyone how to be happy is not an exact science. We are also not mental health professionals. Therefore, we solicited advice from our lawyer friends to share. You may find some, all, or none of it applicable to you, but our strong advice is to continually monitor your happiness and challenge yourself to make decisions that will maximize it. If you are a first-year at a Wall Street firm working a hundred hours a week, this can be difficult, but all the more necessary. If you are a public defender in the middle of heavy case, maybe even more so. Whatever the situation, we encourage you to regularly take time to check in with yourself.

Have an Identity Outside of Being a Lawyer

In our experience, people who are "just lawyers" never separate from their jobs. It's unhealthy and also makes you boring at cocktail parties. It's not about having hobbies (also important and discussed later), rather identifying as something other than a lawyer. Ideally, this identification isn't just internal, it's important for others to see you as someone other than a lawyer as well. Some examples include spouse, parent, musician, author, sommelier, chef, competitive badminton player, mountain climber, or newly minted yoga instructor.

Whatever it is, find something you take pride in outside of being a lawyer. This balance is essential. In our experience, having another identity will make you more appealing as a lawyer, as clients are always looking for well-rounded people who have a multitude of experiences and interests.

Take Pride in Your Work and the Impact It Has on Others

Your work will change the lives of others. Let that sink in for a moment. There aren't a lot of professions like this. No matter what area you practice in and what experience level you are, your work will impact human beings.

That is both a responsibility but also an awesome opportunity. Take pride in what you do. Realize that good work will lead to good results for both you and the people you work for. You can do well by doing good in this profession.

Keep a Continually Learning Mindset

Boredom is a key ingredient to unhappiness, so tilt the equation in your favor. Having a continual curiosity is both healthy for your brain and your clients. We find people who are natural enthusiasts about learning don't suffer from the boredom that others face.

And let's be honest. It's not all glitz as an attorney. There are many days where one is simply grinding out work. We have all been there. But if you can find something, even small, to learn in everything you do, you'll be better off for it. In our experience, no matter how senior of a lawyer you are, you can always learn something at every stage of what you are doing. You just need to be open to the idea and look for it.

Don't Get Too Wrapped Up in Your Work

We've talked about how important it is to empathize with your colleagues and clients. You've heard from clients saying they want partners and people who truly understand their goals. It is possible to get too close to the lab rat, however, and you need to keep a certain amount of healthy distance. These aren't your problems, your businesses, your defense, or your divorce. While you need to sit as a partner with someone, you also need to leave their anxiety and worries in the office before you go home that night.

Disconnecting is healthy for a lot of obvious reasons, but none more so than how this will affect others around you. There are far too many stories of lawyers too involved with their clients' problems who were no longer able to deliver objective advice.

Manage Your Stress

You've had plenty of stress in your life, and however you best manage that stress needs to remain a high priority on your to do list. Realize that stress management is an active, not passive activity. If you think you can do nothing, push the stress down, and internally metabolize it, we are here to tell you that unfortunately you are wrong. Eventually you will burn out. You will start to make mistakes. You may turn to things like drugs and alcohol.

Get a hobby, for sure, but in our opinion physical exercise is mandatory for clearing out the plaque in the brain. Whether you are a high-end athlete, a weekend warrior, or a walker around the neighborhood, get the heartrate up and get out of your chair that you spend all day in while on email, teleconferences, and client phone calls. Your physical well-being is the best way to fight off stress and it's all a matter of willpower and prioritization.

If you are less into the physical side of things, might we suggest watching the Hallmark Channel, which is like Prozac, but cheaper and better for the liver. *Ted Lasso* is also a good call as well and more socially acceptable to tell your friends.

Watch Your Drug Consumption

As a follow-up to the previous paragraph, watch your consumption. Don't let your usage become a crutch, or even worse, an addiction. You will likely be invited to many events early in your career that will involve alcohol and potentially other substances. Moderation is your friend here. And if you aren't a consumer, that is totally cool! Don't let anyone tell you otherwise. Jason will tell you that his COVID find was the world of non-alcoholic beers. Honestly, they rate about 85% to 90% as good as real beers for those times he wants to avoid alcohol.

One key point here: if you are out with a client, don't for a minute think you can do everything your client does. If your client is drinking heavily or doing drugs, don't think because they are consuming that you can, too. Whatever they do, we'd highly recommend doing a lot less of or abstaining entirely. The tales we know of where a lawyer was fired by a client who says, "I can't believe they did that around me. They are supposed to be my lawyer," are numerous. And many times, the client was the person egging the lawyer on.

There are a lot of lawyers who struggle with this. Beware of how you are coping and don't fall down this trap.

Never Compromise Your Value System

We are not here to tell you what is right and wrong. We are not here to judge you. What we will say is whatever your value system is, never compromise it. It doesn't matter what your boss, client, coworker, or anyone says. There are few things in life that are sacred and breaking this contract with yourself will undoubtedly lead to unhappiness.

Nothing is more important than your own integrity. Never give this power to anyone.

Don't Forget to Laugh and Celebrate the Wins

Laughter is good medicine. Don't believe us? Google it. Don't forget to laugh. Find humor in things. Laugh at yourself. Laugh at others. Just work at being happy. It's proven that laughing causes a positive reaction in the brain. Don't forget to do it. If you have a hard time, might we suggest *Schitt's Creek* or *Mythic Quest?*

Also, don't forget to celebrate your victories. You win a trial. You crush an assignment. A client sends you an email telling you that you rock. Celebrate. Take a minute out of the day to smile and reflect. Go buy yourself a gift. Tell a friend. Don't simply move onto the next thing and forget about the wins. It's important to focus on the next problem, but taking stock in victories (large and small) is a key ingredient in sustaining a positive mindset throughout your career.

Failing to enjoy the victories is also frustrating to others in your orbit (particularly those who may not be lawyers). One of Jason's biggest arguments with his wife was around him having a nice outcome on a deal as a venture capitalist. He never told his wife and she learned from a friend of hers. When she asked Jason why he hadn't said anything, he noted that he was fixated at the time having to deal with an issue at another portfolio company. She couldn't possibly understand how Jason got no satisfaction out of a really good outcome and instead only focused on the next problem he had to solve. Jason has since learned. ☺

Internalize the Losses, But Don't Dwell on Them

We talked about this previously but want to reiterate. You are going to make mistakes. Sometimes, you'll make no mistakes but still fail your mission. Maybe the law just doesn't line up with what you are trying to do. Maybe you get surprised with a verdict that even in hindsight you wouldn't have strategized differently. No lawyer wins every time. It's okay. You aren't special.

What is important is how you bounce back with resiliency, not gloom. Be thoughtful about where you could improve or realize that luck plays into a lot of things. But then move on, keep your head up, and don't dwell.

Work with Clients You Really Like

In some ways, this is the most obvious one. In some ways, this is also the hardest one when you are a junior lawyer. But it is super important to keep in mind. As you progress in your career, you'll have decisions of how to spend your time, and we advise to always choose quality of client over quality of the potential payoff or engagement. Even as a junior person, you may have a choice in senior people with which to work. Pro tip: Make a killer first impression as a first-year attorney so you'll be given preference when seeking out and choosing senior partners (and their clients) with whom you'd like to work.

Have a Great Surrounding Team

If you are ever in the position to hire people around you, hire great, not good. Don't hire out of need, hire out of the fact you just found someone who you really want to work with. A great team doesn't just do great work, but also supports one another intellectually and emotionally. It's a happiness chamber in that people inside the team along with the clients are all happy. The reinforcing mechanism is critical in larger organizations.

However, the most important thing a great surrounding team will provide you is what we are going to discuss next.

Set Boundaries for Your Personal Life

This might be the hardest one, especially as the junior person on the team. It's super important that you are not on the clock 24/7, 365.

It happens. Many of us have been there. As a junior person, you are being hit on two sides: clients and senior lawyers at your employer. It's tough and it can be nonstop if you allow it to happen. The work-from-home culture created during COVID may seem cool, but in some ways, it's completely blurred the lines between being home and being at work.

You need to set boundaries that allow you to enjoy your life outside of work. This also may allow you to be present to those around you. As you get more comfortable in your position, you can clearly lay out what you're willing to do and what you are not. When you are on a vacation, you'll need to be able to actually take that vacation or you will burn out. This is why having a great team around you is important as they can pick up the workload you are missing.

Unfortunately, some employer cultures do not allow this. That is a choice that you'll have to consider as you choose employers.

What to Do When You Are Not Happy

Assuming you've taken steps to maximize your happiness, what do you do if you still are struggling? Again, we aren't mental health experts but offer you the following:

1. Ask if your unhappiness is coming from your professional life or personal life. Or both. Sometimes unhappiness gets a little cloudy as to the cause.
2. Try to determine whether this is short-term unhappiness, for example, you dislike a particular assignment or client, or a long-term trend. If short term, maybe you can see the light at the end of the tunnel.
3. Many lawyers choose therapists to help them through rough parts of their lives.
4. If all else fails, it may be time to look for a different employer.

At the end of the day keep one thing in mind. This is just a job. It's not your entire life. You can always use your skills to do something else, and we'll explore some of those options next.

CHAPTER 20

What If You Don't Want to Be a Lawyer Anymore?

In 2014, the American Bar Association completed a study that claimed 24% of people who passed the bar in 2000 were no longer practicing law in 2012. Top among other careers that people chose were nonprofit, education, government, investment banking, real estate, and full-time parenting. According to a 2019 article on FindLaw.com, nearly 60% of lawyers think about getting out of the business altogether.

So, what if you decide today, or one day, that you don't want to practice law? Was law school a wasted effort? We think not. (And not just because one of the authors hasn't practiced in a long time and has had a very fulfilling career.)

Going to law school imparts not only knowledge but a lot of real skills that are translatable to other industries. We personally know of law graduates in a variety of roles including CEO, movie producer, venture capitalist, author, restaurant owner, photographer, product manager, salesperson, business development, policy writer, musician, COO, wealth manager, accountant, CFO, private equity investor, secret service, consultant, entrepreneur, sports and entertainment manager, foundation director, financial advisor, and accountant, in addition to the professions listed above in the first paragraph. And we are sure that we are forgetting many outcomes here.

The bottom line is that a law degree is transportable to numerous other careers.

Some of the skills you learn in law school that are valued by non-law jobs are:

1. Analytical thinking and problem solving.
2. Negotiations.
3. People management.
4. Conflict resolution.
5. Ability to evaluate at lot of information, synthesize, and learn.
6. Public speaking/Communication/Presentation.
7. Research.
8. Organization and management.
9. Ability to work under pressure.
10. Understanding of the law.

Ask yourself: Where wouldn't these skills be used? All make you marketable and helpful in almost any profession. While they may not be sufficient skills for some careers, they certainly range from valuable to necessary.

Okay, so you are set! You have a certain set of unique skills that will allow you to stand out in a crowd for your new profession, right? Well. Maybe.

Some employers will be biased against hiring lawyers for non-law jobs. Interestingly, here is some feedback we got why a lawyer may see bias in their career switch.

1. Lawyers are seen as too risk adverse.
2. Lawyers are prone to "yes or no" and not shades of gray.
3. Lawyers are overly opinionated.
4. Lawyers have overly exaggerated compensation expectations.

In our opinion, some of these biases might be true. Law school does nothing but teach you about situations where things go wrong. There is never a situation where two parties do something and it works out. It always ends up in court. Law school literally beats any risk-taking out of you. Jason believes that this factor makes it harder for some lawyers to go into investing professions, which, by definition, is a risk-taking job.

Additionally, some lawyers are very polar in their thinking. Again, the world is more nuanced than that and when you are no longer playing lawyer, it's about getting things done, not holding things up.

As for overly opinionated, we think this comes from a lawyer's ability to influence better than most others. We are literally taught to exert our will and belief system over others. So, it's not surprising we are viewed as opinionated. In the workplace this can be seen as a negative if one person is overly dominate in getting their way. If any of you have non-lawyer spouses, think about how unsatisfying it is for your spouse to get in an argument with you.

Lastly, lawyers, on average, make more money than most. And when you are looking to make that career switch, hiring managers may see you as unaffordable.

Our advice is to address each of these biases head-on and deal with them, not avoid them. When talking about yourself either on a resume, email, phone call, or interview, highlight risk taking you've done in your life including the fact that you are changing your career. If you have examples of things that you've done entrepreneurially in your past, talk about it. Maybe you don't go all the way back to your lemonade stand as a kid, but what things have you created? What chances have you taken? These can be both professionally and personally.

As for the polar thinking, we'd advise you to keep it in mind and make sure your brain isn't living at the extremes. Showing that you can think analytically, and the answer can still be "it depends," is actually attractive in the nonlegal world, as opposed to the legal world where it frustrates clients. When you are in conversations for that next job, keep this in mind as you craft your narrative or respond to questions in an interview.

As for winning your arguments, remember that outside of the law, winning isn't always winning. Relationships and reputation matter much more, on average, than always winning your argument. Think of it another way: Would you rather win your argument, or would you rather make someone happy and win their trust and respect? Pick and choose your battles. If it truly matters, use your legal skills to get your point across and win. Otherwise, don't sweat all the small stuff and instead be seen as someone who is a good teammate, not someone who dominates all the time. Again, keep this in mind during the interview process.

Lastly, when you apply for another position, make sure you are clear about your understanding of the level of job you are applying for. Let them know that you are willing to take a pay cut (if applicable) to get a fresh start doing something else. Dropping little hints like, "I saved some money being a lawyer precisely so I could take a risk like this later," is very helpful to a person trying to decide if they can afford you. You can always negotiate the salary later after they've offered you a position. You should know a thing or two about negotiation.

If you are scared to make the jump, consider a couple of factors. First, if you keep paying your dues and continue CLE credits, you can keep your bar card. It isn't like you are retiring from a profession and there is no way to return. In fact, many employers that hire lawyers prefer lawyers who have done something else besides law. If your new career doesn't work out, you may have still made yourself more valuable as a lawyer, should you decide to go back.

CHAPTER 21

Let's Sum Up

We hope you enjoyed your journey with us through this book. As you can probably tell, we are very passionate about the issue of how law schools don't prepare their students for the real world. But then again, what did you expect for a six-figure check?

As with any book, we got some things correct, some things wrong, and totally forgot to address topics that you might consider very important. For all of these, we apologize and are happy to take feedback. We hope this book warrants a second version one day and would appreciate your help improving it for future readers.

You can reach us at the following coordinates with a shameless plug for Jason's musical career as well. Alex lost the coin flip in deciding if this would get into the book. (Tails never fails.)

Jason Mendelson

jasonmendelson@gmail.com

@jasonmendelson

Music: as Jace Allen, on all streaming services and Jace Allen YouTube channel for music videos. @JaceAllen_Music on Instagram.

Alex Paul

alex@wealthgatetrust.com

Thanks for reading our book. We really do appreciate it, as we are hoping to make a difference in the world. More than being great lawyers, we hope you all have a great time in the legal profession. We sincerely wish you the best in your future regardless of what path you follow. And despite any vibe you may have gotten, both of us are eternally grateful for our legal background and hope one day you feel the same.

Best,

Jason and Alex

Index

Page numbers followed by *f* refer to figures.